Praise for *Transformed by India*

Drawn to India like a previous life 'avatar,' Stephen regales us with a revealing narrative of his transformative journey of rediscovery of a diverse land that has no parallel – a mesmerizing read.
—**Gaj Singh**, Maharajah of Jodhpur

With an insider's percipience and an outsider's appraisal, Huyler tells the story of Indian folk arts and rituals, predominantly stemming from rural women's worldview. Its soul-stirring anecdotal narrative takes the reader along on his journeys - and once you begin you cannot leave it halfway.
—**Dr. Jyotindra Jain**, Author and Scholar, Former Director of the National Crafts Museum, New Delhi

Stephen Huyler's work and insights are an inspiring, important introduction to India and Indians, and especially to women's identity and creativity in India.
—**Paolo Gianturco**, Author and Photographer Focused on Global Women's Identity and Empowerment

Here is an amazing walk down memory lane spanning half a century of Stephen Huyler's unusual relationship with India. I know of no other Westerner who has traveled as extensively in my country to research art, culture, and history as Stephen. He has devoted his life to building bridges between India and the Western World, and his publications are as valuable to modern Indians as they are to those who live elsewhere.
—**George Dominic**, Founder/Director of CGH Earth Boutique Hotels. Pioneer of large-scale sustainable eco-tourism

As a leading authority on India's rural crafts and popular Hindu sacred arts, Stephen Huyler has travelled throughout its regions for half a century, as at home in remote villages as in great cities. The story of his deep engagement with India is an absorbing one, and he tells it with warmth, insight and candour.
—**Dr. Andrew Topsfield**, Author, Curator of South Asian Art, Ashmolean Museum, Oxford

This is a book of a life richly lived – adventurous, colourful, brave, compassionate. It is a life lived knitting cultures together. In a fragmented world, it can give hope of a shared humanity.
—**Mallika Sarabhai**, Author, Teacher, and winner of multiple honours and awards for her contributions to classical Indian dance, theatre, film, performing arts, and promoting social progress

Stephen's approach is a unique blend of academic rigour leavened with a heart of deep empathy and understanding. What we don't often realise from Stephen's immense body of work is his unflagging commitment over decades to the communities he has studied, remaining engaged in various capacities as friend, mentor, and a special family member. This memoir traces the journey of a spirited, sensitive young man and his extraordinary life experiences as he documents diverse Indian communities, to eventually become a renowned cultural anthropologist, art historian, curator and author.
—**Supriya Rai**, Buddhist Scholar, Retired Director and Dean of the Faculty of Dharma Studies, Somaiya Vidyavihar University, Mumbai

Stephen Huyler has spent a lifetime exploring the peoples and cultures of India's marginalised societies. This engrossing book describes hair-raising accounts of his travels, encounters with village artists, generous mentors and one notably obstructive adversary, as well as the processes of putting together his many successful books and exhibitions and thoughtful reflections on his status as a 'privileged white male' in India.
—**Rosemary Crill**, Author and Scholar, Former Senior Curator of South and Southeast Asian Art, Victoria and Albert Museum, London

Stephen Huyler embraced his dream and followed it by a road rarely travelled. Arriving in India at a good time, he was able to acquaint himself with the length and breadth of India.

Though he may not have realised it at the time, that was also a commitment to a personal journey which transformed his life. Whether you intend to read *Transformed by India* for your own pleasure, or approach this book primarily for illumination and instruction, you can also gain, here, keen insight into becoming a chronicler dedicated to sharing a life lived with passion backed up by intention, research, and skill. He has now shared his journey. And it is an incredible legacy.
—**Thomas L Kelly**, Widely-published photographer, specializing in the Himalayas and Their Cultures

This memoir is a brilliant tapestry of an adventurous life and the threads within it. Stephen's narrative weaves his natural empathy with an ability to both listen deeply and to enhance the visual beauty he has witnessed with soulful and stirring descriptions of his many remarkable encounters in India.
—**Dr Heather Elgood. MBE,** Author and Art Historian of South Asian Art, Former Course Director of the Diploma in Asian Art, London University's School of Oriental and African Studies

Stephen's memoir can inspire young people all over the world to travel and look at India beyond its tourist propaganda—to learn about the rapidly vanishing, simple, and beautiful values of living so cherished by Gandhiji.
—**Sanjit (Bunker) Roy**, Social Activist and Educator, Founder of The Barefoot College, Tilonia, Rajasthan, and of Educational Initiatives to Empower Rural Communities Throughout South Asia and Developing Countries Throughout the World

Stephen's new memoir effectively catalogues his lifetime of travel, field research, and writing about the less-documented aspects of India. As a member of the Meena tribe of Western Rajasthan, I recognize that his books are genuinely rooted in Indian cultural traditions. As a fellow cultural anthropologist, his words and photographs, capture the true essence of rural Indian life, especially the talented women of my country. Whereas tourist photographers have presented

exotic views of India during the last century, reducing my country to images of Sadhus, snake charmers, forts, and palaces, Stephen presents and documents a realistic view of many of the art traditions.
—**Dr. Madan Meena**, Honorary Director, Adivasi Academy, Gujarat

As an avid reader of Stephen Huyler's previous books, I have always admired his expressive way of distilling stories of everyday life and events. In this memoir, Huyler masterfully reveals how a lifelong journey through India profoundly shaped his identity, scholarship, and worldview gained from truly listening to the voices and stories of others. A captivating odyssey of self-discovery and cultural immersion.
—**Chantal Jumel**, freelance researcher, artist and writer specializing in Indian visual and performing arts

Huyler's story is unique and brilliant. At the same time, it speaks for many of us who have also done exhaustive fieldwork in India over the past half-century. His memory of people, places, and events is prodigious, providing an unmatched record of his personal journey and an India that has changed dramatically over recent decades and yet, remarkably, remains much the same. This book will be a classic as are the diaries and journals of other perceptive and enchanted visitors to India over the centuries.
—**Dr. Susan L. Huntington**, Author and Distinguished University Professor, Emerita, at Ohio State University

Open this book and discover in its pages an amazing story. American by birth yet Indian by heart and soul, Dr. Stephen Huyler's extraordinary life has been full of beauty, purpose, and discovery. His memoir traces his amazing journey over decades across India, learning her secrets through a half-century of devotion to her living cultures. *Transformed by India* is precious both as a record of people and places and as a guide to living one's life meaningfully.
— **Minhazz Majumdar**, Author, Curator, and Art Activist

This is a deeply American story of discovery and entrepreneurship. Stephen Huyler marvels at what he has done. But he also marvels at the people who have made it possible for him to do it, and these are almost entirely Indian. We meet celebrated pillars of the arts like Rukmini Devi Arundale, Kamaladevi Chattopadhyay, Jyotindra Jain, N. T. Vakani, and Kaka Kelkar, along with brilliant young coworkers of all castes and both sexes. It's a *Bildungsroman* that keeps on building, with a few hair-raising turns along the way.
—**Dr. John Stratton Hawley**, Author, Scholar of Hinduism and the Religions of India, Professor of Religion, Barnard College Columbia University

Fascinating! I couldn't put it down! Stephen Huyler is one 'who has absorbed India unfiltered'. Through his series of reflections about his long relationship with India, one gets a first-hand view of life and craft, especially of villages hidden in remote forests and terrains.
—**Dr. Asok K Das**, Art Historian, Former Director of the Maharajah Sawai II Museum, Jaipur

Transformed by India is a captivating glimpse into Indian life, taking readers on an entrancing journey into the heart of this country's rich and complex soul. More than just an engaging read, it stands tall as a profound contribution to understanding the resilience and spirit of India's people. Stephen's writing is a testimony to his intimate relationship with India and a reflection of his own growth in the lap of this ancient civilization.
—**Rashmi Singh**, Thakurani and Zila Pramukh of Pali District, Rajasthan

I was delighted and moved by reading this remarkable memoir of a fellow art historian, Stephen Huyler. This aptly titled book is indeed the most unusual memoir by an American scholar about my homeland that I have read in my long career of almost seventy years as a historian of traditional Indian art. I am sure this engaging, insightful and deeply empathetic account of his long and fascinating journey, laced with both pathos and

humor, will become a literary classic about one of the oldest and most enigmatic of the world's civilizations.
—**Dr. Pratapaditya Pal**, Author, Scholar of South and Southeast Asian and Himalayan Art, Former Curator of South and Southeast Asian Art at the Los Angeles County Museum of Art, the Museum of Arts, Boston, and the Art Institute of Chicago

Transformed by India is wondrous! Highly acclaimed Indophile, Stephen Huyler, records in this book (as in all of his publications and photographs) details of our own culture that many of us Indians do not otherwise notice. Huyler's devotion to India unravels so many splendid dimensions of the Indian ethos – cultural, artistic, philosophical, and beyond. His perceptions enrich our understanding of our own lives and those of our countrymen and women. Fascinating descriptions and experiences, both profound and humorous, make for delightful reading. Its amazing personal narrative and exceptional photography make Huyler's latest book enticing.
—**Komal GB Singh**, Television Commentator and Stage Compere; formerly English News Reader on Doordarshan; New Delhi, India

Dr. Stephen Huyler's remarkable autobiography chronicles a life lived fully and richly. The author, a gifted scholar and keen observer of the human condition, weaves together, in Homeric detail, his visual journeys. *Transformed by India* filled with vibrant encounters with charismatic individuals from all walks of life, arcane rituals, and primordial creativity from village shrine to soaring palace. And the amazing thing is that Dr. Huyler's adventures continue unabated today.
— **Mitchell Crites**, Author and Art Historian Focused on the Revival of Traditional South Asian and Islamic Arts and Crafts

Transformed by
INDIA *A Life*

Other books by Stephen P. Huyler

Daughters of India: Art and Identity, co-published by Abbeville (NY) and Mapin (India), 2008

Gifts Of Earth: Traditional Terracottas and Clay Sculptures of India, published by Mapin Press, India, 1996, and distributed in the USA by University of Washington Press

Meeting God: Elements of Hindu Devotion, published by Yale University Press, USA, hardback, 1999; Yale paperback 2002; Korean language edition, Da Vinci Press, 2002

Painted Prayers: Women's Art in Village India co-published by Rizzoli International (NY), Thames and Hudson (UK), Frederking und Thaler (Germany), and Flammarion (France), 1994

Sonabai: Another Way of Seeing, published by Mapin, India, 2009

Village India published by Harry N. Abrams, New York, USA, 1985

Transformed by
INDIA *A Life*

Stephen P. Huyler

Pippa Rann
books & media

An imprint of
Salt Desert Media Group Limited,
7 Mulgrave Chambers, 26 Mulgrave Rd,
Sutton SM2 6LE, England, UK.
Email: publisher@pipparannbooks.com
Website: www.pipparannbooks.com

Copyright © Stephen P. Huyler 2025

The moral right of the author has been asserted. The views and opinions expressed in this book are the author's own and the facts are as reported by him, which have been verified to the extent possible, but the publishers are not in any way liable for the same.

All rights reserved. No part of this book may be reproduced by any mechanical, photographic, or electronic process, or in the form of a phonographic recording; nor may it be stored in a retrieval system, transmitted or otherwise be copied for public or private use – other than for 'fair use' as brief quotations embodied in articles and reviews, without prior written permission of the publisher.

ISBN 978-1-913738-21-1

Printed and bound at Replika Press Pvt. Ltd.

10 9 8 7 6 5 4 3 2 1

For Helene,
whose abiding love has sustained me throughout my life

As an accomplished photographer, it might seem natural that I illustrate this book, but the result would be an expensive volume. Instead, once the publication is in print, I will post a dedicated website with photographs and videos to accompany each chapter.

In the meantime, my personal website has been redesigned to reflect my life's work in India. It includes hundreds of photographs, many films, and separate menus for each of the primary categories of my varied career.

At the bottom of the home page is an interactive Timeline that provides an archival photograph of each key event in my life.

www.stephenhuyler.com

Contents

Foreword 17
Preface 19
Introduction 23

1. Overland 25
At age nineteen, two months of travel alone from Paris through Turkey, Iran, Afghanistan, and Pakistan to India in 1971

2. Transformation 47
Entering India on my 20th birthday, I meet my first great Indian mentor, Kamaladevi Chattopadhyay, and begin initial adventures north and south; first experiences of the women's art and votive terracotta sculptures that will later shape my career

3. Ongoing Change 79
Journeying from the tip of India up the western coast and back to the north in 1972, I encounter difficulties and phenomenal generosity that alter my perceptions of myself and the world

4. Challenges 109
Living with and marrying my life's partner Helene in 1973 gives me a new security, while our subsequent year of travel in the Middle East and India almost ends our marriage in tragedy

5. Decisions 137
Returning to the USA with a rich collection of Indian crafts, I choose scholarship over commerce, subsequently moving to London to enroll in the School of Oriental and African Studies in pursuit of a PhD in South Asian Art and Archaeology. Living in Britain while traveling in South Asia for months during each of our seven years there also informs my perceptions

6. Lessons 151

To avoid the difficulties of Helene's and my first long trip together to and through India, we make the unfortunate choice of a four-month drive through central India in an offensively intrusive car; forays into tribal villages guide my choice of doctoral research

7. Encounters 165

One of the most difficult and inspiring periods of my life is fieldwork among the indigenous tribes of southern Odisha. Unexpected opposition causes me to completely change the focus of my doctoral thesis

8. Abundance 191

Beginning again, I am mentored by Rukmini Devi Arundale, and redefine my research by returning to an earlier fascination with Indian votive terracotta, conducting a survey throughout peninsular India. When not in India, Helene and I spend four years living in Cornwall

9. Grounding 215

Cross-cultural surveys result in my first book: *Village India* in 1985. Tired of being expats, we move back to the USA, settling in Camden, Maine, where I work to improve my photography skills and sow the seeds of a second career curating exhibitions. In 1994, I publish my second book, *Gifts of Earth,* drawn from my doctoral thesis work

10. Impermanence 235

Traveling to gather information on Indian terracottas, I grow increasingly fascinated with women's sacred and decorative art in rural villages. My third book, *Painted Prayers* (published in 1994), is based upon interviews and photographs throughout India, while coordinated exhibitions are displayed in museums in the US, Europe, and India

11. Devotion 255

Changing direction in 1993-2001, I curate *Puja,* a long-running exhibition about Hinduism at the Smithsonian's National Museum of Asian Art. Its success leads to a well-publicized traveling show and book, both entitled *Meeting God*. In 2001, world events require that I yet again alter my career

12. Empowerment..................................281
After interviewing more than 1,000 women throughout India, I compose and publish *Daughters of India* in 2008 based on the profiles and personal stories of twenty individuals; museum exhibitions and a book tour ensue

13. Catharsis....................................293
The experience of knowing Sonabai Rajawar, an elderly central Indian artist, challenges all my preconceptions and changes my life, resulting in a published monograph, a dedicated documentary film, and an innovative exhibition about her: *Sonabai: Another Way of Seeing*

14. Bridges.....................................321
A fourth career, leading tours of India once each year, opens me to new horizons and allows me to share with others much of what I've learned to admire

15. Underpinnings..............................341
My background: how and why my childhood experiences shaped me to spend half a century in India

16. Puzzle......................................371
An attempt to deconstruct aspects of entitlement and privilege that define me as a white, American male

17. Gratitude..................................383
The influence of countless others has informed and enhanced my long life. I credit many of those as I move ahead into new horizons

Glossary..393
Index...401

*Welcomed
into India
for over fifty years.
Seen, heard, fed, and nourished.
Learning to listen,
be present,
notice, and observe,
welcomed to participate.
A foreign guest
transformed
into brother, son, uncle,
even father.
Welcomed through grace
to remain
my own separate self
while melding into
cultures, families, communities.
The Other
becoming so familiar—
almost
an extension of myself.*

THE DALAI LAMA

FOREWORD

Stephen Huyler has compiled this book of delightful photographs and recollections as a tribute to the way his life has been transformed by his long relationship with India. Over more than five decades he has been made welcome all over the country by people happy to share their culture, traditions and way of life with him.

As someone who has also spent the larger part of his life in India, I recognise the warm-hearted friendship he describes. Besides this, my mind has been filled with Indian thought from the Nalanda tradition and my body has been nourished by years of Indian rice, dal and roti. In the face of difficulties, ancient Indian knowledge of the mind and emotions has helped me keep my inner peace. Consequently, wherever I go, and whenever I can, I tell people about the non-violence—*ahimsa*— and compassion—*karuna* that have long been celebrated here.

I share the deep respect and affection Stephen Huyler feels for this ancient land and am grateful to him for the efforts he's made to convey these feelings to his readers.

8 October 2024

Preface

Before anything can be said about the journey you are going to embark on in this book, take a moment ... and imagine different people going through the following experiences:

- travelling alone, at the age of 19, through Paris, Iran, Turkey, Pakistan, Afghanistan and India;
- on your twentieth birthday, pedalling a bicycle rickshaw through the Indian border;
- at that age, being mentored by the legendary Kamaladevi Chattopadhyaya;
- travelling all the way from the southern tip of India up the western coast, to the north;
- driving four months through all of central India in an offensively intrusive car.

These are not disparate experiences of multiple outgoing young people. This is the experience of one person – Stephen Huyler – who knows how to recount them in the most vivid, thoughtful, and evocative way.

One of the most beautiful things about travelogues is the sense of adventure they come with: you are always on the move, there is always something new to see, a unique experience to take in. Wordier travel writers can become monotonous, and lose themselves in trying to describe what they see, rather than what they feel. Stephen does not suffer from this ailment. His book does a fabulous job at making sense of what he saw, deeply rooted in his dynamic approach to life. Moreover, when a travelogue is also a memoir, it doubles up as a treasure trove of insight. It brings to life the generosity of spirit that humanity can invoke, the kind of generosity that ties Stephen so intimately to India – a country he made his own, and a people that have made him their own.

India is a country of sparkling conversations and breathtaking landscapes; of startling social discoveries and homely surprises; of deep flaws and deeper successes. It is, indeed, an ever-ever land. Stephen has been blessed in experiencing it whole – almost in its entirety. In that sense his history is as much India's as it is his own. His changing terms of engagement with the country – first as a young man discovering himself, and later as a reputed anthropologist and art historian – are both a reflection of the changing contours of the nation and his own evolving worldview.

In my own writing, I have spoken of India as a country that is much more than the sum of its parts. Jawaharlal Nehru 'discovered' it through history, civilization, and culture. Ambedkar did that through social reform and the instrumentalisation of law. When Stephen talks of being 'transformed' by India, he is both processing and discovering a country that escapes all conventional niches. Therefore, what you are delving into is a vibrant account of a life of eclectic experiences, lived to the fullest.

Written with warmth, clarity, and candour, this fascinating memoir is one I think you will enjoy. I also anticipate that, as in my case, you will come out of the book valuing your own transformations that little bit more.

Dr Shashi Tharoor
July 2024

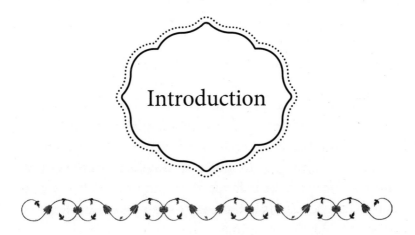

Introduction

When I was sixteen, I chose a single sentence from Herman Hesse's "Steppenwolf" to predict my life's trajectory. "Instead of narrowing your world and simplifying your soul, you will have to absorb more and more of the world and at last take all of it up into your painfully expanded soul, if you are ever to find peace."

Those sentences placed next to my portrait in my high school yearbook summed up the ambition of a sixteen-year-old. Half a century's immersion in India has underscored that. Now, replete in my seventies, I am at last at ease.

Frequently, people question my motives for working in and with South Asia. My answers are varied and complex. Chapter Fifteen discusses my origins, family, mentors, and the environment that helped sculpt my unusual character and choices.

Good fortune shines upon me. It always has. I recognize my privilege. Much of who and what I am was given to me without effort simply because of skin color, gender, and nationality. A tall white American male, one of a majority in my society, and yet a member of a relatively small minority in a world of cultural diversity. Compared with countless others, it may seem that my life has been without effort. Yet, I have worked hard throughout it to make a singular contribution, attempting to help balance the inequities. Efforts can never be enough. It is too easy to slip back into what is comfortable: the trappings of heritage and community.

This book is the story of how India has impacted my entire life since childhood: a process of ongoing adaptation and transformation.

~ 1 ~
Overland

I pedaled a bicycle rickshaw into India on my twentieth birthday. An old man, the vehicle's usual driver, grinned broadly as he held my pack on the seat behind me. I had arrived by local bus from the ancient capital city of Lahore. It was 1971, on the brink of India's last war with Pakistan, my first time in South Asia. To prepare for imminent battle, the two nations had closed all the usual land borders between them. Armaments and troops in full combat readiness, anti-aircraft missiles, and tanks covered with netted camouflage thronged both sides of the road. Only this one lonely outpost provided access to the permitted few.

Once the guards carefully verified my passport and visa, I walked across the border alone and found no buses or taxis to take me further—only that sole rickety rickshaw. I did not wish to trudge the eight kilometers into the nearest small town carrying my heavy pack, but I could not imagine allowing the spindly rickshaw-wala to propel me there. My solution to this dilemma was a novel negotiation and reversal of roles.

So began a lifetime of adventures in India. During the past fifty-two years, I have explored India by rickshaw, bicycle, camel, bullock cart, horse-drawn buggy, elephant, tuk-tuk, scooter, motorcycle, car, bus, plane, boat, and on foot. I have visited almost all the subcontinent's districts, painstakingly documenting their cultures and arts. I have genuinely felt the pulse of the country. Although crises, phenomenal inequities, and injustices in India have also affected my life, I deeply love this nation and its people.

* * *

Seventeen months earlier, in May 1970, I returned home to my small hometown of Ojai, California, after my first year in college. I had never been a good student, either in high school or now at the University of Denver. I loved learning, and read voraciously, but had trouble concentrating. I needed a job for the summer and asked Beatrice Wood if she'd hire me. Beatrice had been a neighbor all my life and was an internationally recognized ceramic artist, one of the original founders of the Dada Movement. An exotic elderly woman, she had always dressed in silk saris after her first trip to India ten years before. I gardened for her, cleaned her studio, and helped her prepare clay for throwing and sculpting. More than that, I was captivated by stories of her remarkable life and travels. Beatrice drew me out as no one ever had. She assessed my interests, discovering a passion for Native American art and culture, and a general interest in craftsmanship.

I was floored when she invited me to join her on a trip through India early in 1971. She explained that many of the rural and tribal cultures of India might hold an equal fascination for me. At school until then I had been interested in everything, but too distracted to focus well on my courses. Beatrice Wood's invitation changed all that. I returned to DU to prepare for our trip, taking courses in Indian art, history, and religions. Within the month, I became an A+ student, finding in one subcontinent a stimulus for all my varied interests. When, after a few months, Beatrice wrote that she had to cancel her Indian travels, I was disappointed but so riveted by my new courses of study that I determined to travel to India by myself later that year. I doubled up on preparatory courses, persuading the university to grant me an interdepartmental major in Indian studies drawn from seven different departments: an ideal match for my talents. As I learned more about Asian cultures, expanding my courses to include the Middle East and Islamic tradition, I decided that the ideal way to get there would be overland from Europe. My new status as a top student helped me persuade my parents that I was mature enough to make this choice.

Although I have some capacity for linear thinking, I have always excelled in a lateral approach to life, exploring how disciplines and practices interweave.

In studying art, I take particular interest in an object's history, why and how it was made and used, and its social and sometimes religious purpose. I improved my skills by writing papers for each course, and my professors appreciated my singular drive. In the spring, the university granted me an unusual privilege for an undergraduate: full college credit for my junior year if I satisfactorily conducted independent field research and wrote creditable papers.

Preparation for the overland trip was not easy. The few guidebooks about the countries through which I would pass—Turkey, Iran, Afghanistan, and Pakistan—described a class of travel far beyond my limited means. Aside from my textbooks, the best material I could find was in old issues of National Geographic: 1896, 1911, 1926, and 1932. They described overland journeys during quite different epochs, but at least they documented some of the indigenous cultures I would visit.

Upon my return to Ojai in May, I received a phone call from Helene Wheeler, a girl with whom I'd fallen in love at sixteen. At that age, we were too young for such a passionate relationship and broke up after several months. Now, three years later, we renewed our bonds. My infatuation with Helene made my decision to travel alone for a year more difficult, but my determination was unflagged.

On September 1st, I said goodbye to Helene and Beatrice and joined a charter plane from Denver bound for Paris. Students from universities in four adjoining states were all headed for their junior years abroad at European institutions. I was the only passenger destined for no fixed university program but intending to travel onward. In many ways, I became an even more different person during the next nine months.

* * *

The rustling of paper woke me from a deep slumber, and I peered over the edge of my upper berth. Ten days had passed, and I was aboard the old, run-down Orient Express on the first leg of my overland trip to India. Below me, my Iranian cabinmate was kneeling on an open newspaper in the middle of the floor while trying to read a compass in the dim light. As our shuddering train curved through a canyon on a mountain pass somewhere in the Balkans, he was desperately trying to find the precise direction of Mecca in order to perform his *Fajr* (dawn prayers) correctly. Our shifting course frustrated his efforts. With a rush of adrenaline, I realized that I was indeed approaching Asia and would be immersed there for the next nine months.

Istanbul beckoned like a veiled but intriguing woman. Nights were spent for less than a dollar in a cheap pension. Days were adventurous exploring the ancient, cobbled streets, many of its hundreds of mosques, and the enormous covered bazaar. The city's magnitude was overwhelming: its numerous lanes heading all directions, each filled with hundreds of shops, many of them glittering with priceless jewels or layered with blue-white-and-red ceramics or richly soft carpets of myriad patterns. Touts and shopkeepers called out: "Meestarrrrr! Come into my shop!" and "Allemagne? Francais? Eenglish? Amerika? Ok?" The odors in the bazaar conflicted and overlaid one another:

perfumes, heavy wool, innumerable bodies, and freshly ground coffees. I stopped in many shops to gaze and was always offered small glasses of delicious Turkish tea, usually consumed by slurping it through a lump of white sugar held in the teeth. Each evening's wander through crowded lanes allowed samplings of arrays of savories and sweets from carts and small cafes. As a foodie, I was hooked.

And then the legendary buildings: The size and rich beauty of the Byzantine Church of Hagia Sofia stunned me. Converted into a mosque by the conquering Ottomans, its roof remains dominated by one enormous dome that was the largest in the world for more than a millennium before the construction of St. Peter's in Rome. The shapes, forms, and interiors of other monuments, particularly the lofty Süleymaniye Mosque and its counterpart, the Blue Mosque, dumbfounded all sense of scale: vast walls of complex yet complementary patterned tiles both heightened and soothed the senses. Hours of quiet contemplation, my back against a soaring column, my bare feet soothed by apparent acres of hand-knotted prayer carpets all pointing toward Mecca. And finally, a full day exploring Topkapi Palace, the former residence and seat of power of generations of Ottoman sultans. For the first time since 1927, the refurbished rooms of the Harem, home to the Sultan's hundreds of wives, concubines, and eunuchs, had just opened to the public. After officials led a group of tourists to see this unveiled wonder, they allowed me to wander through the hundreds of rooms at will and examine in detail anything I saw. The previous year I had studied

Islamic design, but here, immersed in chambers filled with skillfully rendered shapes and motifs, I fully comprehended the creative heights these artists had achieved. In the months and years since that day, all visits have been strictly controlled and limited to specific highlights. The dazzling beauty of Topkapi's Harem remains one of the high points of my life.

While in Istanbul, I received a cable from Beatrice Wood explaining that her trip to India had been reinstated and she would meet me in Delhi. Her personal introductions in that country would prove invaluable.

Eleven days in Turkey whetted my appetite to return to that country someday soon. I found the Turks accessible and friendly. Most women there had been unveiled since the time of Ataturk in the late 1920s, and, even though I had conversations with relatively few of them, it appeared to me that they had gained more social equality than in most other Muslim nations. The savory and complex flavors of Turkish food delighted me. Upon entering a Turkish restaurant and requesting the owner or maître d' to choose the best dishes, more than once I was asked by Turkish patrons to join them and share in their food as they barraged me with friendly questions about my country, and its politics. My study of Turkish history and art the previous year was helpful: each person I met was openly proud of their culture and pleased that I had taken the time to learn about it. They seemed to enjoy setting me straight when they felt I misjudged a particular point, encouraging me into friendly conversational sparring that made me feel right at home. Leaving Istanbul by train and then bus, I continued to feel welcomed into engaging discussions across the country.

* * *

I reached Cappadocia on September 22, 1970. A 1958 issue of National Geographic had piqued my determination to see this series of small villages carved out of unusual stone formations amid the Anatolian Plateau. My room in the town of Göreme was actually cut out of one of the tall conical formations of soft volcanic stone that abutted the community. Surrounding my hotel were homes with brightly painted wooden doors directly set into cliffs. Windows alongside them were adorned with boxes of blooming flowers and even house number plates. Builders could employ the most basic tools to carve the pumice-like stone into rooms and shelters. Caves in Cappadocia were first chiseled into settlements in Neolithic times. Early Christians escaped Roman persecution by hiding out there. The remains of each subsequent era are evident in these villages, some worn away into unusable ruins, others still occupied by the descendants of families who have lived there for centuries.

On my first evening, a few other foreign tourists who had reached this remote area suggested we pool our resources to hire a cab to take us on a full-day tour of other sights. At one point, I requested we stop to photograph a grouping of odd stone cones that resembled the drip castles I had created as a child on a California beach. The position of the sun caused a glare, so I asked the others to wait while I walked through a vineyard and into the shadow of a singular three-story-high cone. Around the corner was a small open-sided barn carved into the base. I saw no one, called out, and received no answer. It was evident that the vintner and his animals were elsewhere on his farm. When I peered inside, I was astonished to find that Byzantine frescoes covered the walls and ceiling of the straw-laden room. I had discovered an unregistered church dating long before the fifteenth century when the Byzantines were ousted. A later search of guidebooks and art histories provided no mention of this building. Today, Cappadocia is a primary tourist site with many fine hotels and tens of thousands of daily visitors. I was lucky to be there before it was well known.

* * *

An overnight train deposited me in the northeastern Turkish mountain town of Erzurum, where the locomotive system ended. Although the network from Europe through Turkey was well developed, train travel into and across Iran and Afghanistan was not possible during that time. A night's sojourn was required before the single weekly bus to Iran departed, scheduled for five o'clock the next morning. I staggered down to the bus station at four thirty to find no vehicle: only the wreck of a Mercedes bus. Other passengers arrived followed by the driver and his helper, who explained that this salvaged junkheap was the only vehicle available for eastern travel for the next seven days. Competent mechanics had managed to make it operable. Most potential passengers wisely returned home. I was on a tight schedule and did not want to lose an entire week waiting for a better bus.

The wreck that had been scheduled to carry us for the full day had recently missed one of the hairpin curves of the pass we were about to renegotiate and had plunged down the mountainside, completely crushing its front end. Apparently, the chassis and both axles remained intact. Combining thrift with Turkish mechanical ingenuity, a local shop had used sheets of plywood to replace the front twenty feet of the long vehicle's body. Small, uncovered windows had been jig-sawed out for the driver to see through, while an entrance door had been hinged and secured with rope. Perched on a wooden stool nailed onto the plywood platform was the same driver who had survived the accident. He navigated the hairpin turns with a wheel that had been spot-welded back into place. His assistant, the conductor, leaned out a small side window in the door to help him keep on track. We seven foolish passengers, three Afghans desperate to get home, two seriously ill Frenchmen, a young Japanese traveler, and me, congregated at the very rear in the undamaged section of the bus as far away from the driver as we could reach. And then we all prayed as we drove for the next fourteen hours up steep and winding mountain passes cresting just below the peak of Mount Ararat. On the same spot where, according to the Biblical story, Noah's ark was supposed to have come to rest, and all the people and animals of the world repopulated, we stopped briefly for bowls of warm soup: our only food during that long day. The only denizens of the place were the bedraggled old cook and his wife—no animals.

That bus trip seemed interminable. We crossed over the border into Iran at three thirty that afternoon. At eight o'clock, in the city of Tabriz, we shifted into a second bus that was undamaged. Somehow, we had survived the first hair-raising portion of the trip! This new vehicle was full of Iranians, and the only seats for us were atop our luggage in the aisle. Every few minutes, the seated passengers on either side of us spat tobacco juice into the aisle, not bothering to try to miss us. It was not a pleasant experience, but, as I was to learn, we seven foreigners were fair game. At eleven thirty that night, several passengers disembarked and, finally, an aisle seat opened up for me. My male seatmate and those around me initially seemed pleasant and asked many questions about America and family life there.

Two hours later, stopping alongside a bakery, I quickly ran outside to buy macaroons. (My only food all day had been the soup eleven hours earlier.) When I reentered the bus, someone had taken my seat, directing me to the only vacant space—next to an old, black-veiled woman. She elbowed me painfully in the ribs and spat on me, at which point all the passengers erupted into laughter. When I asked the same men who had previously seemed pleasant about the reason for her actions, they jeered and refused to answer. My only choice was to crowd myself as far away from the old crone as possible, but exhaustion from that long day overcame me. Any time my clothing touched hers on the narrow seat, she again jabbed me in my side and spat on me, which caused further gales of laughter from the rest of the bus. Several excruciating hours later, the man who had occupied my seat briefly arose to talk to someone else, and I was back there in a flash. He had no option then but to sit where I had just been where he, too, was elbowed by the veiled woman. Two hours later, bruised and unhappy, I reached our destination: the capital city of Tehran.

***

Although expecting to spend several days there, I left after only two nights. The atmosphere of that city was particularly oppressive: abject poverty; homeless families; children malnourished, diseased and starving; and widespread begging. The juxtaposition with the conspicuous wealth of the upper classes was jarring. Chauffeured Mercedes and Cadillacs vied in the heavy traffic with Porsches and Maseratis. Air-conditioned European boutiques lined streets of homeless families, showcase windows displayed furs, elegant fashions, and diamond-encrusted jewelry. I found it revolting. That was, of course, long before American cities began to offer similar views of a blatantly wealthy consumerism that offends our own impoverished citizens homeless on our streets. After my experiences with delicacies wherever I traveled in Turkey, I was discouraged by the food in Iran. I searched for restaurants or cafes serving local recipes but could find none. Most of the fare was disappointing American-style hamburgers, fries, and hot dogs!

My favorite professor at the University of Denver, Dr. Charles Geddes, was partial to Persian culture. Under his guidance, I had spent a year studying Islamic history, culture, and religion. He had prepared me to fall in love with Iran as he had. I did not. Iran is the only country of the forty-three that I've visited in my life that I disliked. My visit was during the last shah's reign—a totalitarian, corrupt regime supported and justified by

America. I sympathized with Iranian antipathy to my country. But in the past fifty years, I've traveled in many nations where our foreign policy has made the people understandably suspicious of and even vehemently opposed to our politics. In each other country, several of them Muslim, I was warmly accepted on my own merits and made to feel welcome. Not in Iran. People from each level of society (the wealthy, the middle classes, and the destitute) were all antagonistically rude to me—not only on that trip but again when Helene and I spent several weeks traveling there in 1974. I admire Iran's ancient cultures and the sophistication of its art, but everyone I met there was offensive.

Interestingly, in the many decades that have passed since, I have met many immigrant Iranians. Without exception, they have been charming, kind, and well-mannered. I do not pretend to understand the stark discrepancy between those inhabiting their native country and those now living beyond its boundaries. I fully accept that the obvious inequities and social strife that prevailed when we visited Iran could cause a shift in character, but that does not explain to me the blatant rudeness of each person I met there—and nowhere else.

* * *

During my bus trip onward to Mashhad, I suffered from my first case of amoebic dysentery. My bus had no toilet, and the Persian desert is flat and endless, with little vertical growth. I had no choice but to request a halt, run out into the desert, turn away from the other passengers, and do what I had to do. I learned an important lesson in humility and that one can overcome one's strongest learned proprieties when circumstances demand. However, I was made more uncomfortable when during each of the six or eight times this situation occurred, the Iranians on the bus pointed and laughed at me through the windows and then jeered as I reentered. In India and elsewhere I have traveled, significant inequities and racial and cultural prejudices certainly exist, but I've rarely observed public ridicule of another's misfortunes. The only bright spot of that eighteen-hour bus ride was during its last third when we stopped to board a farmer and his three prized goats. A beautiful, golden-fleeced goat occupied the seat next to me—a far friendlier companion than any I had previously met in that blighted country.

* * *

Crossing the border into Afghanistan was an almost immediate change of cultural and emotional atmosphere. Afghans throughout the country were friendly, welcoming, and thoughtful. The next two weeks were divided between the three cities of Herat, Kandahar, and Kabul, and I found each attractive, even compelling. Herat was the most traditional of the three: adobe architecture, dirt streets lined with pine trees, herds of goats and sheep, camel caravans arriving and departing, horse-drawn carriages and carts interrupted by an occasional single car or truck. Here, as elsewhere in this ancient, small nation, the men were all turbaned, the women fully veiled, but even though there was a strict division of gender, I sensed a gentle relationship between the people. They were proud of their culture and observed strict Muslim laws of conduct and deportment, but each person I met was direct, generous, and sweet-natured. Although Kandahar and particularly Kabul contained many more cosmopolitan features—paved streets, a few moderate high-rises, motorized vehicles, and even traffic lights—these small cities appeared to blend well the traditional with the contemporary. It was a country that rightfully cherished its unique heritage while in transition toward modernity.

* * *

I was unprepared for the massive influx of young western and far eastern travelers. As yet, there was virtually no awareness in the United States of this eastern migration—what later became known as "The Hippie Trail." Until this point, my transportation in Asia had been local with few other foreigners and no Americans. But on the border, I encountered the first of many overland buses bearing motley assortments of young travelers from countries all over Europe plus a few from North America. Tickets were available in London, Paris, and elsewhere to Delhi or Kathmandu for as little as seventy-five dollars. This realization floored me. Individuals from assorted backgrounds, before learning of the journey's low cost, either had no intention of traveling through Asia or only the vaguest fantasy of doing so. Many seemed startled to find themselves so far afield. It appeared that I was among the few who had prepared for this trip, studying the histories and cultures of the peoples I would be meeting. Many fellow travelers were only interested in easy access to cheap drugs and the exotic, however that might present itself. Many of the men were long-haired and bearded, while both men and women wore a mishmash of clothing picked up en route. Their appearance and morality were a stark and often upsetting contrast to the conservative peoples of our host country. And yet I also espoused many of their philosophies. They injected a cosmopolitan sense of interaction and communication: young men and women from more than a dozen nations who compared travel stories and shared information about the various idiosyncrasies of places throughout the world.

In Turkey, I had been determined to avoid offers of hashish as I traveled—fully aware of the many foreigners lost in prisons there because of their transgressions. However, cannabis products were legal to purchase and consume in Afghanistan, and I gladly experimented alongside newfound European friends. Prudently, I never let myself get lost in drugs. I saw many there and later on my trip who became addicts, derelict, even begging for food. I even knew some who died from it.

My French language skills were moderate and friendships among French men and women were easy to make. Unlike many of these other travelers, I preferred walking out into the city streets by myself, going into cafes, shops, and markets frequented only by the locals and interacting with them. Returning to my hotel, I learned that other Westerners generally kept their own company. By being alone and naturally engaging, I reached out to meet and get to know the people of Afghanistan as much as I could: the beginning of a trajectory that became far more developed in India.

As elsewhere, the hotels I occupied were just above the lowest grade. I met hippies (or freaks as we then called ourselves) whose accommodations were indeed rock bottom. Mine was quite basic, but usually relatively clean with indoor plumbing, if often down the hall. I carried my own sheets (not a sleeping bag because others had advised that it would be too hot). Indigenous food was readily available and delicious in Afghanistan: beef, lamb, or chicken kebabs grilled in coal-burning clay ovens and served with thick, seeded flatbread and a variety of spiced vegetable dishes.

My single backpack was tightly organized: sheets, a cotton sweater, a windbreaker, two pairs of trousers, three shirts, a seersucker suit and tie, underwear, socks, shoes that interchanged with Birkenstock sandals, a rechargeable electric razor, and limited toiletries. A couple of books, prepared notes condensed from a variety of sources, National Geographic maps, my journal, a pad of paper, airmail stationery, and a couple of pens completed my luggage. I wrote Helene almost daily and other friends frequently, remaining constant to Helene, while spurning the many offers of female companionship from new friends. My consequent loneliness resulted in increasingly steamy letters that begged her to join me for at least a couple of weeks in South India during her Christmas vacation. I even made an expensive three-minute phone call to her from Kabul, booked three days ahead, and relayed through a series of operators in Tehran, Istanbul, and Paris before our shouted discussion commenced.

Helene was impressed by the call but discouraged any hope that she might be able to fly to India in December.

Before leaving Ojai, I had pre-addressed and stamped nine sets of envelopes to thirty-one friends and family members and purchased a cheap gelatin copier. Once a month, I wrote a long group letter to them summing up my experiences. When received by my parents, my diligent mother typed it up, copied it, and mailed it to each. The originals, plus my journals, form the basis for the three chapters describing this first trip.

* * *

Before leaving America, I had spoken in detail with two sets of friends who had recently lived in Afghanistan: my cousin Patty and her husband Mick Sullivan, and Dr. and Mrs. Bill Doane, close friends of my parents. Dr. Doane had served a year as a physician to the U.S. embassy in Kabul. When Patty and Mick were first married, they spent two years traveling overland from Spain to India, teaching at military bases along the way. They continued on around the world and were able to end their trip with slightly more money than when they began. All four had loved the country and its people. They had told me that the culture successfully combined the wisdom and insights of ancient traditions with marvelous storytelling and great imagination. I wanted to bring with me something that might unlock these imaginations. In my pack, two treasures from America had been saved for that country: a giant bubble-wand and tray and a large bottle of liquid soap.

I first brought them out in Kandahar. The window of my inexpensive hotel room overlooked a busy night bazaar. Enormous bubbles blew out over the milling crowd of Afghans below. As I had hoped, they had never seen anything like them and responded in pure delight. One bubble flew into the adjoining room's window, and the heads of four Pakistani men peered out, begging me to bring my amazing device into their room. As I created huge bubbles for them, a tiny old man dressed in gold pajamas and a gold embroidered cap jumped up and down on his bed, laughing and clapping his hands. An in-depth conversation unfolded into a two-hour discussion in which we compared our two countries. With success, I repeated my experiment on two different days in the capital city of Kabul. I climbed an old barren tree on a hill in the central city park and began to make bubbles. My efforts drew a large and friendly crowd who stood below me, arms outstretched to catch them. In reflection, I have always been embarrassed by my audacity, but this act succeeded in opening doors. A group of Afghans encouraged me to join them for chai and pastries in a local tea shop and asked me questions about America.

* * *

I left Kabul in mid-October to cross the legendary Khyber Pass by bus, entering Pakistan. It was hard for me to depart. I felt a bond with the Afghan culture incomparable to any previous experience. At the end of my nine-month trip, I rated Afghanistan as one of my favorite countries. If their traditional arts and crafts had been more diverse and complex, and if I had not had such a unique introduction to India, I might have chosen a different path. With long hindsight, I am grateful for the choice I made. But at the time, I was amazed by the thoughtful acceptance of the many Afghans I had met. I longed to return. In my journal, I wrote: "I had heard the myth of Afghanistan long before coming there. I had underestimated its greatness. I speak only of south and central Afghanistan, a country of dust, mud houses, few trees, windswept sun, and the spirit of powerful beauty. Its people are strongly distinct, peaceful with the underlying force of great endurance, extremely proud, coupled with a sense of true humility, permeated with amazing creativity. They are a striking balance of soft and hard, of laughter and sadness, of external poverty and great internal beauty. They have a spark of great LIFE in their eyes, and a great capacity of warmth and understanding in their souls. I give them the greatest compliment I can give anyone: they live unto their hearts."

Certainly, as a naïve nineteen-year-old, I idealized the country. I had little conversation with women there, but those I did meet (not all women were veiled at that time) were friendly and spoke to me without rancor of living in balanced, accepted lives within their communities. It was eight years before the Soviet invasion, more than two decades before the founding of the Taliban, and thirty years before the U.S. invasion in response to the disasters of 9/11. During those later years, political strife untenably affected the majority of the population. The violence perpetrated against them resulted in internal violence and closed-mindedness that has altered the nature of many Afghans, perhaps irrevocably. Whenever I read or hear news about the latest atrocities, my heart bleeds for the Afghans I knew and learned to respect.

* * *

Pakistan was on the brink of war with India. It was not an easy time to traverse it. My original plan had been to visit many of the ancient sites from north to south, but it was evident that if I wanted to enter India, I would have to do so before the imminent war began. In consequence, I spent only one night each in Rawalpindi and Peshawar and three nights in the old Mughal-Sikh capital of Punjab. In the latter, I took the time to explore the majestic Shalimar Gardens and the old Lahore Fort and spent a day in the Lahore Museum, whose consummate collections had been compiled by and overseen by Rudyard Kipling's father. My intention of spending weeks of exploration of Pakistani regions and cultures was not realized then or, indeed, ever. The military was highly visible: sandbagging major monuments, drilling in large platoons, deploying anti-aircraft missiles, tanks, and other weaponry alongside the roads, and covering them with camouflage. Posters and graffiti boldly stated: "Crush India."

It was imperative that I cross the border into India without hesitation, but I had limited choices. The new nations had been adversaries since 1947, when the British unwisely defined new political borders that cut directly through ancient districts of homogeneous inhabitants. In order to create a purely Muslim country, Pakistan, these imperial rulers enforced a deadline that allowed little time to make such a monumental move.

Hindus and Sikhs left almost all possessions they had accrued during centuries of habitation in the region to travel into newly independent India. Those who wished to join the new Muslim nation had similar issues and only days to negotiate their journey. Tens of millions migrated from each side in total chaos, resulting in riots and massacres unparalleled in recent history. India and Pakistan have technically been in a state of war ever since. The impending war was the third escalation to outright conflict in the thirty-four years since partition. To prevent further unconscionable violence, both sides barricaded all the usual crossings along the 2,000-mile border. I was lucky to make it across. To do so, I boarded an early morning bus bound for a remote access point that had only just opened, far from any large and potentially violent community. That is how I ended up entering India alone on my twentieth birthday.

~ 2 ~
Transformation

Beauty surrounded me. I sat cross-legged on a balcony overlooking a large room filled with Sikh devotees in the heights of spiritual ecstasy. It was the evening of my twentieth birthday at the end of my first day in India: October 27, 1971. That morning, I had crossed the border and driven a bicycle rickshaw several miles to the town of Ferozepur in the Punjab, surprised at the clear blue of the sky and the endless golden wheat fields, many being harvested by tractor—an indication of unexpected prosperity. As we approached the town, my legs grew tired, unaccustomed to pumping the bike pedals that pulled the heavy load. Military jeeps, tanks, and trucks carrying missile projectors passed me going the other direction. The drivers honked, while the soldiers waved.

India, too, was barricading itself for war. On the walls of farmhouses and the sides of town buildings, signs bore the ominous words: "Crush Pakistan!" I had no desire to stick around and took the first train north to Amritsar, the sacred center of the Sikh religion.

At the gates of the famed Golden Temple, Sri Harmandir Sahib, a friendly volunteer escorted me to one of the many hostels within the temple precinct. Along with thousands of others, I would be a guest for the next three days. The temple provides free accommodation and sustenance throughout the year to all seekers regardless of religion, background, position, age, or income. I dropped my pack next to my bed in a secured men's dormitory, bathed in a discreet communal shower, and changed into fresh clothing. A second volunteer then ushered me to the vast dining hall for a meal of chapatis, rice, dal, and vegetable curry. Once I had eaten as much as I wanted and cleaned my own brass platter, I finally entered the inner compound and beheld the Golden Temple.

It seemed mythic, appearing to float in the exact center of a large rectangular tank or reservoir. At this distance, its lower third looked pure white, while its upper two stories gleamed in dazzling gold. A wide walkway patterned in marble tiles surrounded the tank. Throngs of pilgrims circumambulated in prayer while others bathed on steps leading down into the sacred waters. I joined in a slow meditative walk to enter a large marble gateway encrusted with gold and inlaid with floral designs picked out in semiprecious stones. Polished brass rails framed a long causeway. The Golden Temple astounded my senses. Finely wrought solid gold plates covered the exterior of the upper floors. Most of the men wore crisp and colorful silk turbans, *kurtas*, and pajamas while the women were dressed in their finest silk saris bedecked with gold jewelry. Together, one mass of multi-hued bodies surged to the left to walk once around the inner sanctum. The white marble walls of this ground floor were also patterned in exquisite inlays of semiprecious stones: lapis lazuli, malachite, jasper, carnelian, and more. Returning to the front door, we entered the temple.

Occupying the center of the room was a plinth, upon which rested an enormous gold-bound book. A turbaned priest sang out the words in an appealing tenor. Other priests on each side constantly fanned this book, the *Guru Granth Sahib*, or *Holy Granth*, believed by all Sikhs to be more than just the word of God, but divine presence itself. Orthodox Sikhs, unlike their neighboring Hindus, do not worship images of Gods and Goddesses. They posit that the Divine takes no incarnate form other than that of the Word and that they are in the presence of God when viewing the *Guru Granth Sahib* and hearing its intoned phrases. Sikh *gurdwaras*, or temples containing versions of the *Granth Sahib*, are scattered throughout India and around the world. But the Golden Temple here in Amritsar is sacrosanct, much as the Vatican and adjacent St. Peter's is for Roman Catholic Christians and the Kaaba in Mecca is for all Muslims.

That evening, as on every day of the year, many hundreds of devotees struggled to be as close as possible to this Holy of Holies. Strong incense was continually wafted through the room by the fanning priests to offset the intense body odors. Oppressed by the crowd,

I discovered that I could climb one floor and sit quietly undisturbed on a balcony overlooking the milling masses, remaining there in a meditative trance for many hours until the last ceremony of the night. Then the enormous book was closed, wrapped in brocaded cloths, placed in a golden palanquin, and carried out of the sanctum with a blaze of trumpets and drums, down the long causeway and into a secondary temple where priests put it to bed for the night. My twentieth birthday had been glorious.

During my hours of contemplation that evening, the murals on the columns and surrounding walls of the balcony intrigued me. They seemed to blend the artistic styles of European illuminated manuscripts with the designs of Persian, Mughal, and Rajput miniatures. I wanted to record them, but no cameras are ever allowed in the temple. The next morning, I determined to find representations on postcards or temple guidebooks, but none existed. Officials explained that the interior had never been photographed or reproduced and never would be. Undaunted and persistent, I applied for information from the temple historian who explained that the current guru of the Sikh School of Art was the son of the last man in a long succession of artists to paint those murals. After searching through the crowded lanes surrounding the temple, I found a studio where a dignified old gentleman, G.S. Sohan Singh, greeted me. His hospitality epitomized that of many Sikhs I was to befriend later. This venerable artist welcomed me in for cups of tea as he kindly showed me his own portfolio. Remember, I had entered with no introduction. His oils, watercolors, and acrylics depicted Sikh historic battles, epic legends, landscapes, and genre scenes. As fine as these were, did he have any of his father's work? In response, he opened boxes containing dozens of gesso paintings by Bhai Gian Singh Naqqash. All were studies that his father had created before painting the same murals I had fallen in love with the previous night. They were fabulous, each appearing better than the last! Asked if he would consider selling any of them, Sohan Singhji seemed surprised. He commented that he was deeply pleased and would be honored to sell me a few. My budget was small with a long and unpredictable trip in India ahead of me. I could not offer to purchase them at that time, but this famous artist agreed to keep chosen paintings until I could return with payment, even with the explanation that it might take several years. This experience was seminal and foretold my future relationship with many Indian artists and artisans. From entering the temple, sitting in quiet meditation, falling in love with its art, searching out and meeting an accomplished artist, and creating a bond that would later burgeon, I was setting the tone for the next half-century. And this was only my second day in India!

    The Golden Temple had given me a benchmark that was hard to top. Dazzled by my three days of deep immersion in the beauty and spiritual presence, witnessing the temple's organization, Sikhism's relative egalitarianism, and the fact that Sikh women are considered equal in power and influence to men—other experiences paled in comparison. I embraced this fundamental change after five weeks in strict Muslim countries where most women were veiled and acted subservient to men, except in Istanbul and some regions of Turkey.

* * *

Before I left the States, many travelers warned me that I would suffer from culture shock in my first days and weeks in India. I did not. I felt at ease in India from the first moment, although I would have preferred to view it initially without the trappings of imminent war. The combination of several factors aided my adaptation. My parents had taken me traveling at a young age and encouraged me to meet and converse with people from many different cultures. My family and community had taught me to place a paradigm on open-minded acceptance of that which I did not know. And I had diligently prepared for more than a year by reading everything I could, taking more than a dozen courses about India, and absorbing information from all I could meet who had been there. Without question, my gradual immersion in Asia had eased me into my current experiences, beginning with Istanbul. Finally, my overriding optimism was abetted by a core belief in positive outcomes. If anything, my culture shock happened months later in South India's Deccan Plateau and then fully when I returned home. I describe both in Chapter Three.

A few days after my birthday in late October 1971, a third-class compartment transported me by train from Amritsar to Delhi, the first of many such trips. My Indian budget of two dollars a day did not allow a higher grade of travel. India abolished third-class trains more than forty years ago. They were extremely basic: not much more than cargo cars fitted with hard wooden benches and metal luggage racks. The bathrooms were repulsive: just a hole in a filthy floor revealing the rushing tracks below, its sides encrusted with the leavings of scores of previous visitors, often with not enough water to flush. The reek would permeate the rest of the car that, in most cases, was so crowded that I would be lucky to carve out a tiny sitting space. The compressed explosion of bodies might have resembled the New York subway at rush hour, except that a journey in Indian third class could last many hours, even days. But I was there to experience India fully, and made the most of it, discovering that each person became friendly when met eye to eye. When asked about themselves and their community, conversations unfolded, and soon I felt among a group of old friends. That was made easier by the fact that India had been ruled by British for nearly two centuries. At least one English speaker came forward in each group I met, often more. Sometimes our communication was rudimentary at first. Still, it usually did not take long for me to adapt to the accent and colloquial constructions and drop into deep conversations.

My first two nights in New Delhi simmered in the soothing luxury of an American diplomat's home. Galen Stone was a good friend of Uncle Coulter, my father's brother. Mr. and Mrs. Stone replenished me with American style food missed during two months away from home.

* * *

I arrived in the capital city just ten days before Beatrice Wood. She had suggested that I call her close friend, Kamaladevi Chattopadhyay, who invited me for tea the next morning at her home in the heart of what had been the British residential area. A walk through the quiet and wide tree-lined streets took me past sets of gates opening into large houses with gardens—so different from anything I had experienced in the past months. Abundant birdsong, not the cacophony of human congestion, teased my eardrums. Kamaladevi, a tiny old woman in a plain grey cotton sari, grimly invited me to sit in her flower-filled garden while she poured us cups of tea. She was a legend throughout India. In the 1920s she had become a non-violent freedom fighter and social reformer, joining Mohandas K. Gandhi's inner circle. In 1930, Kamaladevi was a key leader of the famous Salt March protesting unfair British taxes on the one of the essentials for survival in the extreme heat of India's mainland. She spent five years in prison for her non-violent opposition to British Rule, including one full year in solitary confinement. After the horrific massacres in 1947 during the partition of India, this stoic woman founded key organizations to help provide emergency aid and rehabilitation to the millions of victims. Then, during the first decade of Indian independence, Kamaladevi introduced the country's first handloom weaving centers and crafts cooperatives—initially in major cities, but soon established in virtually every district of the new republic. She also developed the first museums of Indian indigenous crafts. In her late sixties, she still spent much of her year traveling the country, encouraging the restoration and ongoing production of traditional and innovative handmade items. It was she who had invited and sponsored Beatrice's first two trips to India, and she was pivotal to the one that was soon to begin.

To be truthful, I was put off initially by this great woman's apparent brusque and unfriendly manner. Try as I might, I couldn't make her smile or even express herself other than coldly. I was later to learn from Beatrice that Kamaladevi was a profoundly shy woman who continuously had to battle against her own nature to converse with others. She asked many questions, wanting to know the scope of my intended travel and research. I explained that I hoped to make a six-month circle tour of India as the first leg of a cross-cultural survey of traditional Indian folk arts and crafts—a project I hoped would last my lifetime. Kamaladevi asked me to return at the same time the next morning with a map marked with my intended route.

In my backpack, I carried a National Geographic map of India, creased and torn through frequent examination during my months of travel. Back at the Stones' residence, I drew a line with a colored pen following India's comprehensive train system and included each destination I had read about and planned to visit. The next day, this venerable woman offered to arrange meetings with leaders of India's crafts movement in each place I had circled. She even suggested I visit regions that I had not previously considered. Then, in her dry and humorless voice, Kamaladevi informed me that she would write letters to many weavers, artists, artisans, and craft organizers requesting that they host me in their homes. Her generosity provided me with the unparalleled gift of staying in homes wherever I chose to travel and meeting the pundits in my field of study. I have never met any other human being, Indian or foreign, who has been introduced to the breadth of India in this way. On that day, Kamaladevi launched my entire career!

That evening she arranged for me to shift residence from the Stone's home to the apartment of the then-director of the Delhi Crafts Council. I spent several days with her and her husband while they introduced me to other individuals who had made significant contributions to the craft movement. These meetings were integrated with sightseeing—visiting the Mughal palaces and the Jama Masjid (the Friday Mosque) in Old Delhi, the National Museum, and the National Crafts Museum. While viewing the vast and varied collections of folk art in this latter institution, I knew I had chosen the right profession and yearned to learn more. The director, Ajit Mookerjee, whose published work on Indian mandalas I greatly admired, insisted on reading the illustrated essays on the same subject I'd written the previous year for college courses. Although I felt my work was too green for publication, his praise significantly boosted my self-confidence as a writer.

After my arduous overland travel across Asia, I happily settled into Delhi for two full weeks. Kamaladevi moved me to a second home in far south Delhi as a guest of Shami Sawhney and his wife, Teni. Within hours, I had bonded with this couple and their two sons. Their home was spacious and comfortable, decorated with museum-worthy works of art. I was given my own room and told to come and go as I wished. They treated me as a close relative, fattening me with delectable meals and encouraging conversations about a multitude of subjects. The Sawhneys deepened my appreciation of many aspects of Indian culture. As a key member of the All-India Handicrafts Board, Auntie Teni, as I called her, made suggestions that guided my research.

But perhaps this family's most long-lasting influence on me was their introduction of North Indian classical music. Auntie Teni was an accomplished vocal musician, while her eldest son, Nandan, studied sitar with one of India's pre-eminent sitarists: Ustad Vilayat Khan. During my week there, they hosted a house concert: a fully engaged audience of twenty as this celebrated artist played for us alone. Nandan sat next to me, discreetly coaching me in the subtle nuances of his guru's masterful techniques.

Beatrice's appearance shocked me when I picked her up at Delhi's International Airport a few days later and escorted her to the hotel Kamaladevi had arranged. At seventy-nine, she was ill with bronchitis that progressed into pneumonia. I was afraid she would die, but she rested in her room for several days and improved enough to resume her planned activities. Together we visited the Crafts Museum and several private homes with excellent collections of Indian folk art.

Beatrice had the most developed artistic eye I had ever known. She saw everything, and I learned as much by observing her as I did by listening to her fascinating stories. She was a truly open-minded individual, interfacing with everyone, interested in who and what they were. During her two previous trips through India, she had often strayed from the tourist path to marvel at local cultures and traditions. This time her travels were sponsored by the US Information Service. As she flew across Western Asia, she had lectured about American craftsmanship in Istanbul, Tehran, and Kabul. During the coming months in India, she had been scheduled to give similar presentations in cities around India. Before that happened, we would be several weeks together in the far south.

* * *

Back on the road, I spent three nights in the old Mughal city of Agra visiting the famed Taj Mahal, the Agra Fort, and Fatehpur Sikri. It's embarrassing to admit that although recognizing the Taj's beauty and elegance, I had been so impressed by that of the Golden Temple in Amritsar that I was disappointed by this monument. It took me years to recognize that my initial impression was wrong. The two monuments are incomparable, but the Taj is rightfully regarded as one of the world's most perfectly designed structures.

While trying to get from Agra to Varanasi (also correctly known as Banaras) with two new American friends, Jim and Fermin, we were required to disembark our third-class train at Kanpur station and spend several hours sitting in the cold of the platform while we awaited our connection. Discovering a mutual love of train blues allowed us to while away our time by scat-singing harmonies, much to the amusement of the huddled Indians surrounding us. When we boarded the second train, we found only standing room available for the next seven hours of our journey. I climbed onto the jammed luggage rack and stretched my long body over six irregular feet of suitcases and duffels. The curved roof made it impossible for me to relax, and I was only able to keep from falling by gripping the support rail as hard as I could.

I had unwisely refused Kamaladevi's offer of residing in a friend's home in Varanasi, believing I could stay as a guest of an Indian traveler I'd met in Afghanistan. Upon arrival, I discovered that his address did not exist and that he was untraceable. Unfortunately, my mail had been sent to his fictitious house, and all was lost, including a letter from Helene that was crucial. I moved into a basic room with Jim and Fermin—probably the worst accommodation of my long nine-month trip. But for twenty-five cents a day for each of us, it served a purpose. At least there were no bedbugs.

Varanasi might be the longest continuously lived-in city in the world. It was old by the time Gautama Buddha preached nearby in the sixth century BC. The legendary Ganges River flowed just a couple of hundred yards from our lodge. It entranced me from the moment I saw it. Before dawn on my second morning there, I discovered an ancient peepul tree that overlooked the river in an area of the city rarely visited by tourists. From this elevated spot, the broad expanse of water spread each direction. In the predawn dusk, hundreds of tiny oil lamps floated on its luminescent surface. Fading into the distant mist as far as I could see, thousands of worshippers stood on the bank and in the water praying to the soon-rising sun. Nothing suggested the modern age. For the first time, I sensed that alongside this river the veil of time is almost transparent—one had only to squint the eyes to peer back through successive centuries. I have returned to this spot on each of my several dozen visits to Varanasi and always feel revitalized and repossessed by its spell. Tradition states that the Ganges has curative powers, and I joined the tens of thousands of Hindu residents and pilgrims to bathe in its waters. When I mentioned this fact in my monthly group letter, I unleashed an enormous backlash from my parents and their many friends. The Ganges was often described in foreign press then as now as being highly unsanitary. I was judged by that "foolish action" for years. Despite their worries, I did not become ill, at least not there.

* * *

North India's food initially challenged me. After savory but subtle meals across the Middle East, the intensity of exotic spices barraged my tastebuds. I have always been a foodie. I'd spent several summers working in restaurants as a teenager, training as a sous chef to prepare fine dinners. I loved to cook and to explore unusual flavors, but, before this trip, I'd had little exposure to Indian cuisine. Even though I'd been raised in California and liked Mexican food, I realize now that the menus had been considerably toned down for middle-American palates. I enjoyed North Indian tandooris, biriyanis, and curried vegetables, but was unprepared for potent chilis and peppers. Women hosts or their cooks proffered their favorite delicacies, and I ate what they served, but often suffered from indigestion later.

I returned to Delhi by bus and train, stopping en route to visit the temples of Khajuraho. Their sublime architecture gracefully reflects mythic mountain peaks covered with myriad sacred and mundane figures. The site remains at the top of my list of thousands of classical Hindu temples. While there, I explored my first rural Indian village several miles from the monuments, impressed by the amorphous forms of adobe farmhouses that would later become a favorite subject of my field research. Outside the village, the tik-tok-clack of wooden bells around the necks of a herd of goats rang down the hillside. I spoke at some length with the white-turbaned goatherd and was allowed to purchase one of the hand-carved bells. Six months later, I carried it over my shoulder on the international flights home. It rings each time I open one of the interior doors of our house in Maine today and reminds me of that first Indian village half a century ago.

Beatrice was still unwell when I returned to Delhi and Kamaladevi remarked that the cold December north Indian climate and air pollution were not conducive to healing my aged friend's lungs. She insisted that Beatrice fly down to Madras to recuperate in that warmer, less polluted climate and that I accompany her to navigate the airports instead of taking the three-night train south. So, I purchased my first airline ticket since I had left Paris 7,000 overland miles earlier. We were due to depart on December 1. I gladly spent those five nights with the Sawhney family.

The day before we flew to Madras, I stood in line at American Express in central New Delhi, hoping for word from Helene. I was surprised to receive a telegram from Rukmini Devi Arundale, Beatrice's good friend in Madras, informing me that Helene's father had written asking for permission for his daughter to stay as her guest for two weeks in early December. Rukmini wanted me to convey to him that Helene would be well looked after.

My girlfriend was actually coming to see me. When I regained my senses, I pieced together from letters that Helene was indeed traveling to India. She had sent a letter to Varanasi that I had never received. Concerned by my expressed loneliness, and against all odds, she had persuaded her staunchly conservative parents to allow her to spend two chaperoned weeks with me. It was a fantasy come true. Beatrice and I were leaving for Madras the next day, and Helene would be joining us in less than a week. I could hardly believe it.

* * *

Beatrice and Rukmini Devi became friends in the late 1920s. I had met this leading Indian dancer and teacher the previous August while she was staying at Krotona Institute of Theosophy in Ojai. As I was soon leaving for India, Beatrice asked us both for dinner, and I subsequently met Rukmini privately. She invited me to stay in Madras (now called Chennai) as her guest for as long as I liked. Rukmini Devi had founded Kalakshetra, India's largest and most prestigious school of classical Indian music and dance. As a Member of Parliament, she had also been responsible for establishing many of the new republic's national parks and wild animal reserves. By nature, she was Kamaladevi's opposite: charming, sweet-natured, and articulate. When I flew in from Delhi, this elderly dancer welcomed me as a new friend. During the next several years, she became another of my primary mentors. Chapter Eight conveys Rukmini Devi Arundale's remarkable story and her influence upon me.

Hostilities between Pakistan and India had accelerated during the five weeks since I had crossed the border. The geographical and cultural complexities at the heart of the conflict owed much of their genesis to the partition of 1947. When the British had chiseled the Indian subcontinent into separate new countries just before they left that year, they had created the new Muslim nation of Pakistan in two parts. West Pakistan, through which I had passed on India's western border, was a thousand miles away from East Pakistan, created by bifurcating the old state of Bengal in eastern India. Pakistan's primary administration, industrial power, and military strength lay in the West while its most profitable cash crops and largest population were in the East. Unrest had fomented between the two branches ever since their founding. The East Pakistanis, all Bengalis, felt that they were overtaxed and underrepresented in political decisions. A vast majority of East Pakistan's population was now demanding independence.

Violent reprisals from West Pakistan resulted in one of the most hellacious examples of genocide in recorded history. It is still undetermined how many millions of East Pakistanis were slaughtered. Over ten million refugees, most of them Hindu, sought sanctuary in adjacent India. Their host country was already impoverished and could not feed and house them. India requested international aid but had little initial success.

Indira Gandhi, India's premier, realized that supporting East Pakistan's independence was less costly than caring for those fleeing injustice, and she threatened Pakistan with war. In response, Pakistan's government initiated the conflict by attacking eleven Indian airbases on December 3rd, 1971.

* * *

Helene had left LAX two days earlier bound for Rome on her way to India. US news reports had downplayed the possibility of war. The two international carriers, TWA and Air India, irresponsibly neglected to inform her that she was flying into a war zone. She spent a transit day exploring the sites of that capital unaware that, in the meantime, India and Pakistan had declared war. I was with Rukmini Devi and Beatrice in Madras, 1,000 miles from the conflict, but nevertheless biting my nails with worry about Helene.

I panicked at the news that Pakistan's air force had attacked the Bombay Airport just two hours before her transit flight was due to arrive there. A blackout prohibited any further reports. I rushed by taxi to the Madras airport and met every plane that landed, hoping that my girl would arrive safely. When all the passengers from the final flight had come through the gate with no sign of Helene, I was at my wit's end and dejectedly caught a taxi back to my hostel at Kalakshetra. Two miles after I left the airport, I had a strong premonition that I was making a mistake and asked my driver to turn around. Helene descended from the plane in a second group that had been delayed in disembarkation, and I was not there to meet her. When I re-entered the building, my beautiful Helene was in tears. It was not until after our long reassuring embrace that I explained to her that India was at war.

After we were both rested the next morning, I took Helene into a flower-filled jungle in the Theosophical Society compound in Adyar, just south of Madras, and proposed to her. During those stressful, formative months apart, I had fully realized that my life would never be complete without sharing it with her. I was unsurprised that she agreed. As far as we were concerned, our commitment on that day meant that we were truly married in spirit. Our witness was a spider suspended in a web stretched between the lateral roots of an enormous banyan tree. We decided that we would wait to be formally married until after I had graduated from college. The Wheelers, Helene's parents, had only agreed that she be allowed to come to India with the understanding that we would be fully chaperoned throughout our two weeks together. We two lovers agreed that our commitment superseded that decision. Our two weeks were magical. Even though the headlines were full of the travesties of war, Pakistan and north India were too far away to endanger us.

Helene and I were blissfully in love. We spent two nights in a thatched honeymoon cottage on a beach in Mahabalipuram and then traveled by train and bus to Mysore, Bandipur, and Ootacamund. Although we enjoyed the historical sites, the wildlife park, and the old British hill station, we were far more interested in reconnecting with each other than absorbing India. After months of celibacy in the face of many temptations on the famed Hippie Trail, I was glad for these physical and emotional pleasures. We understood that soon we would be separated for another five months.

For twenty-five years since independence, India had considered the United States a good friend. In many ways, our governments appeared well aligned, and US economic policies often aided India in crises. However, America changed allegiance during the buildup to the current war, and India justifiably felt betrayed. President Nixon's government had long underwritten Pakistan's military and economic expansion in the false belief that the US needed them as allies in the chess game with the USSR. Now the US had extended support to India's enemy. Helene and I disagreed with what we viewed as US imperialist politics. As we traveled in south India, we wanted to disguise our nationality. Several times Indians confronted us, angrily asking us how our country could justify this perfidy. In one town, a group of young men even threw small rocks at us, not to cause hurt but to demonstrate their animosity. We were frightened.

India's well-organized and armored military force completely overwhelmed Pakistan's defenses. The enemy only held out for thirteen days. On December 16, 1971, the new nation of Bangladesh emerged from the tatters of what had once been East Pakistan. The western nation of Pakistan not only was defeated, but it was also impoverished. It had also lost two-thirds of its population. India was jubilant. We were sad that we had only three more days together before Helene had to leave Madras to fly back to California. I was heartbroken as my fiancée left, torn between the dread of the lonely months ahead and the thrill of unknown adventure. That emotional dichotomy was to underline our relationship for decades to come.

* * *

I stayed in the international hostel at Kalakshetra for three weeks. My comfortable but unadorned room opened onto a small casuarina forest. Nearby a thatched fishing village abutted more than a mile of unpopulated sand beach. I body-surfed each day in the perfect waves and fell in love with the dance and music school, eating simple vegetarian fare with the students and watching the classes in fascination. Young girls and boys began to learn the complex rhythms and movements at age seven and eight, and as they grew older their expressive grace was mesmerizing. I also began to absorb my lessons in classical Carnatic (South Indian) music, different from the more familiar north Indian style I had heard in New Delhi. This resonance drew me back to work at Kalakshetra years later.

During those three weeks, Beatrice and I had many adventures together. I learned as much from her unusual perception as from the accomplished individuals I met through her. One day we shared a taxi into the city and split up to shop separately, promising to meet for afternoon tea at the Connemara, a well-known hotel that had been a landmark of British society. The facade was a little dilapidated and stained, the carpet at the entrance slightly frayed. Inside was the faded elegance of a well-thumbed Somerset Maugham novel. I arrived before Beatrice and sat down to wait in one of the sets of wing chairs that occupied each corner. Over the upholstered arms were old, somewhat stained antimacassars.

Across from me, in the opposite corner, an elderly English woman served tea to her friends. It appeared that they met every week like this: the last remnant of a previous empire. In front of her was an ornate silver tea service on a silver tray. With careful and precise ceremony, she poured out a cup of tea into a flower-figured porcelain cup, gently requested of her friend whether she wanted it with lemon or milk, offered sugar, and handed it to her guest with just the slightest hint of a tremor in her liver-spotted hand. She then signaled the turbaned bearer to serve a small plate of cucumber sandwiches, the crusts removed. Next, she turned her focus toward the friend in the next chair, serving her, discussing the weather and the problems with servants. I watched this ritual for over half an hour as the Englishwoman conversed with poise and animation, laughing over the anecdotes of one woman and tsk-tsking over the story of another.

The whole situation was overlaid with poignancy—for, you see, in truth there was only one old lady sitting across from me. She was the last. The bearer told me that her friends had all died over the years, but the hotel didn't have the heart to stop her. So, each Tuesday, this lone remaining Englishwoman arrived at the Connemara to maintain this custom of the Raj and to discuss the days before the empire was lost.

I purposefully had tea at the Connemara on Tuesday afternoons for the following two weeks, watching in a kind of macabre fascination, and then left Madras. When I returned several years later, the hotel had changed. The facade was gleaming white, the red-carpeted entrance regal, and the lobby redesigned with white marble floors and no wing chairs. Of the elderly Englishwoman there was no sign, and when I asked the receptionist and the bearers, they said they'd never heard of her. They were all new employees. With the renovation, the ambience has changed, and the Raj is now preserved in a form of showy nostalgia. Even the ghosts are gone, overcome by the noisy purposefulness of tour buses and determined shoppers. I like the cleanliness and efficiency of India's new hotels, but I miss the mysteries of the layered past.

* * *

Christmas and the New Year came and went. I grew restless to begin exploring south Indian villages. The previous year, Mary Lanius, my professor of South Asian art history at the University of Denver, had loaned me a museum catalog portraying the ritual art of Indian tribes and villages in a groundbreaking 1968 exhibition in at the Philadelphia Museum of Art. I became fascinated with images of painted Tamil terracotta horses assembled under sacred trees, ostensibly proffered as mounts for gods to ride as they protected rural communities from evil. I found the concept enchanting and wanted to know more but could find little information about them. This subject was one of the two projects of field research I had proposed to the university. When I explained my goal, Rukmini Devi introduced me to K. Srinivasulu, a contemporary painter who taught studio art at Kalakshetra. He offered to take Beatrice and me on a two-day excursion by car to search for examples of these sculptures in remote areas of the local state of Tamil Nadu. Alongside the highway several hours' drive south of Madras, a large stucco horse placed in an outdoor shrine stood majestic against the blue sky. Soon we ventured off onto smaller side roads where groupings of terracotta horses edged almost all communities. Some were life-size, others tiny. The assemblages included cows, occasional elephants, and human figures. Beatrice and I were exhilarated: the figures we found were charming, diverse in form and style, and expressive of the personal whimsy of each sculptor. I learned that most had been fashioned as votive offerings to the deity that protects the boundaries separating one village from the next. Although each community had its own name for this God, he is generally known as *Ayyanar*, viewed in legend as the son of the two supreme Hindu male deities, Shiva and Vishnu (the story of Ayyanar's conception is fascinating). Indian Terracotta vessels and sculptures in fact became the focus of my doctoral thesis.

When we stopped that night at a local guest house, we were amused when Srinivasulu innocently ushered us both into a single room containing one large, canopied bed. The manager proudly told us that the first prime minister of India, Jawaharlal Nehru, had once occupied this same room. We waited until our host had closed the door behind us before bursting into gales of laughter. After we both had returned to the States, Beatrice created an artwork for me entitled: "Honeymoon Night in Nehru's Bedroom," an abstract of the two of us in flagrante. It hangs in my home to this day.

The next morning this same manager guided us to a disused Ayyanar shrine in a nearby forested region owned by a mining corporation. Under an ancient tree was a refuse mound of ancient sculptural fragments. It was raining that day, and the ground was soft. With permission, I took a sharp stick and dug up some of the buried treasures, uncovering a fragmented female torso that appeared to be an Indian version of the Venus de Milo. She remains a highlight of my private art collection.

* * *

Soon after we returned to Kalakshetra, Beatrice and I parted for the next four months—she to begin her lecture tour through major Indian cities, I to travel by third class train throughout Tamil Nadu. I visited cities famous for their monumental temples carved from granite in the tenth to sixteen centuries: Kanchipuram, Chidambaram, Kumbakonam, Thanjavur, and Tiruchirappalli. Each was magnificent, deepening my appreciation for and understanding of classical Hinduism. But it was the homes I visited, arranged by both Kamaladevi and Rukmini Devi, whose impact was strongest. In each, I was an honored guest, treated with generosity and thoughtful kindness. I frequently felt undeserving of their gifts: I had done nothing to warrant them. But in each case, I was made to feel perfectly at home, a member of the family. Many of my hosts had been freedom fighters, some close compatriots of Mahatma Gandhi. Others were individuals who had committed their lives to establishing crafts cooperatives and art centers, correctly believing that Indian traditional arts were in danger of being dominated by contemporary technologies. Their determined dedication was humbling.

One of the benefits of staying in these many homes was the opportunity to observe and begin to understand family and societal dynamics. I was invited to watch as the mother in one of these homes lovingly washed each of the sculptures in the family's household shrine, then dressed it in a clean silk garment, adorned it with fresh flowers, lit lamps and incense, and made her puja, or ceremony of worship, for the health and welfare of her family. I learned firsthand about personal, family-based Hinduism—not just that of temples and brahminical hierarchies, but the spirituality of the home, which is the true basis of all Indian belief systems.

Tamil food was delicious. After the north, I appreciated menus that were less rich and oily. My diet felt healthier, but I found the use of hot spices more challenging than elsewhere. The care with which my hosts created our meals was inspiring, and I began to savor subtle flavorings, but often found these canceled out by chili peppers that would leave me gasping for something to soothe my burning throat. It took me several years to overcome this reaction, but I am glad that now I can eat and fully enjoy almost any recipe. In many ways, Tamil food has become my favorite.

* * *

I am a light sleeper and one morning the noises of people moving around woke me long before dawn. I climbed to my feet, splashed water on my face from the jug next to my cot, changed into fresh clothes, and staggered out of my room to see what was going on. The sounds came from just outside the house's front door. There in the dim dusk, the mother of the family was sprinkling water from a brass pot in her hand onto the dirt road directly in front of the door. Trading the pot for a small metal bowl, she bent straight from the waist and began to mark out a grid of dots on the damp earth with pinches of white powder. Then she began to connect the dots with sinuous, fluid lines and, as I watched, stems and leaves, flower petals, and birds began to cover the ground. Finally, she took several other bowls containing colored powders and filled in the designs with color: purple, pink, bright red, and two shades of green, redefining her painting with color. What did this mean? Why was she doing it? As the predawn light began to open my view down the street, I saw women, young and old, in front of every house, all painting designs. Each painting was different in form, in size, and in palette. The dirt street became a huge mural. As a woman finished her painting, she would walk along the road to observe the others' handiwork before re-entering her home to care for her family's needs. Then, as the sun rose, and the day's activities began, families began coming out of their houses: men on their way to work, children walking to school, women going to the market, and all stepping directly onto these beautiful powder paintings and scuffing them into the dust. Within a short while the paintings had all disappeared.

When I returned to the house and questioned the family members about the meaning of this extraordinary process, they said that new paintings were created each day in every home. Most of the *kolams*, as they call these daily artworks, were mandalas: concentric forms that replicate the sacred diagrams believed to protect the home from evil and to encourage benevolent spirits to enter, bringing luck and good fortune to the occupants. What an extraordinary culture! This discovery made me want to see more. As I continued throughout this state of Tamil Nadu, I arose early each morning to witness the creation of these kolams. I learned that they were freshly made daily in more than a million homes and that the women took pride in never repeating a design. How could that be possible?

For the previous eighteen months, I had been studying mandalas as keys to interpreting many of India's complexities. I wrote papers for different university courses about the mandala as an ancient political paradigm, its symbolic use in history and in Hinduism, Jainism, and Buddhism, its Jungian psychological interpretation as a human archetype, its adaptation in the late twentieth century as a psychedelic touchstone, and other forms. Here in Tamil Nadu, I found an almost endless source of material for future documentation. Years later, I returned to Tamil Nadu to document it further and to photograph the making of kolams for my second book, *Painted Prayers: Women's Art in Village India*. I now have thousands of photographs of these ephemeral designs, far more than I can ever use, and yet their ingenuity continues to bewitch me. Whenever I find myself arising in the pre-dawn Tamil light, I always walk along the streets to discover new designs and record on film this exhilarating example of human creativity.

* * *

Despite my positive learning curve and my excitement with much of what I experienced, not all was easy. I found the poverty, disease, and malnutrition I witnessed oppressive. Lining the streets outside many of the temples were beggars, some of whom exhibited the open sores of leprosy and the swollen limbs of elephantiasis. I found begging children the most upsetting. What was I to do when faced with a young girl, barely more than a toddler herself, carrying an infant, both filthy and covered with flies? How could I help? I remember one time in Madras with Beatrice when we came upon an old woman lying in the street suckling a baby to her flattened breast, both unfortunate beings withered and distorted with extreme hunger. When we asked the Indian friend with whom we were walking how such an elder could still nurse, he stated that she was probably in her mid-twenties, no older. Her starvation had totally dehydrated her. We gave what we could and continued our way. But India was challenging me. As difficult as I found these experiences, I realized that to remain in this country, and particularly to focus my profession on surveying its cultures, I would have to find ways to steel myself. Since then, I have tried to blend compassion with a certain personal strength that is not always easy to maintain. In recent years I can no longer turn a blind eye, and I have begun to acknowledge more fully the injustice of inequality and human inequity.

* * *

I caught a train from Tiruchirappalli to the pilgrimage temple of Rameswaram, an enormous stone edifice on a peninsula close to the island country of Sri Lanka. After spending several days there, I had intended to take a ferry across to Colombo and spend ten days exploring the cultures of old Ceylon. However, just before I was to move on, I met an Englishman who had recently arrived from the north. He decided that he had seen enough of India and was ready to leave the country. He had purchased a six-month first-class circle tour ticket of India that he wanted to sell me for $100 cash. I would have to leave right away since the ticket was scheduled for a train due to depart for Madurai in one hour. I paid him from the pouch that hung around my neck, ran as fast as I could to my hotel, retrieved my backpack, and rushed to the station just in time to jump on the departing train. I was nervous that the conductor would identify me as an imposter and throw me off the train. That never happened. Suddenly I was traveling in relative luxury.

From that moment on for the rest of my trip, I could board any train I chose, produce my first-class pass, and occupy a priority seat in a comfortable compartment, often by myself. I could not believe my good luck. In some ways, my ongoing journey was lonelier: I met far fewer train travelers—yet those with whom I shared my compartment were invariably nice. I always had my own berth upon which I could fully stretch out. I welcomed the cleanliness of my compartment and of the bathroom down the hall, sometimes with its own shower! It was on that first long train trip to the temple city of Madurai, alone for the first time in months of travel, that I began scat-singing train blues to the accompaniment of the varying percussion of the moving locomotive. I could sing for hours at a stretch—a hypnotic ritual that lasted for years until I fully replaced train travel by other modes of transportation.

When Indian travelers asked what I was doing in their country, some reacted negatively when I explained that I was attempting to document the folk arts and crafts of India. Time and again, they accused me of wanting to take India backward. Educated Indians would tell me that they strived to discard their traditions, that they served no positive functions. India, they stated, needed to modernize, not preserve its past. In most cases, individuals were friendly, not hostile, but, almost without exception, they believed that the arts and crafts that I found so appealing were emblems of South Asia's downfall. Luckily, when I exited the train and contacted the individuals in each destination that Kamaladevi and Rukmini Devi had provided, they encouraged my efforts. It was as if two opposing groups existed. The vast majority believed that the only way to overcome the poverty and inequality left in the British Empire's wake was to rapidly become a modern, industrialized, self-sufficient nation. The few, including my Indian mentors, maintained that progress could only be made by harnessing the innate talents and insights gained through millennia of knowledge and skill, blending those with contemporary technologies.

Stimulated, challenged, open, and adapting, I reached India's southern tip and the painted sands of Kanyakumari at the end of January.

~ 3 ~
Ongoing Change

White feet sinking into pure black sand, soft and finely grained. As a small wave covered them, then receded, I pulled one and then the other up to reveal bright yellow sand that trickled from sunken prints in patterns over the black. A short distance away, iron-red sand interspersed with the black and yellow, creating its own designs, then blue, dark purple, even green sands. Not all the colors were as stark as the yellow and red, but their intermingling shades captivated my senses. I was at Kanyakumari, India's tip that juts out into the Indian Ocean, with the Bay of Bengal to my left and the Arabian Sea to my right. Hindu parents tell their children that a local Goddess was betrothed to the God Shiva, who didn't turn up on their wedding day. In her divine wrath, she spilled her multicolored wedding rice on the ground, thereby creating the beach. Forever after, she remained a virgin, a *kanya kumari*, and is worshipped as such in a temple named for her. Science states that the multi-hued sand is composed of various minerals, each of a different weight, which cause the streaks and whorls of color as the beach shifts with the tides. Although long fascinated with rocks and minerals, I preferred the legend's explanation.

From this southernmost spot, I had nowhere to go but north up the western coast, and soon crossed the Tamil border into the State of Kerala. After the flat alluvial plains of Tamil Nadu with their endless bright green rice paddies, Kerala is densely jungled. Coconut palms and fruit-bearing trees are ubiquitous. Waterways, canals, and rivers intersect this long, narrow strip of land. In the early seventies, highways were not yet fully developed, and transportation was more accessible by boat than by bus or train. I was glad of the change. My first several nights in Trivandrum were hosted by a well-known art critic, K.P. Padmanabhan Thampi, a friend of Rukmini Devi. Thampiji shared with me his passion for Kerala's art, particularly its classical murals. In his funny little car, we sped through tree-lined lanes to visit palaces and local temples where he spent hours explaining the complex iconography and the stories of local legends. The *Nayar* matrilineal system, where property, title, and possessions were traditionally passed solely from mother to daughter intrigued me. Men worked the farms, fought the battles, and served as primary business agents, but the women ruled the home, raised the children, and made all the important decisions. In 1972, more than eighty percent of the population, men and women, were literate—more than any other state. Kerala provided most of India's doctors and nurses. Even today, Indian medical professionals working in the West are more likely to be from that culture than from any other.

* * *

Hundreds, perhaps thousands, of carved granite cobras stood under trees in a dense jungle a few hours to the north. Each tree had a collection at its base; some obviously ancient, others newer, all daubed with yellow turmeric paste and vermillion. Many had garlands of flowers hanging over their heads while, beneath them, sticks of incense wafted sweet perfume through the forest. Some depicted the venomous snakes erect with hoods displaying up to five viperous heads. Others portrayed a male figure standing in front of its body that proclaimed it to be the *Nagaraja*, the King of the Snakes, or a female representing the *Nagini*, the Snake Goddess. I was visiting the remote temple of Mannarasala, famed for its healing powers. Most of the many devotees there were women, praying for fertility or for the Divine Cobra's intervention in healing a loved one. Thampiji and I were exceptions. The few other male devotees, like me, were shirtless and wearing *dhotis* (a white, cotton cloth about the waist). Stitched, zipped, or snapped clothing was considered impure and offensive to the resident deities.

Together we worshipped within the beautiful wooden temple, giving offerings of trays of fruit and flowers, blessed by the priest. The traditional wooden architecture of Kerala contrasts with buildings found elsewhere in India—curved eaves and latticework walls reminiscent more of the Far East than of other temples in this diverse country. After our pujas, we walked the long and winding path through the forest of carved stone Nagas (cobras), taking our time as we stopped to visit each one. Thampiji instructed me in the correct manner of worshipping. He pointed out the holes in the roots of most of the trees and explained these were entries into dens that held living cobras. In front of these holes were offerings of fresh eggs and milk for the snakes to eat at night. Although we encountered no living snakes, my host explained that if families feed cobras that live under their houses or beneath the trees nearby, the snakes are not considered dangerous. These vipers would never attack a child or member of the household that protects them.

    A second ancient wooden building housed the leader of this unique sacred center. Mannarasala is the only important temple in India governed by the ministrations of a high priestess, the *Valai Amma*, considered by Hindus to be a saint. She was a direct descendent of brahmin priestesses who trace their lineage back thousands of years. The present Valai Amma was the closest emissary of Nagaraja, the only one in full contact with Him. Thampyii and I stood in line for almost an hour to reach the shuttered window that let us view into a small room. In its center, an elderly, simply-attired woman sat cross-legged on the floor. As she glanced up, I felt that I was being seen, not just as a young foreigner, but as the person I was and could become.

As we walked away, Thampiji helped me understand this transformative experience. Locals believe that just by catching a glimpse of the light in the Valai Amma's eyes, a devotee might be healed. My elderly host also told me that a giant cobra hundreds of feet long with the diameter of an elephant lived in an enormous cavern beneath that building. At a festival once each year, worshipers pour wagonloads of offerings of his favorite foods into the cave. The Lord of Snakes feasts upon them and is sated. Rukmini had predicted how significant this brief meeting would be for me and arranged for this visit on my last day with Thampiji.

Since that initial visit, I have returned to Mannarasala at least a dozen times. Wealth from Kerala's citizens working in the Gulf States and elsewhere has changed the economy of this state. Grateful devotees have given generously to this temple, believing that their lives were improved because of Nagaraja's beneficence. The temple and residence remain much the same, but the thousand or more granite Nagas have all been collected from under the sacred trees throughout the forest and placed in stacked rows along a well-maintained stone walkway between the two buildings. I still find it inspiring to visit and have succeeded several times again in having *darshan* (eye-to-eye contact) with the current Valai Amma, the successor to the one I met first.

* * *

Padmanabhan Thampi delivered me to a jetty in the port town of Alleppey, where I boarded a ferry for transportation a few hundred miles north. The exotic beauty of Kerala's backwaters charmed me. Abundant fruit-bearing trees hugged the shores of the wide rivers and canals. Flowers accented waterside houses: some, traditional thatched huts; others, fanciful cement and stucco homes. Women wearing saris in a full spectrum of colors washed themselves, their cookware, and even their animals in the moving stream. Boys and men with fishing poles calmly cast their lines. Thousands of domestic ducks swam past as we chugged along. Patchwork square-rigged sails propelled long, deep-hulled *wallams*—wooden boats with prows evocatively curved into spirals—which carried a variety of cargo up- and downriver. Today, imaginative entrepreneurs have converted these same vessels into thatch-roofed houseboats that comfortably cater to the burgeoning tourist trade.

In Kottayam, I caught a bus that traveled through miles of rubber plantations before winding up a jungled mountain pass and into rolling hills of tea and coffee plantations. My goal was the newly established Periyar National Park and Wildlife Sanctuary that had been founded through the efforts of my friend Rukmini Devi Arundale when she had served in parliament. I presented a letter from her to the park's newly appointed wildlife preservation officer, Mr. K. Nanu Nair, who invited me on a private tour of the sanctuary the next morning. Just after dawn, I walked several miles into the park along a road lined with enormous first-growth trees filled with exotic birds and to a fifteen-foot motorboat docked on what appeared to be a river. The elderly boatman explained that engineers had converted the Periyar River into a lake by damming it many miles to the south to power a hydroelectric project. The easiest way to view wildlife was from the lake's edge. I was soon joined by Mr. Nair, his wife, and their two young children, who had recently settled into new accommodations in nearby Thekkady. None of them had yet seen the sanctuary; we five novices were to explore it for the first time together.

The boat's small outboard engine putt-putted slowly through miles of narrow lake. The marshes on its banks teemed with birds—hornbills, parakeets, flycatchers, thrushes, and storks—and small mammals such as otters, martens, and a lone mongoose. In the grassy meadows beyond were wild boar, bison, sambar deer, and two king cobras standing on their tails in the sinuous dance of a mating ritual. Large families of monkeys (lion-tailed macaques and Nilgiri langurs) scampered through the dense jungle of teak, sandalwood, rosewood, jacaranda, tamarind, mango, banyan, fig, and bamboo that covered the steep hills. As we rounded a bend, an enormous bull elephant with massive tusks looked up from his foraging and saluted us with his trunk.

On a further hillside, we encountered a herd of five female elephants and their three young, silhouetted among the trees on its summit. We watched them as we ate sandwiches before continuing further down the lake. After several hours of exploration, we returned on the same route. As the sun began to set and the surface of the water changed into pinks and oranges, we looked again for the herd of elephants. They were no longer on the hilltop, but swimming across the lake in front of us: nine grey backs rising and falling like dolphins, heads underwater, but trunks held up to breathe like a series of periscopes. The old boatman cut our engine, and we drifted about thirty feet offshore.

One after another, the huge mammals lumbered onto the far bank and began to grab sand with their trunks and throw it onto their backs in order to dry, until the lead female, a monumental specimen, noticed us out there in the water. Displeased, she trumpeted at us loudly and then urged the other adults to create a solid wall facing us with their young behind them. Our navigator began to pull at the starter but the engine flooded. When we did not move, the lead elephant reached down to the bank with her trunk and pulled out by the roots a small tree that she flailed at us in anger before throwing it toward us. It landed in the water not far away. Our engine still would not engage. She stomped around in increasing anger, then reached into the hole where the tree roots had been and picked up a large rock that she threw at us. It landed in the water about two feet from our boat's edge. With no further warning, she gathered her strength and charged us just as the old man finally started the boat and threw it into reverse. We backed up about ten feet and narrowly avoided a massive projectile: four-and-a-half tons of furious pachyderm landed right where we had been moments before! The wave swamped our boat, but we did not sink. All of us bailed out the water using whatever we could find. We didn't talk much during the hour's journey back to the dock. We were all just glad to still be alive.

* * *

I next spent five days investigating the engaging seaside city of Cochin (now Kochi). The streets and buildings that frame this enormous deep-water port reflect the overlay and interplay of untold centuries of international trade with China and Southeast Asia to the east and Arabia, Africa, Venice, and Portugal to the west. The Phoenicians sent ships to this Malabar Coast long before the Portuguese, guided by the global adventurer Vasco da Gama, founded Cochin Harbor in the late fifteenth century. It was the prosperous spice trade of this region that compelled Columbus to set out in his misguided voyage, resulting in his claim of discovering America. It has long been said that the fragrance of Cochin's spice markets can be scented far out to sea, long before land is sighted.

An overnight train trip landed me in Bangalore (Bengaluru), then a relatively sleepy small city in the heart of Karnataka, the state just north of Kerala. I received a letter there from a University of Denver friend saying that the Peace Corps had assigned him to live two years in a remote village in that same state. I contacted him, and we agreed to meet in the town of Hubli in a few days. First, I traveled by train and bus to visit the ancient temple sites of Belur and Halebid.

* * *

Months of eating highly spiced food had caused my intestines to revolt. I had been thin before I left home. Now I subsisted on bananas and papayas supplemented only occasionally by cooked meals. Something I ate in those temple towns violently disagreed with me, causing my second case of amoebic dysentery. On this sixteen-hour third-class train journey, no seats were available, so I carved out a space on the floor so small I had either to squat or sit tightly cross-legged. The toilets were almost impossible to reach, backed-up, and non-functional. My only choice was to return to my tiny spot and deal with explosive diarrhea the best that I could. Reaching my destination, I had a high fever and was covered in my own repulsive filth.

I staggered onto the platform, soiled and deeply ashamed, and sought the stationmaster for help, careful to keep my distance from him. All I required was a moderate hotel near the station and a porter to carry my pack there. There were no taxis or rickshaws available at this early hour. I did not have the strength to carry this pack myself. The stationmaster gave me the information and appointed a typically red-shirted porter to help me, telling both of us that I should pay no more than one rupee for the service.

The hotel was several hundred yards down the road, and even though it was only 6:30 a.m., the day was already broiling hot. Following the porter, I weaved weakly down the road to the hotel where I gave him five rupees in consideration of the heat and the weight of my bag. He refused it angrily, demanding ten. When I tried to say that he had received five times the going rate, he berated me. Leaving the five-rupee note at his feet, I took my pack from him and walked into the lobby to arrange for a room. He followed me in and began to complain loudly to the receptionist. The hotel man told him firmly that the amount I had given him was way more than he should have received and asked him to leave. I then signed in and received my key.

My room was across the parking lot from the lobby. As I approached it, the porter was still there shouting invectives at me. I tried my best to ignore him and, with difficulty, climbed the stairs to my room, went in, and wretchedly began to peel off my foul clothes to take a shower. Doors nearby resounded with banging and loud arguing voices. Outside my window, the porter was pulling sleepy Indian neighbors out of their rooms and haranguing them with a story of how this rich American kid had cheated him. In my delirious state, all I could think of was to defend my country and myself. I pulled on my revolting clothes again and staggered downstairs. The porter, two inches from my face, screamed a long list of insults—and I just lost it. Reaching back both my arms, I pushed him violently with all my strength. He was a little man, short and wiry, and he flipped completely over the car directly behind him, landing in a daze on the other side. Shaken, he got to his feet and left. The event was over, and the crowd quickly dispersed.

I returned to my room in complete shock. The porter could easily have hit his head. Had he remained in front of me, I was angry enough to have pummeled him. In either case, I might have seriously injured or even killed him. In such a remote Indian city, I could have been tried and spent years in jail. How was this possible? I knew that my anger was justified: the situation was untenable. Nevertheless, the experience forced me to reassess my character. I had never been violent. I had eschewed every physical fight in my childhood and adolescence and believed myself to be totally passive. My response was visceral, impulsive. Who was I now?

That incident destroyed a layer of my naiveté and altered my self-image. I remain non-violent, and hope that I never again strike another living being, but India continues to teach me the depth of my passions and that within us all is a dark side we must recognize if we are to live in balance. I was learning to love the culture and people of India deeply, but some aspects challenged me then, and still challenge me. I remain dedicated to the concept of ahimsa, of trying never to harm another being in word or action, but now know that great internal strength is sometimes required to refrain from outrage.

Luckily, I was able to rest a day in the hotel before I met my friend. Although I was still weak and unable to eat much, we had a good reunion and great discussions comparing our life-changing experiences since we had last seen one another. The next day, stronger still, I took the train to Goa.

* * *

Beginning in Afghanistan, whenever I met other young foreigners, I heard tales of the wonders of Goa. This narrow strip of land in the center of South Asia's western coast was touted as a Hippy Mecca or, as we would say then, "a haven for freaks." Until India had annexed it just eleven years earlier, Goa had been a Portuguese colony for almost four-and-a-half centuries, the trade capital of their empire. Although the Catholic hierarchy there had forced conversions to Christianity and installed a brutal inquisition centuries before, Goa in the twentieth century had become known for its easygoing, laissez-faire manner. Young travelers found its sixty-five miles of near-perfect beaches alluring. Without the censorship of more conservative Hindu and Muslim India, they could live cheaply, yet well. Goa gained a reputation for plentiful, inexpensive drugs, free sex, and unrestricted nude, or almost nude, swimming. I wanted to check it out.

My train arrived in the old port city of Vasco da Gama in late February followed by a bus north to Calangute. I'd become friends with many French in Herat, Kandahar, and Kabul. I'd given them my mailing addresses in India, and Michel Bongoat had written that I might find him and his girlfriend Marie-Claude somewhere near that coastal village. I booked a room in a beachside hotel and was invited by scantily clad Europeans to join them in smoking ganja (the Indian word for cannabis leaf). Soon thereafter, I found myself bodysurfing on near-perfect waves wearing only a loincloth—basically a G-string. Lying on the beach were well-tanned, sexy young European women, most topless, some completely nude. I'd never seen anything like it. Most of the men had long hair and beards. Mine, too, had grown longer during my months in India, but was still clean-cut compared to many. Several women openly propositioned me, but I resisted the obvious temptation. I am naturally monogamous and remained devoted to Helene.

Through word of mouth, I easily tracked down Michel, a French friend I'd met in Afghanistan. He and Marie-Claude were living with another couple in a three-bedroom bungalow in nearby Baga alongside a river just one hundred yards from the beach. Their large Portuguese-style house had a wrap-around verandah where, when they weren't swimming, they would spend much of each day in comfortable easy chairs. They paid a rent of $25 a month. Fresh seafood: lobsters, prawns, and fish arrived daily to their front door and cost almost nothing. Regular vegetable and fruit vendors came too. Aside from rent, they could live well on $10 a month per person. They never wore clothes in the house or on the porch. When they went into town or the market, the two men wore only loincloths and perhaps shirts if they wanted to keep the sun off their backs, while the two women wore only sarongs tied around their necks. As we smoked ganja together, these two couples tried to persuade me to join them. They had an extra bedroom, and I would be welcome. I resisted. All of us were wanderers, but I had a purpose: to learn about India and conduct research. Goa was deeply beguiling, and I could not allow myself to succumb. Three enticing days later, my travels resumed. If I stayed longer, I might never leave.

* * *

My next stop became a favorite. At that time, Badami was a small town nestled at the open end of a canyon of tall granite cliffs. This area had little annual rainfall, and the roofs of the single-story houses were flat, used as drying surfaces for crops of wheat and bright red chili peppers. A large reservoir (called a tank in India) filled the apex of the canyon. Lines and layers of ancient stone steps (ghats) led from the community's edge down into the dark green water. Millennia of use had worn these granite ghats into cascades of geometric shapes. Beginning in the early morning, hundreds of sari-clad women stood in the water or squatted on its edge to wash clothes and scrub their cooking utensils. The varying percussion of laundry beaten against the rocks reverberated and echoed against the canyon walls. On one side, the cliffs were perforated with a series of open-faced caves that had been carved into temples in the sixth and seventh centuries. Cresting the cliffs on the other side were eleventh century temples constructed of blocks of the local stone.

The local government guesthouse was cheap. As I perused the town's open streets, inhabitants warmly welcomed me as the only tourist there, Indian or otherwise. They invited me into their homes for cups of sweet, spicy tea and homemade snacks. I spent hours sitting on the steps down into the tank engrossed in the ongoing spectacle of washing. Many of the women smiled openly at me, even coyly flirting with no suggestion of enticement. I inspected the cave temples and the variety of carving on the walls, columns, and ceilings: compelling depictions of Gods and Goddesses, appealing decorative designs, even mandalas that I photographed and sketched for use in my ongoing study. Weeks before, I had been swept away by the magnificence of Tamil stone temples, but in comparison, I preferred the simplicity of these rock-cut ones. I climbed up fissures in the cliffside set with series of granite steps, bending and twisting to maneuver overhangs and narrow spaces. The cliff tops opened into spectacular vistas of near and distant stone monuments and the rocky plain that abutted the town. From the edge, I could look down into the town's active life without disturbing it: children playing cricket in the street, women pausing to gossip, old men stretching their aged limbs as they passed around a lighted chillum of tobacco, and the constantly changing array of clothes washers on the long expanse of stone steps into the water. A highpoint was watching two farmers as they herded seven or eight water buffalos into the verdant liquid, and the grey-black animals submerging like a line of happy hippos.

* * *

Dr. Dinkar G. Kelkar was a tiny old man with twinkling eyes. At a time when most traditional Indian decorative art was undervalued and increasingly discarded, Kaka Kelkar, as he was known, was besotted by it. He had an uncanny ability to uncover unusual works of art and to charm their owners into either giving them to him or selling them at notably low prices. Over the previous decades, he had amassed India's largest private collection, some 15,000 pieces by the time I met him. He had enticingly displayed this collection in an ever-expanding museum in the city of Pune, a few hundred miles west of Bombay. I had traveled there from Badami via Sholapur and Bijapur. When I arrived in late February, Kaka was working hard on negotiations with the government of his local state, Maharashtra. He wanted to give the museum and all its contents to the Indian people as a legacy, but in return, the government had to agree that they would keep it open to the public in perpetuity. Just three years later, he realized his lifelong dream. The Raja Dinkar Kelkar Museum remains a state-run institution to this day.

Kaka and his wife Kaku (translated as Uncle and Auntie) charmed me. He could not have been more than five feet tall, and she was shorter. In their late seventies, they both radiated energy and generosity. I appeared without warning carrying a simple letter of introduction from an American Fulbright student I'd met in Kerala. The Kelkars insisted I move right into their home, giving me an art-filled guest room with a carved Goanese rosewood canopy bed. Kaka had traveled throughout India, avidly collecting anything of note. Each of his many galleries was filled with hundreds of creative works, most rare, each different from the next, and organized by category: lamps, nut cutters, containers, cooking utensils, jewelry boxes, cosmetic and perfume vessels, ritual items, sacred images, puppets, dolls, textiles, and costumes. One room opened into the next, and each was entrancing and informative. For me, it was like an Ali Baba's cave of endless resources—and Kaka willingly shared with me whatever I wanted to know.

I stayed there five days. While Kaka explained the backgrounds and stories of each piece, Kaku squatted in her kitchen to create an array of mouthwatering Marathi vegetarian delicacies. Each generation in her family had passed down precious recipes. I had never tasted such food. So strong became my bond with this elderly couple that Kaka kept asking me to remain with him so that he could train me to become the director of his museum. As flattering as his offer was, I knew I was too young to accept such a position and that I must return to the United States. But during those days, his insights became primary to my understanding of Indian art. Kaka also wrote a letter of introduction to N.T. Vakani, an artist friend in Ahmedabad, Gujarat, whom he felt could be helpful to me in my research there. That gift alone was worth the whole trip.

* * *

I spent the next five days holed up in a room in a basic hotel in Colaba, Bombay (Mumbai). I worked feverishly to compose one of the two papers I had promised the University of Denver. "The Mandala: A Link Between the Folk and the Classical" synthesized my research on kolams in Tamil Nadu and on other mandalas I had recorded in temples and shrines. I wrote the text longhand and created careful pencil drawings based upon mandalas I had seen. A package of the pages reached my mother, who had offered to type them for me. Helene had processed and printed all the films from the first third of my trip and sent relevant ones to be included as corroborative illustrations. Together these two loving women compiled for me a finished paper that they sent on to the university. I received top marks.

* * *

High stacks containing tens of thousands of antique embroideries and appliques surrounded me: an unbelievable array of riches. Many were priceless, and I was about to learn to decipher their hidden treasures. Here in the center of the old city of Ahmedabad, Gujarat, I was being tutored by N.T. Vakani, who became an invaluable mentor, and guide. He was strikingly good-looking, with long greying hair and a full, unkempt beard, and always dressed in traditional khadi, the handspun, handwoven cotton cloth that had been popularized by Gandhi. That great leader's ashram remained only a few miles away on the other side of the city. As a young man, Vakani had been a dancer and actor. Now he supported himself as an artist while he lived with his elderly auntie in the traditional family house.

I stayed in a hotel but spent all of my waking hours with this man, who had dropped all activities in response to Kaka Kelkar's correspondence. My original intention had been to spend just a few days there and then explore the craft villages of the highly artistic state in which it was centered. Vakani ascertained my fascination with textiles and invited me to visit treasure houses of inventory deep inside one of the most ancient parts of this venerable metropolis. His friends, brothers Manubhai and Becherbhai, had founded a thriving business, Saurashtra Handicraft, by purchasing old textiles at inexpensive prices from rural communities throughout Gujarat. Village women had created most of these fabrics as essential parts of their dowries: bed and pillow covers, quilts, wall hangings, door coverings, bags, purses, skirts, blouses, veils, caps, and shawls. Many pieces were generations old and had been sold willingly by family members in exchange for extra cash. The two brothers had created a niche market exporting handmade toys. In a factory adjacent to the warehouse, they employed hundreds of women. Some cut bolts of plain cotton cloth into set pattern pieces. Others stitched and stuffed these shapes into elephants, camels, horses, cattle, and human dolls. A third group scissored embroidered textiles into small pieces, while a fourth sewed them onto the toys. The workers created thousands of these hand-embroidered toys each week. The export department crated and inventoried them before shipping them to dealers, stores, and markets throughout the world. I often had seen them in import shops in the United States before I left but hadn't realized that the legacies of generations of women had been decimated to create these fripperies.

Despite his friendship with the owners, Vakani deplored their wanton destruction of so much historical beauty. He had no ability to stop the trade, but he was permitted to use the inventory before they dismantled it to teach me about western Indian textiles. He suggested that I might even be able to purchase fine examples at a low cost. We arrived at the warehouse early each morning and stayed until dusk. Manubhai and Becherbhai provided two boys to help us. We would point at a stack of several hundred embroideries, and one of the boys would climb to the top and throw them down to us one by one.

Vakani's encyclopedic knowledge of textiles floored me. I would open each while he explained to me what village it came from, who the people were, what the motifs represented, and what stitches were used. The variety was vast—outstanding classical pieces next to bold folk designs. Some appeared to be ancient, some in almost mint condition, while others were torn and tattered. As we went along, Vakani asked me to tell him which were my favorites, and we would put those aside. The second boy refolded each textile to create two new piles, one of favorites, the other of discards. Occasionally, my mentor would suggest that he disagreed with my choice and would explain why. My learning curve was steep. When we had gone through perhaps 400 or 500 textiles, and my mind and eyes were spinning, we would stop for cups of sweet-spiced chai while Vakani continued to tell me stories of the crafts and the people who fashioned them. Then we returned our focus to the next pile. In that way, we progressed through thousands of textiles each day, many exquisite, some gaudy or poorly constructed. We would leave at sunset to return to Vakani's home in Saraspur Char Rasta for a tasty and filling meal prepared by his auntie. I then went back to my hotel to collapse in dreamy exhaustion, only to meet him at the warehouse early the next morning. This education was unsurpassable. I was learning far more by remaining in that warehouse with Vakani than from traveling through the villages where the textiles were made. My host offered to continue teaching me as long as I wished to stay, and I remained under his spell for two full weeks.

Each day, my pile of chosen textiles grew. On my last, Manubhai joined us and provided prices. My travels so far had been so inexpensive that I had managed to save a fund for purchases. These works of art were dirt-cheap, and we winnowed the selection down to about sixty excellent pieces that I paid for directly. I took a few with me in my suitcase, and the factory owners arranged to ship the bulk of them to California for me. One of my favorites was a large, fully beaded textile created to frame a double doorway. The tiny glass beads had been woven by needle into a series of colorful panels that portrayed Hindu Gods and Goddesses and mythical beasts as well as common symbols of local daily life. Mounted on the wall, it was spectacular, but the full doorway could be folded into a bundle about twelve by five inches square. For me to carry the heavy artwork home, Manubhai commissioned a handstitched shoulder bag. That night at dinner, Vakani showed me three rare paintings that he encouraged me to purchase at minimal prices. He wanted me to take them to sell in the States and insisted that they were valuable. Beyond that small payment, a pittance of their true worth, my mentor would accept nothing from me. As with so many others on this journey, Vakani's kindness humbled me. I departed Ahmedabad the next morning with my mind filled with new knowledge, my suitcase loaded with art, and my spirit vibrant with gratitude.

* * *

My long adventure was beginning to wind down. Only a few weeks remained before I would leave India. My original plan was to explore the subcontinent until mid-May but increasing longing for Helene had changed my mind. I had decided to surprise her by arriving on her twenty-first birthday. I booked a flight to leave Calcutta for Rangoon on April 20. On March 16, I entered Rajasthan by train. The lakeside city of Udaipur allured me from the moment I first saw it and I have returned countless times. I was the guest of the Samar family, friends of Kamaladevi who ran a local museum of indigenous folk art. That first evening before dinner, I walked and walked through narrow cobbled streets, admiring the frescoed walls of houses, the numerous shops of local crafts, the colorfully veiled women, and the men's large bright turbans. Children called out to me from every corner. At first glimpse, the fabled Lake Pichola was framed by three looming arches. Women washed clothes on rows of steps leading down into the water. I crossed a nearby bridge and stood at sunset to face a cityscape encompassing a full kilometer of interconnected royal palaces reflected pink in the opalescent lake.

Both Kamaladevi and Rukmini Devi were in town to participate in a local festival. It was like an abundance of riches to be able to meet with each of them as they questioned me about my travels, the people I had met through their kind invitations, and the research and insights I had gained. They invited me to join them at a keynote concert by world-renowned sitarist Ravi Shankar and his equally famous tabla accompanist, Alla Rakha. Thousands had gathered for this event—tickets had been sold out for weeks. Upon arriving at the outdoor concert hall, to my utter embarrassment and thrill, I was ushered directly onto the stage, introduced to the musicians, and then asked to sit cross-legged just ten feet away to one side. Only six of their favored students were up there with me. Kamaladevi and Rukmini Devi sat front row center, flanked by Rajasthan's Chief Minister and other political leaders. I was numb with awe throughout the long concert, fully aware of my unbelievable privilege. I could see clearly the fingers of the two maestros as one plucked his sitar and the other intoned his tablas. I watched the expressive joy in their eyes as they riffed off one another. I recognized the *raga* they had recorded the previous August during their friend George Harrison's Concert for Bangladesh at Madison Square Garden.

Aside from exploring the many craft shops in that city, I spent my days perusing the folk art collections at the Bharatiya Lok Kala Mandal. Founded in 1952, only a few years after Indian independence, this interactive museum and center for folk art, music, dance, and puppetry served as a prototype for many museums of indigenous Indian arts that were to become popular throughout the country. My host, the director, Dr. Devi Lal Samar, opened the reserve collections and patiently answered my many questions about Rajasthani traditional arts and customs. This institution still exists but has been eclipsed by others with better funding and more flash in Udaipur and elsewhere. Nevertheless, at that time, its concept was innovative: live artists and artisans displayed their current production techniques alongside exceptional exhibitions. This experience was to influence my own future museum exhibition career.

* * *

The city of Jaipur is also enchanting. Unfortunately, I again became ill there. I could not figure out what was wrong with me. Despite an increasing fever, I explored its fort and palaces, unique eighteenth-century observatory, and streets filled with crafts shops. I had to wait to return to Jaipur with Helene a few years later to truly appreciate the city's unique wonders.

The last leg of my overland journey was the train to Delhi. I arrived there depleted, almost delirious, intending to stay with the Sawhneys, who had hosted me so graciously more than four months earlier. But Mr. and Mrs. Stone, the diplomat friends of my Uncle

Coulter, insisted that I come directly to their home where I could be examined and treated by the US Embassy doctor. He diagnosed malaria. I was quite ill, but instead of hospitalizing me, the Stones thoughtfully took care of me themselves in their lovely Lutyens home. I had a comfortable room to myself and was treated daily by the American doctor. The combination of strong antibiotics, chloroquine, bland, nourishing food, and days of deep rest was effective. Within a week, I had recovered, although I remained frail. As is typical with this disease, I relapsed biannually for the next several years until it finally worked its way out of my system.

The super-guru, Sathya Sai Baba, was coming to Delhi. Millions of devotees descended on the capital city to hear and, hopefully, be healed by him. Sai Baba was a self-proclaimed messiah, a living reincarnation of the Hindu God Krishna. He was renowned throughout India for his miracles, healing the sick and infirm, and bringing enlightenment to the masses. The Stones told me that the American ambassador, Kenneth Keating, had requested an audience with the great man. As deputy chief of mission, second in India only to the ambassador, Mr. Stone was invited. He declined, but Mrs. Stone expressed interest and asked me if I would like to join her. I was thrilled: an opportunity to meet one of the world's foremost religious leaders. Ever since I had heard Maharishi Mahesh Yogi a few years earlier and been introduced to Transcendental Meditation, I had wondered if I might find my true spiritual teacher in India. I still practiced daily those meditation techniques and found that they helped me become more peaceful. Mrs. Stone and I were invited to the ambassadorial mansion for tea with Sai Baba. I went with an open mind, hoping to find the answers to my lifelong quest for truth.

Only four of us were with the guru: Ambassador and Mrs. Keating, Mrs. Stone, and I. Sai Baba, a man in his early forties with a prominent Afro haircut, wore a saffron silk kurta, pajamas, and a raw silk vest. We sat in elegant, upholstered armchairs in the formal drawing room as tea was served in china cups and saucers. Sai Baba spoke in a mellifluous voice and openly answered all the questions the three others asked him. I was quiet and observant, not saying anything beyond the required niceties. After all, this man was reputed to be God. His words seemed gentle, wise, and insightful.

At the end of the hour's meeting, Ambassador Keating asked the guru if he might receive a memento of this profound occasion. Although I didn't know it, this request was protocol. Sai Baba raised his right hand and, from thin air, produced white ash in the palm of his hand, offering a small pinch to each of us. This ash was sacred *vibhuti*, believed by Hindus to be the material essence of God. In a similar gesture, he also produced a printed photograph of himself that he presented to the Keatings. I might have been as astounded as the others had I not been trained to notice details that others might miss. In my adolescence, my goal was to become a stage magician. I studied books of magic and spent dozens of hours at magic shops learning sleight of hand and other tricks but was never good enough to be an accomplished performer. Nevertheless, I knew well the art of deception and how to watch for visual misdirection. I clearly observed Sai Baba palming both the ash and the photograph. I did not tell anyone of my discovery. Many adored this man, and I had no desire to destroy their illusions. I also had heard and read about the many fine charities that he supported: hospitals, orphanages, and schools for the poor. But I could not believe that God incarnate would have any need for parlor tricks.

For years thereafter, I kept that story to myself, only occasionally telling it to others who had expressed doubts as to that guru's authenticity. More than three decades later, a French documentarian filmed Sai Baba creating his miracles. He then slowed that film down to prove that the guru had done precisely what I had witnessed. The Frenchman exposed him as a fake and published the film on YouTube.

I spent my last few days in Delhi as a guest of the Sawhneys, feeling better and profoundly grateful to the Stones. The friendship these two families showed me was just the beginning. I now have a wide circle of close friends in that city. I felt at ease then in Delhi—a sense of well-being that has lasted. Even though the capital has grown exponentially in the past half-century and its air pollution requires restricting my time there, it remains one of my favorite cities in the world.

* * *

Calcutta was my final stop in India. I had read much of its history and was apprehensive. Instead, what I discovered was a highly intellectual, cultured city that had been overrun in recent years, particularly in the previous twelve months, by impoverished immigrants from East Pakistan/Bangladesh. The conditions of poverty, homelessness, and starvation were upsetting. Beatrice Wood was already there when I arrived. As elsewhere, I met the cream of the art society through her. We had interesting discussions comparing our months of independent experience, and then it was time for me to leave. I was more than ready. By this point, I had already been traveling for more than seven months, usually alone. Although I had encountered remarkable individuals throughout South Asia and had cemented new friendships that would last my lifetime, I was now worn-out and lonely.

I had initially planned to fly the least expensive way home—via the West, changing planes in Europe. But my parents thoughtfully offered to pay for me to continue flying east around the world. They wrote that I had well proven my dependability and that my trip so far had been a resounding success. My return itinerary would take me through Rangoon, Bangkok, Penang, Singapore, Hong Kong, and Tokyo, three nights in each. It was a mind-opening opportunity. Those experiences, too, further informed me about the world's wide diversity.

It was wonderful to see Mom and Dad when they met my flight at Los Angeles on May 4. We drove from there to Newport Beach to spend a night in a motel near the Wheelers' home. At eight o'clock the next morning, early on Helene's twenty-first birthday, I knocked on her bedroom door. It took her a while to register that I was not a mirage. We had a joyous reunion. It was healing to be with Helene again. I had missed my family and friends and many aspects of my life in the States. Those people and places that I loved resuscitated me. My favorite foods, most particularly crisp, green salads, began to nourish me. My frequent illnesses and growing aversion to highly seasoned food had resulted in a tremendous loss of weight. I was six-foot-one-inch and weighed only 138 pounds! On the day I returned, my fiancée discovered that she could reach around my waist and touch her fingers together.

Culture shock plagued me. The commodity-oriented nature of American society was truly upsetting: the newness, the mass-production, the fast life of good cars, modern buildings, and efficient businesses, and the easy availability of anything I might want if I had the money to purchase it. After India, my native society appeared too clean and antiseptic. A week or so after I arrived, Helene took me into a large department store to look at potential place settings and silverware that her parents had offered to give us as a wedding present. After the shops and the endless variety of handmade crafts in India, the store's wall-to-wall carpeting, its canned Muzak, and its row upon row of perfectly placed, brilliantly lit, mass-produced china and silver were too much for me. I ran outside and had to decompress in the fresh air.

Friends, family, and acquaintances looked wonderful to me, and I could never get enough of gazing at Helene. But initially, I found the appearance of most white people bland and the lack of racial diversity boring. I had spent so many months in India as the only Caucasian, rarely encountering other white foreigners, that I had grown accustomed to and even preferred brown and black skin tones and the infinite variety of genetic types I encountered there. I had grown so comfortable with being the anomaly that I felt awkward with my own people in what seemed an endless sea of relative racial conformity. I adjusted over the following weeks and months, but during the next years, it was as if I was divided, if not quite schizophrenic. I felt as if I had two different personalities: the man at home in America and the one at ease in India. It was a tremendous relief when, decades ago, I recognized that these two sides had melded into one. For the past forty years, I have been the same person at home in either country.

I had flown to Europe, traveled overland 9,000 miles, and continued flying around the world. In eight months (239 days), I had visited seventeen countries. Except for the return flight paid by my parents, my total expenditure was $2,400. Of that, I only spent $960 on travel and living expenses. The folk art and crafts that I brought home were indeed valuable. I had collected well. Over the next year, I sold some of the finest pieces, many of which I had purchased through Vakani, to art museums and collectors. For example, the Denver Art Museum bought the beaded doorway for $3,500. I had purchased it for $60. Of the pieces I had collected by spending $1,440, I sold one third, gave a third to friends, and kept a third to become the basis of an unusual collection of Indian folk art. My sales totaled $14,600, with which I paid all my expenses for my last year-and-a-half in college.

It indeed was the trip that changed and made my life. I have never been the same since. Of all the many experiences I had, the most profound were due to Indian generosity. That, for me, is the true pulse of the Indian people. I have spent half a century since then learning more about it.

~ 4 ~
Challenges

"My prognosis is bleak. It is likely that your wife will not survive." After a five-hour operation, the surgeon had come out to meet me in the waiting room. His face was ashen. It was January 28, 1975, and I had just been told that the love of my life, twenty-three-year-old Helene (Hi) Huyler was dying. We were in Bombay during our next trip to India after seven months of travel.

During my nine-month adventure in 1971-72, I had been loyal to Helene. I returned even more determined to spend my life with her. She accepted my proposal of marriage with the agreement that we would live together first for a year and a half in Denver. That spring and early summer, I worked for two months for Beatrice Wood. My fiancée moved from California to Denver to live with me in mid-July—a choice that we made openly, but that deeply challenged the morality of our parents. Without question, it was for us the best thing we could have done. I continued my intensive course of study, still taking classes about India from seven different departments. I believed then, as I still do, that I could not possibly have had a better undergraduate education anywhere else in the world. I graduated with honors just a couple of weeks before Helene and I were married on December 20, 1973.

We remained in close touch with Beatrice. She regularly penned us wonderfully illustrated letters. Helene asked Beatrice if she would be her maid of honor at our wedding. We were married in a wild oak grove in a secluded mountain valley above The Thacher School. As of this publication, we have been married fifty-one years, and I can honestly state that Helene is my best friend and the only person I physically desire. If that is not good fortune, nothing is.

We spent our honeymoon in New Orleans and Martinique, and then moved back into our tiny house, converted from a garage, just a block from the University of Denver campus. I spent the next months preparing for our upcoming trip, wanting to share Middle Eastern and Indian wonders with my wife. We would leave in the summer of 1974 and spend four months traveling overland following the same route I had taken but doubling the number of days in order to explore and absorb those ancient cultures more thoroughly. Once in India, I planned to conduct a further seven-month cross-cultural survey of Indian folk arts and crafts. I realized that I would need access to a viable reference library during our travels, a confounding issue at a time long before the advent of the internet. We would be traveling with only one backpack and one small suitcase between us, so I condensed thirty-eight books of Indian history, religions, sociology, anthropology, and arts into abbreviated spot notes that I typed into a single slim bound volume that could easily fit in my pack.

Between my two trips, Beatrice asked me to serve on the board of a museum of international folk art that she was trying to establish. The other board members were leaders of the southern Californian folk art and craft world. Impressed by my scholarship and determination (for years Beatrice jokingly referred to me as her "Egghead"), the board requested that I direct the proposed museum. Equipped with letters of introduction, new business cards, and a letterhead, Helene and I departed in mid-July for the trip's first week in Europe. I wrote ahead to make appointments with museum directors and curators in cities and cultural centers in Eastern Europe, the Balkans, Turkey, Iran, Afghanistan, Pakistan, and India. Even though I was young and professionally naïve, each individual welcomed me. Once again, through Beatrice, doors opened for me everywhere. Even though the museum itself never materialized through lack of funding, and the endeavor was dissolved a couple of years later, the experience taught me immeasurably.

***

Our overland trip together was deeply informative—in part because it taught us how arduous travel can challenge a relationship. By the time we reached Amritsar in early November, we were exhausted physically and emotionally. However, many of our experiences along the way were wondrous. Helene was as awed as I had been by the glories of the Golden Temple. We met with the artist G.S. Sohan Singh and purchased seventeen rare studies painted by his father and seven watercolors and acrylics of his own—a collection that I recently gave to the Museum of Art and Photography in Bengaluru.

For the previous two-and-a-half years, I had been extolling the charms of the Sawhney family to Helene. We both looked forward to spending two weeks in their home in Delhi—a means to recover from some of our travel weariness and stay in comfortable, easygoing accommodations. Uncle Shami and Auntie Teni embraced my wife as they had me. Their son Nandan was then studying at Delhi University, and we spent each evening together, securing the bond of a close friendship that lasted decades. During the days, we explored the palaces, mosques, tombs, parks, gardens, and museums. Our time there further cemented my attachment to that city and introduced me to academic colleagues and art enthusiasts who remain friends to this day.

My mentor Kamaladevi Chattopadhyay had founded Central Cottage Industries near Connaught Circle in New Delhi. The crafts cooperatives and production centers she had helped establish in each state supplied their finest items. The rooms of this enormous emporium unfolded one into another, each devoted to a specific form of craft from regions throughout the country: boxes, vases and vessels, china and terracotta, papier-mâché, brass sculptures, stone carving, wood sculptures, architectural pieces, paintings, prints, frames, handmade papers, furniture, clothing, upholstery fabrics, silk and cotton yardage, shawls, bedcovers and pillowcases, tablecloths and tea-cosies—each fashioned by hand. The standard was not uniform: many objects were beautifully crafted, others appeared to have been created in production lines. Nevertheless, Cottage Industries was an excellent introduction to the vast diversity of the field I had chosen to study—as it still is today.

The twenty-eight Indian states also had their own crafts emporiums that stood side by side on one street a few blocks away. We visited each one to learn about its indigenous handicraft industries—so different from region to region. There, too, we discovered an uneven level of quality: the products of some states were diverse and well-chosen for their artistry, while other emporia appeared to favor more commercial, mass-produced items. Collectively, however, these shops provided insights into the distinct character of each cultural subset and augmented my previous research.

Although Helene fully participated in our activities in Delhi, I did not comprehend how much the intensity from four months of travel had drained her. I am adaptable and gregarious, thriving on seeing new things and having new experiences. Unlike me, my wife is naturally shy—an introvert who genuinely prefers peace and quiet to noise and crowds. Much of the time, she would rather be alone or in the company of just me. Despite her enjoyment of many of our experiences, the constant demands of travel, of changing environments and meeting new people in each place, the intensity of noise, the press of humanity, and the pressure of always being the focus of attention—

all of this drained Helene's reserves to the bone. We were in love, and not mature enough to recognize that travel was undermining our relationship.

In retrospect, we should have left India then to return home, but we were committed to our itinerary and too inexperienced to recognize the seriousness of our issues. Instead, we left Delhi in the beginning of December for a seven-month circle tour of the subcontinent. We took a train to spend three nights in Agra. I was grateful for Helene's response to the Taj Mahal. Although we are both visual and artistic, and our tastes are usually complementary, we often react to stimuli differently. When I returned there with Helene, her rapt appreciation of its sublime design and decoration helped me realize my earlier myopia. I had seen so many photographs, paintings, and representations of it that I was jaded at first sight. The Taj Mahal's global reputation is well deserved.

We discovered that we could escape the crowds (minimal by today's standards) by wandering the extensive formal gardens and sitting on the grass at the far side to view the building obliquely. We also explored the jewel-like Mughal palaces of the Agra Fort and Fatehpur Sikri. But the beauty of the Taj Mahal and its mythic history provided the romantic focus of our visit. We returned there several times during our stay: at dawn when fog from the adjacent Yamuna River faded and the monument's massive marble walls began to glow with increasing heat; at midday, when it stood solitary and magnificent against a cerulean blue sky; and in the evening as the setting sun picked out details of the inlaid Koranic calligraphy that surrounds the overreaching arched doorway. Then, in the dark, the only ones there, we spontaneously waltzed around the platform's smooth terraces by the light of the full moon, its soaring luminescent minarets and dome bearing noble witness to our frivolity.

My excitement about what we were experiencing had so occupied my attention that I failed to notice that Helene's energy was flagging. I witnessed her positive response to the beauty and romance of much of what we were viewing and ignored the fact that she was suffering from culture shock. For all its glories, India also confronts visitors with much that is unsavory. My optimistic nature and increasing ability to compartmentalize combined into insensitivity to this sensitive young woman's personal responses to poverty, beggars, filth in the streets, and many other factors. I encouraged her to focus on the bright side. In doing so, I ignored her feelings. I was the only one to whom she might have been able to unburden, and I discouraged those conversations. We returned to the pace of travel we had set through the Middle East.

Venturing into Rajasthan, we traveled first by bus to the ancient walled town of Bundi in the southern mountains of that state. I wanted to introduce Helene to the essence of Rajput culture in its relatively unadulterated form before she saw its more illustrious versions. After a few days of exploring the frescoed palaces and ancient lanes of this old-world community, we continued to the capital city of Jaipur, one of the most splendid royal centers of India.

In the mid-seventies, before the rapid rise of tourism twenty years later, Jaipur's glories had receded. It was a dirty, polluted, and overcrowded city, and the storied pink facades along the wide boulevards were peeling and stained. Urban planning appeared nonexistent, and Jaipur was becoming a hodgepodge of mismatched buildings that began to define many Indian cities. With my strong filters in place, I focused on what it once had been and, for the most part, ignored what I found distasteful. Helene absorbed our surroundings unfiltered. She found much of it appealing and much that disturbed her. In the early eighteenth century, Jaipur had been India's first fully planned city to use the contemporary concepts of wide, open streets. As a royal center of a progressive and far-seeing monarch, it prided itself on the architectural homogeneity and beauty of its buildings.

We first visited the incomparable Amer Fort several miles outside the city. Constructed in the eighth century and extensively enlarged and improved over the following thousand years, Amer had housed the royal family, court, and retinue for centuries until, in 1727, the progressive Maharajah Jai Singh refocused his reign on the new city that bore his name. Amer's palaces spill in a cascade of colonnaded terraces down a steep mountainside. They contain some of India's most breathtaking architectural ornamentation: a showcase of sumptuous design. By this time, we had viewed many of the wonders of the ancient middle east and north India, but nothing excelled what we saw in Amer. Local artistry reached its peak there in the seventeenth and early eighteenth centuries—a perfectly balanced blend of Turkic, Persian, Mughal, and Rajput motifs and forms that even reflect some aspects of the contemporaneous illuminations of European manuscripts. Intricate tiny mirrors cut into flower petals were inlaid in marble columns carved to complement the floral motifs while nearby frescoed flowers repeated the forms and enlarged the scale. The designers had blended planes of negative space with the resplendent decorations. The result intensified and soothed all the senses at once. Gardens interlaced with bubbling fountains underlined the effect.

Helene felt a strong sense of déjà vu as soon as she entered the fort. After we had thoroughly explored the palaces, she wandered off by herself and climbed to one of the highest terraces for the view. In a dream-like state, she turned a corner and, seeing her reflection in a mirrored wall, did not recognize herself. Helene had an apprehensive response: who was that strange white woman dressed in Indian clothes? When we met a short while later, she was stunned. She stated that for the first time in her life, she had what she could only assume was a spontaneous past-life regression. My wife became convinced that at one time, she must have lived in Amer Palace as an Indian woman, perhaps a princess.

The successful sales of objects and textiles I had purchased on my previous Indian trip had inspired me. I believed I could support my future academic career through finding, exporting, and selling fine Indian crafts. The artistry and craftsmanship of Jaipur were legendary and diverse. Helene enjoyed canvasing textile bazaars as much as I, finding detailed old block prints, embroideries, and appliques. We discovered marvelous antique marionettes, painted masks, and carved architectural ornaments. Jaipur has long been famous for its stone-cutting and gold and enamel jewelry studded with gems. Although we purchased only a few small pieces, we visited well-known jewelers who bedecked my beautiful wife in glittering emeralds, diamonds, and freshwater pearls befitting the princesses described by Scheherazade. When I expressed my fascination with rare textiles to one of the jewelers, he brought from his vaults the finest embroidery we had ever seen. It was a yard long and ten inches high, depicting seventeenth-century court scenes stitched in gold and colored silks. Its needlework was so delicate that unless one looked at it closely, one would swear it was a miniature painting. The royal family wanted to sell it discretely. With further research, I recognized that this was the best and largest example of only five known pieces of an entire sub-school of royal art. Although its price was more than we had intended to spend, this masterpiece left Jaipur with us. Years later, that same jeweler unsuccessfully attempted to purchase it back from us at ten times our cost. In the late nineties, we sold it to the Virginia Museum of Fine Arts, where it remains on permanent display.

The crowds and the sheer mass of humanity affected Helene everywhere we traveled in India. Except behind the closed doors of our hotel room, privacy was rare. Once in a while, we could find a corner of a garden in which to sit or a table in a quiet café. Still, almost invariably, we would be discovered by one and then more curious bystanders who felt it imperative to ask us questions. I was at ease with these circumstances, but Helene was shy and required privacy. Open and undaunted staring was an acceptable norm for much of the Indian populace in those days—they had not been taught, as we had, that it was rude. (That tendency to stare at strangers is no longer often evident in South Asia.) We two young Americans were like magnets that drew a crowd of starers wherever we went: one, then two, three, ten, then twenty people standing near us just staring open-eyed. Rarely was their gaze hostile or even aggressive, but it was an almost constant presence when we were in public. Its effect began to shatter Helene's composure. Perhaps because of overpopulation and close living, many Indians have a different sense of personal space than most westerners. Whereas in the Americas and Europe, individuals strive to place comfort zones between themselves and others, the Indian public often seems at ease in close proximity, talking right in your face. People frequently crowd together, push and shove in situations that don't necessarily warrant it. While in my first seven months in India, this closeness irritated me, I grew to accept it as a cultural norm and adapted to it. It increasingly invaded Helene's vulnerability.

Udaipur was our next destination. The Lake Palace had captured my imagination when I spent an hour there on my first visit. I had booked a room for ten nights, including our first anniversary and Christmas, 1974. Our sojourn exceeded my dreams: an escape into luxurious, secluded fantasy. When we arrived, the manager gave us a five-room corner suite with walls inlaid in decorative lotus patterns of pink, green, and pale blue glass. Besides our enormous bedroom, we had a sitting room overlooking the lake, a domed corner room with oblique views, a well-appointed dressing room, and a luxurious bathroom—all for just $32 a night. Today that same suite is fully booked months in advance at a starting rate of $3,450. The high season can be almost double.

The Lake Palace was constructed in the eighteenth century in the middle of man-made Lake Pichola for the sole purpose of catering to the private pleasures of Udaipur's *Maharana* and his *zenana* (or harem). At the time, its design and decoration employed the most refined artistry in the land. The many rooms, gardens, and pavilions had been enlarged and improved over the centuries. When, after independence from the British, the revenues of India's previous monarchs were greatly depleted, the Lake Palace was the first royal property to open as a luxury hotel, just five years before we arrived. We had read Pearl S. Buck's romance novel *Mandala* about the metamorphosis of this uniquely beautiful property. Our ten palatial nights were pure heaven! Helene loved it as much as I: isolated, protected, phenomenally beautiful, and romantic.

We arrived soon after the Taj Mahal Hotel Group took over its management and before they had upgraded the hotel to world-class standards. Over subsequent years, the Lake Palace has grown to include sixty-five rooms and eighteen suites, all elegantly furnished and decorated. We visited recently, and the complex is truly epic, but its earlier version had an indefinable character that seemed closer to its original spirit. When we were there, it was as if the specters of previous kings and courtesans still inhabited and overlaid our activities. The palace was not full, even in the holiday season, and we wandered at leisure through the chambers and public rooms, and alongside the lovely lotus pond.

Sunset in our corner room became a favorite pastime. Nothing blocked our 180-degree view of the lake as it stretched out to the forested far shore and the green mountains beyond. The population of Udaipur then was one-quarter its current size, and the city had not yet spread far beyond its ancient boundary walls. As the sun crested the far hills, the lake turned shades from dark blue and green to bright yellows, pinks, and purples. Right outside our multiple-arched windows, fish would rise to the surface to feed, their scales flashing and reflecting the lake's colors as they jumped above water.

A motor launch from the Maharana's private jetty accessed the mainland. Most days, we would cross over to climb the steep lane through two of the five monumental palaces that were interconnected along the lake's edge. Some days we explored the wonders of the city palaces, examining in detail inlaid glass mosaics and historical frescoes, moving from spectacular mirrored royal bedchamber to tiled audience hall. We were almost always alone—long before the current situation where hordes of tourists jam narrow access passages and stairwells. We would spend hours each day meandering along the full mile of the crafts bazaar that stretches down into the center of that age-old town, from handicraft shop to painting gallery to textile emporium. We gladly accepted cups of sweet chai as we got to know the shopkeepers, enquiring about their businesses, their children, and their heritage while they asked about us. Each time we also learned details about the art they sold.

Spellbound for hours, we watched a painter of miniatures delicately dip a single-haired brush into pots of pigments ground from semiprecious minerals and apply minuscule lines to paper to create the face of a princess or the leaves of a forest. Another afternoon we watched cobblers use hooked needles to pull silk thread in a looping embroidery stitch to decorate the tops of curved-toed leather shoes. The bell sound of ringing hammers drew us into the studios of Udaipur's silversmiths as they pounded thin plates of silver into floral-shaped steel dies. They pulled fully formed silver petals and blossoms from these metal blocks to solder them into earrings and necklaces displayed on racks sparkling in the sun. Each place we went, we absorbed a deeper understanding of the fundments of Indian artistry as we selectively purchased items both as gifts for each other and friends and as investments for our future. Three years later, when we next returned to Udaipur, we were amused when we were besieged with calls all along the market street: "Mister Stephen! Mister Stephen! Mister Stephen!" The many hours of getting to know vendors and artists had been well spent. Some of these individuals and their extended families remain close friends to this day.

In the evenings, back in the Lake Palace, we were served dinner in the formal dining room. Long before the current internationally trained chefs prepared the delectable meals now on offer, the fare was basic, even mediocre. Each evening, we would order from a menu of daily specials, mouth-watering descriptions of some new dish—Vegetables a La Russe, or Legumes Parisienne, or Shanghai Surprise—only to find that it was yet another variation of the same two vegetables: carrots and cauliflower, with little difference in their preparation or seasoning.

For our first anniversary, the staff prepared a private table on one of the top terraces of the Lake Palace. White linen, silver, candelabra, and fine china accented the special occasion. We will never forget how rays of the setting sun illuminated an amber-colored crystal finial that rose from a perfect onion dome on one side. The sky above and around us turned deeper and deeper shades of pink while the lake created a perfect reflection of the long row of legendary palaces that faced us. Helene was radiant in a brocaded gold tissue sari and a set of enamel jewelry we had purchased in Jaipur, while I wore a white raw silk Nehru jacket. We were young and much in love. Little did we suspect that our joy would be short-lived.

Five days later, we celebrated Christmas. At our request, the hotel gardener procured a potted, wispy casuarina pine that we decorated with small folk dolls and toys, strung with colored paper chains. My mother had sent us a candy cane, and when we tried to affix it to the top, the tree bent over like the one in *A Charlie Brown's Christmas*. We spent a romantic morning lazily opening gifts we had hidden from each other.

Too soon, we were on a train bound for Ahmedabad. At that time, many Indian locomotives were still coal-fired. The extreme heat of our compartment on that late December day forced us to open the windows. The coal smoke blew in, creating a film throughout, including our lungs. Helene already had a minor cold. She had always been susceptible to sinus allergies that often developed into respiratory ailments, and the excessive carbon proved too much for her. By the time we reached Gujarat later that day, she had developed a bad cough. By the next, it had progressed into a fever.

For one scheduled week we stayed in the relatively upmarket Cama Hotel on the banks of the Sabarmati

River. Helene took antibiotics and I believed that her health was improving. N.T. Vakani, my beneficent mentor, came to meet us the night we arrived. He offered the gift of guiding us through the rural Gujarati communities that I had been unable to visit three years earlier. Instead of three weeks on the road, we remained in the city of Ahmedabad taking care of Helene. Vakani facilitated our move into a far less expensive, fairly basic hotel—comfortable but with no frills. Helene was weak and rested in bed nursing what we believed to be the aftermath of her bronchitis. As the hotel had no restaurant, Vakani helped me find delicious local foods that I spent part of each day ordering and fetching.

Anchored there, but with a young man's energy, I returned each day to the warehouses of Saurashtra Handicraft. Yet again, Vakani and I sorted through tens of thousands of old textiles, selecting the finest for purchase. Over those weeks, I built up an incomparable trove that eventually became what might have been the single finest private collection of Indian textiles in North America. Each day, I returned to our room with treasures that I spread out for Helene to view and help choose. (More than a decade ago, I gave ninety-five percent of my Indian art to Mingei International Museum in San Diego where it is regularly displayed.)

During those weeks, I also met and became friends with three crucial individuals: Haku Shah, Dr. Jyotindra Jain, and Dr. Jutta Jain-Neubauer. Hakubhai was a diminutive man with large bushy eyebrows that overhung eyes radiating wit, humor, and intelligence. A renowned graphic artist, he also had documented more village and tribal arts in Gujarat than anyone else. His own collections and those that he built for museums were unexcelled, and his published research with Dr. Stella Kramrisch had introduced me to much of what I would spend my life studying. Jutta and Jyotindra Jain, both elegant, engaging characters, were to become two of my best friends—individuals whose scholarship, dedication, and distinctive gifts of insight have infused the complete field of Indian art. Jutta's specialty is the architecture of stone step wells in western India, among other subjects. Beginning in Ahmedabad, Jyotindra has created the finest museums of Indian craftsmanship, folk art, and decorative arts. He is also one of India's most prolific, diverse, and original scholars and authors.

The children and grandchildren of the cotton mill owner and business magnate Ambalal Sarabhai are among India's leading philanthropists, scientists, architects, art historians, teachers, musicians, and dancers. Following my introduction by Beatrice Wood in 1972, two legendary Sarabhai doyens offered me essential guidance during these weeks we stayed in Ahmedabad. Giraben Sarabhai, an avid follower of Mahatma Gandhi, had founded the incomparable Calico Museum with its inventory of thousands of Indian textiles, its research fellowships, and superb publications. She invited me to explore her museum fully and allowed me the rare privilege of examining its extensive reserve collections. In 1947, with the help of Maria Montessori, her sister Leena Mangaldas, the renowned choreographer and exponent of bharatanatyam, had established the Shreyas Foundation as a beacon of liberal education. The Shreyas School blends forward-looking thought with an awareness of indigenous Gujarati traditional values and technologies. Its museum of regional arts and crafts was designed and curated by Dr. Jyotindra Jain. Leenaben and Jyotindra openly shared with me their progressive visions and goals.

Gira and Leena's niece Mallika Sarabhai was to become a good friend. Her father was the late Vikram Sarabhai, India's leading nuclear physicist and rocket scientist, while her mother, Mrinalini, was one of the nation's leading classical dancers. Together her parents had established Darpana Academy of Performing Arts, a landmark institution that Mallika would later run. Over the years, my friend has become a leading dancer, choreographer, actor, playwright, and teacher. She has modeled outspoken women's empowerment and rights throughout her life. Mallika and her husband Bipin Shah founded Mapin Press, the art publishing house that has produced three of my books. Decades after we first met, her insightful editorial guidance helped me create one of the achievements of which I am most proud, my book *Daughters of India: Art and Identity*.

While I kept productively busy each day getting to know these individuals and conducting my research, my young wife's illness increasingly mystified me. I was self-centered and immature and wrongly blamed her lack of improvement on hypochondria. When Helene complained of backaches, I countered by arguing that she was bedsore from inactivity and that if she only exercised, she would regain her strength and feel better. Finally, the Sarabhais set up an appointment for an examination by their own physician, who ordered chest x-rays. My beloved wife had only one half of one functioning lung, while the other had collapsed!

She suffered from untreated pneumonia that, without proper care, had infected her pleural cavity. The doctor diagnosed advanced tuberculosis and advised that we fly that night to Bombay for intensive specialized care.

Our Indian Airlines flight caused Helene extreme pain. Every air pocket made her feel like she was being kicked in the lungs. Upon our arrival and transfer late at night to the recommended hospital, we were told that they could not admit Helene. Her condition might be highly contagious and cause an epidemic. We knew no one in that major city. In desperation, I called Uncle Shami Sawhney in Delhi for help. He had retired as India's director of Burmah Shell Oil Corporation and still maintained business connections throughout India. After a sleepless night in a mediocre hotel in Colaba, we received a cable from Uncle Shami saying that he had arranged Helene's admission to Breach Candy Hospital, one of India's finest private medical institutions. Once she was given an ocean-facing room, specialists administered two intensive days of examinations.

India had a lot of bad press in the West at that time. International news often reported statistics about unsanitary conditions and death by disease. When we told friends and family that we would be traveling in India that year for seven months, many had expressed concerns that our health might be compromised. When Helene had first contracted bronchitis back in Ahmedabad, she had made me promise that I would not inform anyone in our families or any friends back in America. She did not want to worry them unduly. Over the subsequent weeks, she had repeated that demand many times and I had reluctantly agreed. I was now frightened more than I had ever been in my life and could confide my fears to no one.

Finally, Breach Candy's doctors ascertained that Helene did not have TB, but instead had empyema, a rare disease of the pleural cavity. The pleural cavity is a membranous sac that encases and protects the lungs. Helene's untreated pneumonia had caused an infection that produced viscous pus that filled this cavity, leaving no room for her lungs to function. Using a long needle, specialists attempted to draw off the liquid, but it had been allowed to fester so long it had solidified. The only option was immediate lung surgery scheduled for the morning of our third day in Bombay. We were in shock, and felt adrift, lost, and terrified. I first placed a call to Charlie and Katie Wheeler, my parents-in-law, and then to my own. To my immense relief, the Wheelers booked the next flight from Los Angeles to Bombay. I would not have to go through this agony alone.

In the meantime, while Helene's parents were in the air, the long and delicate operation began, led by India's leading lung surgeon, Dr. Farokh E. Udwadia. To get access to her pleural cavity, he had to open a space between the ribs in Helene's right side, cutting the muscles to gain access. He could then reach in with his whole hand and manually remove the thick accumulation of pus. The theory was that once her pleural cavity had been cleaned out and she was stitched back together, her lungs would gradually reinflate, and she would be able to breathe again normally. I sat by myself for hours in the small waiting room, my gaze fixed on the door into the surgery theater, praying. Finally, when Dr. Udwadia emerged, he came and sat next to me, took my hand, and gently told me that he doubted that my beloved wife would survive. The next few hours would determine the outcome.

By this time, it was late afternoon of January 28, 1975. I had to drive by taxi to Bombay's international airport to pick up my parents-in-law. Just before I departed the hospital, a nurse came running out to tell me that my beloved's vital signs were looking better. Dr. Udwadia hoped she would survive.

By the time I met Katie and Charlie and accompanied them to Breach Candy, their daughter's condition was stable. I burst into tears when I saw my beautiful young wife that first time after the operation. The infection had been eradicated, her ribs replaced, and reconstructive surgery completed on the muscles and tissues of her right side. Two long tubes, the diameter of a narrow garden hose, extended from her side to drain any additional build-up in her pleural cavity. Oxygen, blood transfusions, and various drips fed her body. Her recovery would be slow and painful, but her prognosis was good. She would live!

The next week was a confusing whirlwind. When we left the hospital, the Wheelers checked themselves and me into the five-star Taj Mahal Hotel. They occupied a lavish suite overlooking Bombay Harbor, while I had a room just down the hall. Staying there was both an incredible blessing and totally surreal. Each day I would spend all possible hours with Helene, while her parents came and went. It was unlikely that they would ever have come to India under any other circumstance. They had never wished to travel there. Their daughter's health and recovery were paramount, and they did all they could to ensure it. I was both grateful for their company and crushed by the events that had just occurred. I blamed myself for my wife's initial illness and for being so callous that I had not recognized its progression. My guilt and self-condemnation seemed insurmountable, and I vowed that, if she survived and did not leave me, I would do everything I could to become worthy of her.

A week later, Helene's condition had improved enough that the Wheelers decided to return home to Orange County, California. They generously promised to pay all medical bills and my continued expenses at the Taj. The following six weeks focused on Helene's slow recovery. After two weeks, Dr. Udwadia removed both drains from her side and sutured the holes. By this time, my wife had been taken off constant oxygen and was slowly rehabilitating her lungs. Although each physical movement exhausted and pained her, the nurses had her up and walking as soon as possible. Her final two weeks in residence were purely cautionary. By this time, Helene was desperate to get out of there, but her doctors believed that she still was too susceptible to reinfection to leave her antiseptic confinement. A negotiation between her medical team, the hospital, and her parents permitted her release with the explicit understanding that she would stay with me in the Taj Mahal Hotel until her lungs had sufficiently healed. In 1974, that hotel was one of the few in India that could boast of a fully filtered, centralized air system. Katie and Charlie Wheeler kindly offered to continue footing all our bills there for the next six weeks, explaining that the expense was a fraction of what they would pay for a hospital room in the States.

Our experiences at the Taj were incredible. During the first two weeks, Helene was confined to our luxurious room. We could order whatever we chose from the astounding menus of six different hotel restaurants. After that, as long as she did not go outside, we could wander together through the arcade of shops or dine in any of the restaurants: Chinese, Indian, Western café, Western gourmet, bar food, or pan-Asian mix. After our four months of arduous travel across the Middle East and the mélange of encounters and challenges in India, I found these weeks both beguiling and preposterous.

When I was not with Helene during the two-and-a-half months that she was hospitalized and recovering, I had plenty of time on my own to explore museums, galleries, and shops. I built bonds with canny dealers and shopkeepers and learned lifelong lessons about the pros and cons of India's fine art trade. That knowledge was to inform essential decisions upon our return to America. I continued to collect art with the intention of selling it in the United States and, before we left, shipped a large crate back to Ojai of treasures accumulated in Northern and Western India.

Just before I sent those items, I invited Kaka Kelkar to take the train from Pune for a day's visit with us. On our original itinerary, we had intended to spend a week with him and Kaku in their beautiful home and museum, but the operation caused us to cancel our plans for a circle tour of India. Kaka's reaction to our luxurious accommodations was typically humorous. This tiny, elderly man, dressed as always in his traditionally modest white cotton dhoti, khadi kurta, and vest, could not stop laughing at all the nouveau riche extravagance. He giggled in the elegant lobby, guffawed at the stuffiness of many of the hotel patrons and staff, mocked the glitzy objects in the glass-fronted shops and galleries, and chortled as we stood in the mirrored, brass-inlaid elevator to ascend to our room. I had spread out all our finds for him to see: the Golden Temple paintings, the sculptures, puppets, and boxes from Rajasthan, the royal gold embroidery from Jaipur, all the varied textiles from Gujarat, and the decorative art I'd found in Bombay's shops.

Kaka avidly examined each item, exclaiming with glee at the excellence of our purchases. I ordered hot spiced chai from room service and, as I poured it from the pot, he noticed its price: five rupees. In 1975 the standard cost of a cup of chai from a street vendor in India was twenty-five paise, one twentieth the price of the Taj tea. Kaka thought that was the funniest thing he had ever seen: "Five-rupee tea!" he exclaimed. "Five-rupee tea! This man has just paid five rupees for a cup of tea!" He dined on that fact for the rest of his life. Each time we met in future years, he would mercilessly rib me about it. Whenever he served me tea, he would tell me he would soon be giving me a bill for 500 rupees or 1,000 rupees, each time inflating the price further. I have never known another man who filled his days with such genuine enjoyment of life. I miss his almost constant laughter.

On April 20, Helene was strong enough to fly to Delhi. Her doctors had persuaded us that the prolonged travel back to North America might endanger her. They insisted that we wait a further month before we returned home. For ten days, we were guests of the Sawhneys. Reuniting with that family was always anchoring. We then flew up to the Vale of Kashmir for a blissful two-week holiday on a houseboat on Nagin Lake. Auntie Teni and Uncle Shami introduced us to Ghulam Mohammed Major, the owner/proprietor of the New Peony Houseboat. We thought we had landed in heaven. Constructed and paneled with fragrant deodar wood, our houseboat contained two comfortable bedrooms and bathrooms with showers, a pantry, a large living room, a sheltered back verandah, and a full open roof deck: all just for us. The beds were comfortable, the water piping hot, and the rooms tastefully furnished in antiques and beautiful Kashmiri crafts. The price for all expenses was $121 a week. Our vessel was moored alongside its sister boat on a quiet lake far from the intensely crowded areas where most other tourists resided. Between them was a smaller one that contained the residence of Mr. Major, his staff, and the kitchen. The cook created three delicious meals each day plus high tea, all served by our personal bearer, also named Ghulam. Each day a flower vendor, Bulbul, paddled up to the boat in his long dugout filled with fresh spring flowers: tulips, crocuses, hyacinths, daffodils, and lilacs. Mr. Major provided as many vases as we wanted, and we filled each room with fragrant blossoms, replaced afresh on the second or third day.

Whenever we chose, Ghulam would call for us a shikara, or canopied gondola-type boat with the front two-thirds filled with a mattress, silk bolsters propped against a backrest, and soft lap blankets. We reveled in Kashmir's cool mountain breezes after Bombay and Delhi's increasingly hot temperatures. Behind the screened backrest, our boatman propelled his craft with a heart-shaped paddle. Often Ghulam sat with him as our guide, answering our questions about what we were seeing. We glided from clear-water lake to wooded river through hundreds of lotus pads, usually quietly by ourselves. The only sounds were the gentle swish of the paddle as we moved forward and the ever-present chorus of songbirds. Surrounding us were the incomparable snow-capped mountains of the lower Himalayan range.

Our goal one day was the romantic Mughal gardens of Shalimar. After we had viewed the rows of fountains surrounded by beds of blooming flowers, Ghulam spread an embroidered cloth on the grass and served us tea in china cups, with fresh hot biscuits and lotus honey. On another, we visited Nishat Bagh, also a resplendent Mughal garden. We ventured into town several times, once to explore a shop filled with more than a thousand intricately hand-painted papier mâché boxes, vases, lamps, and tables of every color and shade imaginable. On a second, we visited the studio of one of Kashmir's most famous shawl makers and watched men embroider the softest wool with tiny flowers or rows of mango-shaped paisleys.

May 5 was Helene's twenty-fourth birthday. Although we had innumerable choices for inspiring outings, we chose to stay by the heated woodstove in our oriental-carpeted living room reading books, listening to good music, and enjoying each other's company. Occasionally, we would hear outside the sing-song voices of vendors trying to catch out attention. Mobile shops—shikaras or dugout canoes—filled with a selection of local crafts would sidle up to our back deck offering carved walnut boxes, antique shawls, silver jewelry, or more mundane items such as drugstore sundries.

After our ordeals of the past months, this romantic sojourn in Kashmir was deeply healing for us both. At the end of a restful day, we sat for tea on the back verandah, watching bright blue kingfishers dart in and out of the water. As the sun began to set over Emperor Babur's fortress on a distant hill, we felt peace suffusing our hearts and minds. A week later, we flew back to Delhi and readied ourselves to return home. Our experiences in Western and Southern Asia had challenged us to the core. Our naiveté and immaturity had endangered us both, but our experiences had strengthened our commitment to one another. We returned to America thoughtful and determined to be more attentive to one another's needs.

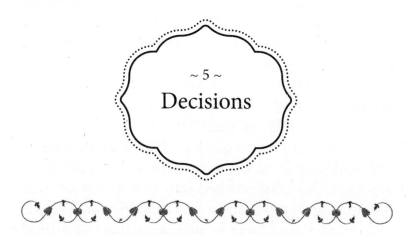

~ 5 ~
Decisions

Patience, humor, and dogged determination: three qualities required to travel well in India. All three were necessary simply to mail a package. It used to take an entire day for such an endeavor.

Whether I had one package or more to send, the length of time was almost the same. Since it took so long, it seemed better to wait until I had several to mail. First, of course, boxes had to be procured. That might seem like a simple affair, but in the seventies, before India relaxed its massive international trade restrictions, all commodities were highly prized, and almost everything was recycled. Durable boxes were hard to come by, and it took diligence to find just the right ones.

Let's assume that I began the postal day with the necessary containers already in hand—otherwise, hours might be added onto the morning. The first place to visit with the boxes was the cloth merchant where bolts of strong white cotton were unrolled and examined, the sizes of the containers measured, and the appropriate lengths of cloth purchased and cut. Remember that all transactions in India at that time were accompanied by at least one cup of tea and all the necessary small talk. Things did not happen quickly. I had to locate a tailor, one willing to do such a menial job, and without delay. The cloth was hand-stitched into a wrapping for each box, leaving the top open for later examination. A needle and strong thread were bought, sometimes at a third shop, and taken with me to the post office.

It would have been foolish even to consider mailing a package at a town or small city. The time involved would have been quadrupled, and that package might never reach its destination. I would only mail in large cities. Of course, Indian urban centers are subdivided according to profession, as are most old-world towns. Tailors are in one street, cloth merchants in another. Neither was near my hotel, and both were almost always far from the main post office, which is usually in the business center. Carrying my increasing bundles, I would have to take a bicycle rickshaw to my destination. And up to this point, the whole process was relatively easy.

The post office was another matter: a sea of people, all crowding into disorderly lines. Indians learned their love of queuing up from the British, but the demands of the hierarchy and inflammatory natures had altered the concept of the polite, straight queue. Many would stand patiently in line, but the sense of personal distance can be different in India, and people tended to push and jostle one another constantly. Others demanded seniority through a form of entitlement. They believed that they had the right to push directly to the front of the line, shouting for the clerk's attention. This action may or may not have produced overt resentment from those others who have been standing for hours. Some just chalked it up to karma, others screamed in rage. A post office was rarely a quiet place.

Arriving amid this confusion, I had to first locate the queue for customs forms. This line might be relatively short. Once at the front, I would take five copies of three different forms for each package, and then retire to a dark corner of the building, or perhaps to the steps outside, and painstakingly fill out all the forms. Each was required to be written individually; carbon copies were unacceptable. I wrote and signed a list of all the contents and values, a statement that they were not antiquities, included my passport and visa numbers and their dates of issue and expiry, my address, and that of the destination: fifteen times for each package. Then on to the line for customs examination. That line might well take an hour or more. Remember that India is often hot and muggy. Standing in line, even for a young man in his twenties, was never comfortable. On reaching the counter, I had to present my passport, open the box for examination to prove that the contents were not restricted for export, show my invoices, and give all the papers for checking. One of each was kept by the customs official, who assigned a peon to accompany me to the sealer's queue.

At this point, I had a choice. I could either return to my corner or steps to sew up the cloth, always under the watchful eye of the peon who made sure that I did not alter the contents, or try to juggle them while standing in line, attempting to complete the sewing by the time I reached the sealer. The sole occupation of this invariably aged bureaucrat was to heat red sealing wax over a candle flame and drip it onto all the sewn edges of each box. He then pressed a brass seal into it at short intervals along the edge to prevent the package from being reopened. Once I paid the sealer for his services, I would tip the peon who could now return to his post. Now that the parcels were sealed, I used a ballpoint pen to laboriously print the destination and return addresses onto the white cotton of one side. For each box, I also had to roll eight of the remaining forms into a single tube, tie several loops of thread around it, and sew it to one edge.

It was now necessary to have the packages weighed. Of course, the clerk who manned the scales had his own long queue which might take me an hour or more to wade through. Once reached, this clerk placed each package, one by one, in the left-hand dish of an age-old scale with various bronze metric weights added and subtracted from its counterpart until the needle was precisely centered. Then he counted all the weights and wrote the appropriate figures in ink onto the cotton cloth of each parcel. I could then move to the end of the line for the postage calculator. That clerk would read the weight amount of each and figure out the cost of sending the packages (we would discuss whether they would go by air or sea), and, after that, mark the amount onto the cotton. The next queue was for the stamp vendor who, when paid, would hand out a collection of stamps for each box. Indian stamps never seemed to be in large denominations. Consequently, each box usually required several dozen stamps.

It might appear logical that the process was over at this point, but that conclusion would be based upon the assumption that Indian stamps were manufactured with glue already on them. They were not. It was always necessary to find a piece of scrap paper (often newspaper) and use my fingers to dig a dollop of white paste from the ever-present mound on the nearby counter. Then, precariously balancing packages, remaining forms, stamps, and glue, I would try to find an empty space at a counter (not an easy feat in such a crowded place). Paste smeared with my forefinger onto the back of each stamp allowed me to messily affix it directly to the cotton. Often the stamps covered more than one side. I took one of the remaining contents forms and similarly pasted it to the side opposite the address, difficult on small packages.

Finally, I was ready for my last queue: the canceler. Once reached, this man would take a large round bronze seal, pound it onto a red ink pad, and cancel all the stamps, tossing the package into a bin behind him. I had finished.

In general, it might take me between eight and ten hours to mail a group of packages. As I only had one set of arms, I could only manage between six and eight on any given day. In my first six months in India, I sent sixty-seven packages home: some handicrafts to be given as gifts to family and friends, others the basis of my first collection of Indian art. Because the itinerary of my second trip with Helene was greatly foreshortened, we mailed only thirty-two and shipped the rest in crates by sea from Bombay and from Delhi (via Bombay). But on the upcoming third trip, we posted more than ninety.

India has modernized and significantly changed during the past five decades, and mailing packages is far easier. Boxes are readily available and are strong enough to endure rough handling without disintegrating. Cotton covers are no longer necessary. Packages are not sealed with wax, stamps are sold with glue on the back, and only three forms are required for each parcel sent. In most cases, customs inspections are far more manageable. Today I might only take an hour or two to mail a package and find it almost as efficient and reliable to do so in a town as a major city. Sometimes I wonder what happened to the people who filled all those minor jobs: the customs peons, the sealers, and the weighers. Perhaps they have graduated to much more exciting occupations? The Indian bureaucracy is still ingrained, and India still teaches me the lessons of patience, humor, and determination. Nevertheless, I am glad of the changes. On mailing days, I luxuriate in the many free hours I now have for other activities.

* * *

A field day of opening and examining awaited us on our return to America. Our purchases were varied and wondrous. As before, we had stockpiled many as gifts for friends and family. Some were intentional additions to our growing collection of Indian art, but most we had acquired for the sole purpose of resale.

In the months that followed, I had a crisis of conscience: I discovered that I was uncomfortable as a dealer. Over my two long journeys through India, I had become a good bargainer. I enjoyed the whole process. Unlike many other academics, I bonded with shopkeepers and gallery owners. Some were canny, others ruthless, but the game was like chess: its moves, countermoves, and complex strategies intrigued me. Nevertheless, while I was a shrewd and clear-sighted negotiator and enjoyed giving purchases away, I became too attached to the artworks to feel at ease selling them. Suddenly and unexpectedly, we were left with an enormous inventory, and our private collection grew exponentially.

Back in Denver for thirteen months, we moved into a larger but still modest house away from the university. During our travels the previous year, I met with museum directors in the Middle East and India as part of my efforts to help Beatrice build a museum of international folk art. I continued to work with that organization and to write grant applications for the museum. At the same time, I also applied for the postgraduate program at the University of London's School of Oriental and African Studies. My primary advisor and favorite professor at the University of Denver, Charles Geddes, had received his doctorate at SOAS and strongly recommended it. In this highly esteemed college, 115 different post-graduate curricula focus on the cultures and languages of more than sixty countries in Asia and Africa. The SOAS Library is globally acknowledged as one of the world's finest repositories of published Asian and African knowledge. The India Office Library south of the Thames had almost nine miles of shelves containing 70,000 books written in English about South Asia. It also held most of the ledgers, diaries, and letters of civil service officers and their families from the British East India Company and the subsequent British Indian Empire. (The new British Library has since absorbed these archives.) The British Museum is a block away from SOAS, and the unparalleled Indian collections of the Victoria and Albert Museum are easily accessible by the Underground.

Dr. Geddes's advice made sense. SOAS accepted me into their post-graduate program, and Helene and I began to prepare for several years' residency in Britain. Both sets of our parents were thrilled at our opportunity to live in London but were sad that we would be so far away. Beatrice was proud of my choice yet protested our decision. Her dream of a museum of international folk art in Ojai never materialized due to lack of sponsorship and strong leadership. Yet, not much later, one of our board members, Martha Longenecker, formed her own organization: Mingei International Museum near San Diego, based upon similar principles. I have remained closely connected to that institution since its inception. It was to become seminal to salient aspects of my later career.

* * *

Upon entering SOAS, I had intended to major in Indian anthropology with a focus on art and craft. I hoped I would be able to continue my lateral interdisciplinary approach. Enrolled in the autumn of 1976, I soon discovered that SOAS's Department of Anthropology did not value cultural anthropology. If I chose to study under its auspices, my course work would be focused purely upon social or physical disciplines. I found that viewpoint too limiting and transferred to the Department of South Asian Art and Archaeology. This program accepted my integrated point of view as long as I took the courses it required.

Real estate costs in London were so low at that time that, for a small investment ($40,000), we were able to purchase and furnish a row house in North London (Muswell Hill). Five days a week, I took the Tube down to SOAS and attended demanding lectures on various Indian subjects, perusing the library between classes. The smell of old books, the feeling of their spines and covers, and the textures of paper and print have always struck me as sensuous experiences. The library stacks were open, and, as elsewhere, I learned as much through discovering books adjacent to those I found through the extensive card files. My learning curve was huge. Today, in the twenty-first century, I see many advantages to the internet and regularly explore its wonders, but it will never replace my love of physically handling and reading books.

London pulled us into its web of stimulating experiences. We explored its streets, shops, garden squares, parks, and, above all, museums and theaters.

Over centuries, the East India Company had stockpiled enormous quantities of Indian art—some of it looted from a variety of sources, other works acquired legitimately. In 1801, the company constructed the Indian Museum to house them in London. After parliament disbanded the EIC in 1858, the British Empire absorbed India and established the Empress Victoria at its helm. The Indian Museum dissolved in 1879, and its vast collections dispersed to several museums and institutions. The South Kensington Museum, later renamed the Victoria and Albert Museum, agreed to house all the Indian decorative art temporarily. One hundred and forty-two years later, the collections remain there and in vast storage houses south of the river. While I was at SOAS, and until just a few years ago, the extensive reserve collections of South Asian textiles remained in one large storage room in the center of the V&A. I spent several days each week during my first eighteen months in London examining and making notes about the 60,000 textiles in store. These hours provided an incomparable education. Many embroideries, brocades, silks, and cottons had been accessed in the early nineteenth-century and their provenance was unassailable. I learned the touch, feel, weight, and smell of fabrics hundreds of years old. These experiences, combined with the lessons I had absorbed through weeks of examining textiles with Vakani in Ahmedabad on each of two trips, helped develop my eye and awareness.

We also stretched our minds by attending London's antique markets each week. Early Friday mornings before sunrise, we would bundle ourselves down to Portobello Market, where hundreds of vendors set up their stalls for trade only. Everything of quality was for sale: furniture, paintings, prints, porcelains, kitchenware, tools, clothing, jewelry, ornaments, stained glass, bric-a-brac, fine art, folk art, crafts, and utensils—perhaps 100,000 items fetchingly displayed. Each week we scoured the wares, asking questions, handling, inspecting, and learning to discern age, quality, content, and rarity. On Fridays, the dealers traded among themselves. On Saturdays, the market was open for retail. By our third year in London, Helene's and my visual awareness had been so heightened that we could tell when the inventory of the hundred or more dealers that we frequented had changed. We learned to spot a reproduction quickly. This new awareness complemented our ongoing exposure to the abundant diversity of Indian arts and crafts.

* * *

For three years at SOAS, I studied the Urdu language and continued learning Sanskrit, but most of my courses were in Indian art history. The specialty of my primary professor and advisor, Dr. John Burton-Paige, was pre-Mughal Sultanate architecture, and I attended an excessive number of lectures about that. I bonded with two classmates who remain close friends today: Heather Marshall (later Heather Elgood) and Steven Cohen. Heather later went on to expand and rewrite the full syllabus of SOAS's South Asian Art History and Archaeology Department. Because of her, its scope is now far more broad-minded and interdisciplinary. Steve became one of the acknowledged world experts on early Indian textiles. His partner, Rosemary Crill, was, until her retirement in 2016, senior curator of South Asian textiles and decorative art at the Victoria and Albert Museum. A third friend, a Canadian, John Silverstein, lived with Helene and me in our Muswell Hill home for several months in 1977 and then moved into his own flat not far away. He and I shared many interests and approaches, and, at my encouragement, he audited many of my classes. Helene and I invited him to accompany us for two months during our next trip to India.

In the late seventies, London was becoming a focal point for studying Asian textiles, including those of India. Although I remained fascinated by them, my stubborn wish to work in a ground-breaking field forced me to look for another subject for my doctoral thesis. In preparation for our return to India in early 1978 to resume our postponed circle tour, I canvased the libraries to learn all I could about Indian tribal cultures.

Scholars believe that many of the diverse Indian tribes descend directly and indirectly from India's earliest human inhabitants. Although India has the largest indigenous population of any country in the world, little documentation existed about them at that time. The field remains inadequately studied. Most Indian tribal people (often generically called *Adivasis*) have their own language roots, religions, rituals, customs, and social orders that differ significantly from those of mainstream cultures. Although Adivasis exist in almost every Indian state, they generally live in remote regions—those areas previously considered undesirable for development, such as forests, jungles, high mountains, and inarable lands. My sources for information were old district gazetteers, a few published researches, unpublished British documents, and the papers of post-independent Indian surveys. The more I learned, the more I found parallels with the ways that white Americans had betrayed, subjugated, annihilated, and ignored Native Americans and the people of First Nations. However, tribal Indian cultures are unique, and I realized it would be a mistake to compare them too closely to those of

North America. Nevertheless, this field of study echoed my childhood fascination with Plains Indian cultures, which had been encouraged by the Laubins (Lakota friends of my parents, referred to in Chapter Fifteen). In changing the subject of my doctoral thesis to tribal Indian material culture, I determined to find one or more tribes in Central India whose documentation might be my focal point. I based my rationale on the theory that these people's ancestors had engendered the original roots of Indian culture. Numerous cultural invasions and societal adaptations had overlaid and altered these primary customs over the millennia. I would start from this central core and gradually expand my vision and understanding outwards.

~ 6 ~
Lessons

Often the gesture is so simple and quick that unless I am watching for it, I will miss it. It may be touching with fingers the forehead or the eyes, or placing the right hand on the heart, or a rapid bow of the head: small motions of acknowledgment and prayer. Throughout India, in cities and countryside, are places considered sacred to the gods: trees, rocks, hills, ponds, rivers, and crossroads upon which a shrine or temple has been built. Sometimes the spot itself is almost imperceptible to the outsider, but for the local it has a presence that must be honored. Whenever I am walking or driving with someone else, either slowly on the street or rushing by in a car or bus, I try to notice these little gestures that affirm the abiding presence of the Divine and one's integral relationship to it.

* * *

Almost three years after our previous trip, in January 1978, Helene and I flew back to Delhi and resided again with the Sawhneys while I arranged for a car and driver. After our earlier ordeals, it might seem insane that Helene was traveling again with me in India, but honestly, neither of us considered any other option. Helene was eager to put her negative experiences behind her and investigate India's cultures that she had not been able to enjoy on the previous trip. Also, our role models influenced our decisions. I had been raised by intrepid parents, both of whom loved low-budget travel and prided themselves in adapting to foreign lifestyles without frills. Other couples in my family had traveled extensively. I had been guided into my overland trip by my cousin Trish and her husband Mick, who had spent two years journeying around the world while living simply. We even met several of my married colleagues where both husband and wife equally engaged in field research in challenging environments. Helene was doing her best to be the brave explorer she wanted to be and believed I would prefer.

This time we would travel in relative comfort, resuming much of our previous itinerary, but booking a higher grade of hotels to avoid some of the problems we had encountered earlier. I was determined not to repeat the same insensitive mistakes. As my wife suffers in extreme heat, I thought an air-conditioned car was essential. Yet at that time, few were available in South Asia. During the first forty years of independence, all imports were heavily restricted as a national endeavor to support local production. India manufactured only two models of automobiles: the small Indian Fiat and the Ambassador coupe, based on the British model of a 1950s Morris Oxford. Neither had been upgraded or changed in any significant fashion in decades, and neither offered air cooling. The only air-conditioned cars in the country were those few legally imported by diplomats and notable foreigners. Some of these had been sold to Indians by their first owners. I made the mistake of hiring a large white 1960s American Ford Fairlane with blue upholstery. How could I have been so blind to its implications?

At twenty-six, I remained naïve and unconscious of many of the issues that plagued my wife about travel in India. Helene is naturally introverted and shy. Although private transportation and better hotels helped her to isolate and be more comfortable, our enormous American car drew crowds wherever we traveled. Most had seen anything like it: twice as large as any Indian vehicle, with big white fins and a shiny chrome grill. We couldn't have been more conspicuous. Helene was profoundly affected by all the staring, the ubiquitous litter on Indian streets, the heat and mosquitos, and our ongoing encounters with the extreme poverty and disease of much of India's disenfranchised population. On top of that discomfort, our driver, Surat Singh, had never traveled outside of regions close to Delhi. Once we left Rajasthan, he was increasingly uncomfortable, complaining volubly that everyone we met was boorish and untrustworthy. The primary reason we had chosen that ridiculous automobile was for its air conditioning, but throughout that long journey, it constantly malfunctioned. Although Helene remained healthy during those four months, our experiences once more drained her reserves.

The trip had many high points as we traveled again through Rajasthan, more extensively through Gujarat, down through Bombay and Maharashtra, and into Andhra Pradesh. I continued documenting all the craft and folk art (material culture) that we saw: from rural community layout (the configuration of the streets) to differences in house construction and the materials used—flooring, walls, columns and beams, roofing, and all the elements that furnished the house from its kitchen to its living spaces. I was interested in the how and why: what tools were used, who the artisans were, and how their societies treated them. It required comprehensive and exhaustive research. I knew, of course, that I could only brush the surface on this trip, but my intention was to spend my life in its pursuit. I absorbed and documented as much as I could.

On my first two trips, I had carried a Pentax 35mm reflex camera and each time recorded a few thousand images on print film. I was untrained as a photographer, and most results were discouraging. I had prepared for this third voyage by beginning to learn the craft of photography. In the months before departure, I had worked in the SOAS photo lab and received more training. This time I brought a 35mm Nikon, improved lenses, and a larger number of transparency films, to make a photographic survey. My results were slowly improving.

I documented both rural Hindu and tribal communities in western and central/south India. Although many of the tribal cultures were intriguing, I was looking for a group that had not yet been documented. During those first two months of my long drive with Helene, I began to find two non-tribal subjects particularly fascinating: wall and floor decorations by women and terracotta sculptures given to sacred shrines.

Just walking into an Indian village would soften my soul. Even though we crossed India in a sleek white monster, we had far more ability than before to stop and explore wherever and whenever we chose. I soon discovered that the best strategy was to park the behemoth so that it was blocked from sight as much as possible, perhaps amid trees, or behind a building. We would then walk off the highway into the countryside on a random dirt road, leaving Surat Singh to polish off the most recent dust and insect splatter, fuming by himself outside the car, scowling at any passerby. More often than not, we would soon approach a village: a scattering of mud huts roofed in locally fired tiles or thatch. In eastern Rajasthan, we found dark red walls painted in intricate white floral and figural patterns. Further west, I photographed walls patterned with geometric bands and squares of bright colors that resembled a canvas by Dutch abstract artist Piet Mondrian. The more villages we visited, the more I realized that women in rural communities throughout South Asia decorate the walls and floors of their homes with ornamental designs, most of which are in one way or another sacred. I yearned to know more. These observations were the seeds of a project that has occupied more than forty years and resulted in three books and many exhibitions.

As we arrived, children ran to welcome us, reaching out to hold our hands, pulling us up the street. A farmer or a headman, often turbaned in a swirling pile of colorful cotton, put his hands together in a *pranam*, all smiles, asking us to sit for a cup of tea. We perched on the clay shelf-porch outside his front door, or he asked us to enter into the courtyard where he straightened a rope-woven wooden cot (charpai) for us to sit. Giggling shyly in a corner, one or more brightly veiled women nodded at us, raising their gauzy face-coverings to reveal bright smiles and striking silver or gold jewelry piercing their noses and ears. Usually, they began to prepare hot chai by boiling milk and water to which they added black tea powder, ground ginger, cardamom seeds, and plenty of sugar. Often, they served us this delicious concoction in simple terracotta cups made by the local potter.

Surrounding us inside an invariably clean enclosure gathered all the life of a farming household: goats tethered to a stone post, a cow nursing her calf, a string of laundry stretched out across two edges of the roof from tile to tile. The painting we had seen on the outside walls was often repeated in different patterns inside, complementing and enhancing the space. As we drank our hot chai, I drank in the peaceful environment, noting and photographing its individual personality that told stories about vision, creativity, and custom. I felt at home myself, put totally at ease by these thoughtful people. Experiences such as this underlined my earlier observations about the inherent generosity and graciousness of rural Indian people.

Back in our car, as we sped along the roadside, I began to notice shrines at the base of large sacred trees, rock outcroppings, and boulders. I was particularly attracted to these ancient, gnarly trees, their trunks and branches wound with bits of bright cloth and adorned with glass bangles by devotees. We stopped to discover clay sculptures placed as votive offerings beneath them, often small and easily overlooked, but occasionally grouped in large assemblages. Most often, these terracottas represented horses given symbolically for the Gods or guardians of a community to ride in their efforts to protect local inhabitants from malevolence. They were charming, often whimsical. As we saw them repeatedly, I began to recognize that this practice was almost universal in India, although the forms and sizes of the sculptures, the deities to whom they were given, and the inherent rituals were as disparate as the individual subcultures. A few years later, this subject became integral to my career. Aside from photographing these shrines, I began collecting cast-off clay sculptures. We purchased a luggage rack and a large box that we began to fill with objects.

* * *

We spent a week with Kaka and Kaku Kelkar in their joint museum/home near Pune's center. Again, I was able to work closely with him, examine his extensive collections, and gain further knowledge and insight from his encyclopedic understanding of Indian decorative art. The elderly couple gave us their largest guest room, equipped with a suite of furniture that included a grand four-poster bed. Each piece had been carved of black-stained rosewood elaborately decorated with dragons, mythical beasts, and flowering vines.

The ancient capital city of Bidar, Karnataka, was famous for its black enameled metalware inlaid with silver wire. As we walked its streets, I enquired in a local brass shop for old examples of this unique craft. The owner suggested I check his scrap metal and poured from a filthy gunny sack a mess of blackened brass intended to be melted down and recycled. Picking through it, I found no enameled *bidriware*, as it is called—but I did discover a finely wrought brass box and a cast bronze figural lamp. I recognized that both would be valuable once polished. I purchased them for their weight alone: twenty-five rupees per kilogram when the exchange rate for one US dollar was twenty-seven rupees. I bought both items for less than three dollars! This discovery launched an obsession.

Our friend John Silverstein joined us in the city of Hyderabad. With my guidance, he had left London several months earlier and completed the overland trip I had taken twice, wending his way down to Andhra Pradesh through several Indian states. During these travels, he studied Indian folk art and collected pieces for himself. John is an easy-going, good-humored, adaptable man—an equal friend to both of us. He moved into the front seat next to Surat Singh, even closer to our driver's constant moaning, swearing, and angry gesticulations at pedestrians and other drivers. But we three passengers developed an ongoing banter and fascinating conversations, often humorous, that helped us while away the endless hours of driving.

Soon after he joined us, John became as excited as I with my discovery that brass shops had scrap piles which often contained fine old bronzes and brassware discarded for melting down. Much to Helene's dismay, we began stopping in towns and small cities along our route several times each day. John would take one end of the street while I took the other, canvassing all the brass vendors asking to see their "*puraana peetal*" (old brass). We purchased dozens and dozens of fine works of art and craft, many of them centuries old, at the going rate of twenty-five rupees per kilo, each for a few dollars at most, all rescued from imminent destruction. Our heavy collections on the roof grew.

Typically, as we drove, I would watch the road's right side while John would scan the left. We took note of all we saw. When either of us found a roadside shrine, particularly one with a sacred tree, we usually stopped and examined it. I began documenting the inspiring diversity of regional images of deities and their forms of adornment. And in many of these shrines, we found ritual terracotta sculptures, usually small horses, sometimes cows, elephants, or human figures. All of these I photographed. When possible, I would interview a priest or a devotee to identify the deity and local customs. Often, we were invited to walk off the road into a village to visit the local potter who had created the clay sculptures or to see other aspects of the community that fascinated us. The unfettered kindliness of the people kindled our hearts. Sometimes, we were given terracotta sculptures to take with us or purchased ones at the cost of a few pennies. These we added to the multiplying boxes on our roof.

Once we'd reached India's east coast and turned northward, we began to skirt more closely one of the primary tribal belts. A range of mountains, the Eastern Ghats, stretches inland along the Bay of Bengal for a thousand miles. Dense forests prevented access until recent decades, protecting a natural enclave for diverse indigenous Indian populations. These people and their scant documentation had beckoned me during my research in London. The region seemed ripe for exploration and a possible focus for my doctoral thesis. I had booked a series of good hotels scattered alongside the beaches, not far off our route. As our continuous road travel was taxing Helene, we began leaving her for a day's rest in our hotel room while John and I rose early for a long expedition over mountain passes and into Adivasi villages. Each day we would visit different communities, each inhabited by a distinct tribe. We noted the varied styles of household construction and decoration, dress, and personal ornamentation, and, when possible, met and interviewed tribal leaders. We returned to our hotel late that night, and then usually took the next day off to rest. Helene, in the meantime, read copiously and waited for us to get back. These excursions were intensely stimulating to John and me. But while we were active, the resting time intended to be refreshing for my wife often bored her.

We were surprised at how engaging and forthright tribal women were. Unlike typical females in mainstream or even rural Hindu or Muslim India, these women boldly approached and asked us questions. With flowers in their hair, tattooed arms and faces, and simply wrapped blouseless saris, they remarked on what odd beings we were. More than once, they enquired if we came from as far away as Delhi as they had heard that the people there had paler complexions and were taller than they. Their isolation was so complete that they did not even know that other races and countries existed. The individuals we met were different from anyone else with whom we had come in contact in South Asia. The more I experienced, the more I was sure that this was the path I wanted to follow.

Although I hoped that this trip would persuade Helene to love travel in India, I still doggedly misunderstood the fundamental difference in our natures and motivations. I loved challenge and adventure and did not let the many difficulties distract or dissuade me. My dear wife continued to enjoy much of what we experienced but found the constant travel demands and the invasiveness on her personal space overwhelming. In some ways, John felt caught between a rock and a hard place. He loved our discoveries on the road, and our solo field trips but implicitly understood Helene's growing unease.

Our driver, Surat Singh, had become an increasing burden. He had no navigational skills, could not read a map, and could not remember directions. He was constantly lost, having to stop and ask for guidance frequently. He had become venomous in his hate of the people we met. For the first time, I began to understand the depth of India's cultural distrust and institutionalized racism: the fear of the other. Surat Singh genuinely believed that Southern Indians were stupid and that their darker skin and facial differences were ugly and inferior. His constant judgments were offensive, annoying, and often undermined our pleasure. Had we been savvier, we would have cut our losses earlier and sent this incompetent, narrow-minded man back to Delhi, but we did not.

Further north in the State of Orissa (recently renamed Odisha), we passed mud houses with walls enchantingly covered with white floral designs.

We stopped to discover that they had been painted seasonally by household women as invocations to deities. As often as once each week during the annual months of festivities, these unrecognized artists resurfaced their exterior mud walls with fresh wet clay. They ground rice from their fields into a paste that they painted onto these fresh canvases, creating new designs each time. They dedicated most of their artwork to Lakshmi, the Goddess of Abundance and Prosperity, and their homes displayed her auspicious symbols: lotuses, peacocks, and elephants. I was charmed by the creative excellence and variety of these paintings and determined to document them more fully when I had time.

Wending our way through West Bengal, we recorded dozens of terracotta shrines that marked the verges of our route. Our training in the museums, markets, and theaters of London to observe details and record subtle differences often unseen by others was paying off. As we continued through Bihar, eastern Uttar Pradesh, Madhya Pradesh, and back up to Delhi, our experiences began to shape my vision of the future. The sheer scale of diverse creativity could be boggling, but I was increasingly aware and stimulated by ranges of subjects that others had ignored. Local individuals regarded me quizzically. The art that I found astounding was so commonplace to them that they questioned why I would be interested. But they became proud of their endeavors once they realized how much I appreciated it. As before, when I met educated Indians—not those of Kamaladevi's or Rukmini Devi's viewpoint, but individuals who considered themselves "modern Indians"—they often accused me of attempting to lead India backward into its past rather than celebrating its technological future. When I tried to explain that Indian progress could be enhanced by understanding its history and traditional cultures, they ridiculed me. This criticism only further inspired my determination, encouraged by those many Indian mentors whose work I admired.

By the time we reached Delhi, Helene had realized that she had neither the interest nor the stamina to be a constant companion in my fieldwork. That comprehension was a sad blow to us both. While this trip had reconfirmed my commitment, it had also helped us realize more fully that we could pursue separate interests and still spend most of our time together. After this, I would return to India alone or be accompanied by my wife for shorter, limited journeys. When we flew home to London, I began intensive preparation to return the next year to Orissa's tribal mountains. Although I had not yet selected a specific tribe on which to focus, I had chosen the geographic region of my doctoral thesis.

~ 7 ~
Encounters

It took more courage than I had ever summoned to leave Britain for India in 1979. Fear of the unknown had rarely dominated me. Now I would be cut off from everything that I knew, or for which I could fully prepare, and I was terrified. I had spent most of a year learning about tribal cultures in Orissa. That state contained India's second-largest Adivasi (indigenous) population: twelve million. I had chosen to document Koraput District, a region with one-and-a-half million tribal people who were either scantily documented or not at all. Although Koraput was one of the nation's largest districts at the time (the size of Maryland), it contained only ten towns and no cities. This heavily forested, narrow finger of land jutted down from southern Orissa between two states: Andhra Pradesh and Madhya Pradesh. All the leaders and merchants of this district came from the three different dominant cultures of these states. In contrast, Koraput's major population was composed of sixty-two distinct Adivasi groups who spoke a total of thirteen primary languages. Koraput District appeared to be a petri dish of civilizations—a blend of isolation and rich cross-fertilization that fed my fascination for the interplay of cultures and disciplines. I believed that this region might provide the perfect springboard for my professional career.

Never had I been so far off the grid. Some of my meager resources described tribes who had massacred English adventurers barely more than half a century earlier. One tribe, the Kondhs, was even recorded as having condoned human sacrifice as a part of religious rituals. Few foreigners had ever traveled there. I would be going alone, cut off from communication, far from mainstream Indian culture, and distant from telephones and telegraph, long before the internet's immediacy. Would I even survive this encounter? Would I disappear there, as Michael Rockefeller had eighteen years earlier in the tribal jungles of New Guinea? My fears seemed well founded, yet my determination was unabated. With a six-month initial plan for exploration, I minimized my trepidation to Helene, our families, and our friends, and flew from Heathrow to Delhi in early January 1979.

At the recommendation of others, I acquired a research visa for the first time, rather than a tourist visa. I had written Kamaladevi Chattopadhyay about my intentions, and she was expecting me. This elderly stateswoman wrote letters of introduction by hand to all of the primary officials in the central and the state governments that she believed could ease my ability to work in Koraput. Over the next ten days, I met some of the nation's most relevant political and diplomatic leaders in India's capital: the Home Secretary, the Minister of Home Affairs, and the Commissioner for Scheduled Tribes, as well as the Orissa Chief Minister, among others. Each provided me with official letters of authorization for my work.

Introductions in hand, I flew to Bhubaneshwar, Orissa's state capital. Although it is one of India's oldest cities, filled with ancient monuments and temples, Bhubaneshwar's new legislative and business center includes wide, open streets and beautifully designed contemporary buildings. Foreign tourism was minimal in Orissa, and few services existed to supply its needs. I resided in the State Guest House, a simple but comfortable accommodation catering to government visitors. On the street, I met a young bicycle rickshaw wala, Anand, who offered to pedal me to my various destinations. This young man's radiant smile and open nature drew me in, and although his English was sketchy and my Oriya only rudimentary, we cobbled together intense and fascinating conversations. Over the next days, we began to build a friendship.

I hate navigating India's hide-bound bureaucracy, but my letters from Kamaladevi helped me reach my goals. Twelve days of knocking on doors and waiting in offices, eventually resulted in meetings with the State's top officials in charge of legislating Koraput District, its tribal affairs, and its security concerning foreigners attempting to work there. I was lucky that the Home Secretary of Orissa, Sitakant Mohapatra, was a poet himself, passionately interested in documenting his State's tribal culture, and a published author of several books of tribal poetry. He eagerly encouraged my research. With new permissions from the leading State officials in hand, I arranged for Chand, a driver of a local Ambassador car, to transport me 330 miles to Jeypore, the largest town in Koraput District. As Anand was willing and capable, and a natural linguist, I hired him to accompany me as interpreter/assistant for my field research. On the morning of January 30, 1979, we began our sixteen-hour drive.

Sitakant Mohapatra had recommended I stay at the local Maharajah's guest house, as no hotels existed in Jeypore, and secured permission to rent it by the month for a nominal fee. I planned to canvas the indigenous villages throughout the entire district over the next month or two, using this building as my home base from which to make forays out for days or a week at a time. I could return there to get my mail and restock provisions before heading out again. Once I had chosen the tribe or tribes for the focus of my thesis, I expected to retain this rental for occasional R & R.

Although the guest house sounded like an exotic accommodation, the reality was disappointing. When Chand dropped us off late at night, and the *chowkidar* (guard) admitted us, Anand and I found that the dwelling comprised one room caked in filth, a single wrought iron bed (no mattress), and a sole hardwood straight-backed chair. The bathroom was repulsive. The next morning, we searched the few shops in town, buying scrub brushes, mops, a broom, disinfectant, detergent, scouring powder, bedding, mosquito nets, towels, a gas camp stove, cooking pots and utensils, teapot and cups, plates and glasses, a large cooler, and all the staples we needed for the next week. Unlike many, Anand had no scruples against arduous, dirty labor. He and I set to work that afternoon on our hands and knees, scrubbing all the guesthouse surfaces. It took us two full days to get the grime off.

On the afternoon of the second day, I showered, dressed in my coat and tie, and hired a local taxi to drive less than an hour up a mountain pass to Koraput Town, the district's administrative headquarters. As instructed, I went to present myself to the District Collector, a title carried over from the British Empire. This official was the highest-ranking administrator in this political division of each state government, combining the offices of district magistrate and principal revenue officer. Protocol stated that I must receive his blessing before attempting my research. Higher-ranking officials in Bhubaneshwar had assured me that he would grant permission easily.

It turned out that the Collector was "out of station" and would not be returning for three weeks. Nevertheless, his junior officers could not have been more cordial and welcoming. They helped me plan my itinerary for the next three weeks, giving me names and letters of introduction to individuals who could aid me wherever I went. I would spend one week in Malkangiri Tahsil to the far south, a week in Kashipur Tahsil northwest, and the third week in northeastern Bissam Cuttack and Chandrapur Tahsils before returning to meet the Collector in the same office on February 26. I was blissfully happy as I drove back to the guesthouse.

A day later, three of us packed tightly into the front seat of a small American Willys open jeep that I had hired from a local service. This vehicle was dented and rusty, but serviceable—perfect for the rough dirt roads that the driver, Ramana Rao, would need to negotiate. Anand and I had layered the rear of the jeep with a tent, mosquito nets, bedrolls (each with a lightweight mattress, sheets, blanket, and pillow), the portable cooking gear I had purchased, and sufficient staples and food to supply our needs for a week. We headed south into Malkangiri, a wide-open valley interspersed with and surrounded by ranges of jungled mountains. I soon discovered that we did not need our tent: we could stay in government guesthouses built for traveling officials. Their qualities varied throughout the district. The condition was often basic, but better than the Maharajah's guesthouse when we first arrived in Jeypore. Occasionally, we set up our cookstove and fed ourselves, but, usually, the accommodation had its own caretaker/cook, and sometimes our meals were surprisingly tasty.

During that week, we entered many Adivasi villages, sometimes two or three a day. As my purpose was to document each community's individuality and contrast it to others, I attempted to visit as many different tribes as possible: Bhumia, Paroja, Gadaba, Kondh, Koya, Didayi, and Bonda. Most of Koraput's Adivasis are divided into totemistic clans, each named after a particular animal, place, or object regarded as sacred. Indigenous women had much more freedom than women elsewhere in India. Their societies permitted open social exchange between the sexes, and women worked, ate, danced, and sang alongside men.

A vibrant marriage festival commanded my attention upon entering a Gadaba village. Long, low-roofed mud houses festooned with garlands of green leaves and flowers crowded either side of a wide dirt street. A line of brightly dressed men and women snaked through the road in a shuffle dance accompanied by drums strung around the necks of male musicians, the blare of locally-cast brass horns, and the high-pitched hum of simple two-stringed instruments played with bows. The dancer in front carried a sheaf of peacock feathers that he waved to direct the group's movements behind him—about twenty participants looped arm-to-shoulder. Participants and spectators laughed uproariously. Geometric tattoos decorated the women's faces and arms, their necks hung with necklaces of colored beads, their bare breasts natural and beautiful. These people appeared to welcome me gladly into their midst, offering me fresh palm wine served in a leaf cup, joyous that I could witness this pledge between two of them.

Adivasis are intensely communal and cooperative; to show concern and take responsibility for the other members of the tribe was considered of paramount importance. Children partook in almost all activities and accompanied adults wherever they went. The young were regarded as mature beings at an early age and learned to accept responsibility through example and practice. Although both state and central government supposedly protected the fundamental rights of tribal communities, Adivasis were politically autonomous as far as their own internal affairs were concerned.

In the dark of one evening, as Anand, Ramana, and I sat on the verandah of our unelectrified PWD (Public Works Department) bungalow gazing at the thousands of stars that illuminated the sky, we were serenaded by a local minstrel. A Koya boy, probably a late teenager, sang us ballads, his earnest, handsome face lifted to the sky. Wearing only a loincloth and a striped cotton shawl, he asked nothing of us. He only wanted to share his exhilaration in the evening's beauty. Luckily, the old cook who cared for the bungalow spoke both the Koya language and Oriya and translated the singer's evocative words. The boy sang of the forest and its animals, and the love between a young man and woman on a starlit night like this. We three visitors felt caught by his spell.

Of all the Adivasis, the ones that most fascinated me were the Bonda. These shy, intensely private people lived in secluded villages high in the mountains. Criticism, ridicule, and suspicion by other inhabitants of this district had contributed to the tribe's remoteness. An ancient custom prohibited Bonda women from wearing clothes. They completely shaved their heads and then covered them with woven straw bands. Tall stacks of large aluminum rings enclosed their necks, and copious amounts of beaded necklaces partially covered their breasts. For modesty, they wore a narrow band of fabric around their waists that just managed to cover their genitalia, but still gapped at the back to fully reveal the buttocks. Bonda men excessively drank palm wine and were reputedly aggressive, defending their women, even frequently murdering their opponents. Except for their appearances at the weekly market, the Bonda remained apart and did not welcome visitors.

Two factors influenced my choice not to document them further: the tribe's unwelcoming nature and wish for privacy, and published treatises about the Bonda by other foreign researchers. I was determined to work with an undocumented tribe.

The day before I drove out of Malkangiri Valley and back to Jeypore, an extraordinary event happened. I had just left the Bonda market when a thundering fleet of enormous olive-green helicopters landed in an adjacent field. Weapon-toting guards leapt out first, spreading defensively. Then, to my utter surprise, Indian Prime Minister Indira Gandhi stepped from the largest copter into the field, surrounded by an entourage of women in colorful silk saris. They moved toward the tribal market. It took me a while to find out what they were doing. Mrs. Gandhi was on a mission to teach the indigenous women to dress with appropriate female modesty. Accompanied by bales of cotton blouses, she was traveling between communities throughout that tribal region, attempting to persuade the descendants of these ancient traditional cultures that their habits were obscene. They would be far happier, she declared, if they began covering their breasts. I found the Adivasi women and men's insouciant acceptance of their natural bodies refreshing. Recent surveys have shown that most women in Odisha now wear blouses.

After a brief overnight in Jeypore, we headed northwest to Kashipur Tahsil. The few mentions I had found through my research in London described dense mountainous forest, splendid waterfalls, abundant wildlife, and unknown tribes. It sounded like an ideal region upon which to focus, but I arrived too late. A foreign-funded lumber company had clear-cut all the old-growth forest. Miles and miles of stumps populated the recently lush hillsides. I visited village after village of shell-shocked victims. The corporation had vivisected their identities. For centuries, possibly millennia, these people had lived harmoniously with their environment. They told me that the trees held their deities and their sustenance—their food and their livelihoods. Songs and poetry had all been about these forests. I saw no wild animals, no birds—all had fled. It was total devastation. I found one hillside of about thirty acres of new reforestation. An insightful tribal elder explained that officials had photographed this stand of saplings from all angles. When collated, the images suggested that the whole forests had been replanted. The foreign investors were satisfied, and the Indian middlemen pocketed the difference. After three days, I had had enough. I was no war correspondent. I could not bear the pain of that tragic region and left earlier than expected to travel east to Bissam Cuttack and Chandrapur Tahsils.

My first view of the Dongria Kondh will remain with me forever. A tall, well-built young man approached us on a narrow dirt road into the mountains. His long hair was curled back from his forehead and held in place by a decoratively carved wooden comb. While his pickax rested on his right shoulder, he lifted his left hand gracefully to hold the fingers of an elegant woman. A garment embroidered in red and yellow fell from her right shoulder. White cloth was gathered around her neck, covering her breasts, and a second piece of embroidered fabric encased her lower body. Several thin disks of solid metal encircled but did not confine her neck. Together the postures of this young man and woman resembled those of eighteenth-century European courtiers.

For seven previous days, I had explored Kuttiya Kondh, Jatapu, Paroja, Lodha, and Kol Adivasi villages throughout these two tahsils. I found each interesting in its own right. The Home Secretary, Sitakant Mohapatra, had suggested I meet S.K. Mohanty, the Special Officer of the Dongria Kondh Development Agency. By this point, I had talked with many government officers. Most were scathing in their attitudes towards the indigenous peoples, openly hostile about what they perceived to be the Adivasis' stupidity and laziness. (I found them hardworking.) Most local officials thought I was foolish to want to spend time with them. Mohanty was open-minded, engaging, and passionate to learn more about one of the least known tribes, the Dongria Kondh. He represented the DKDA, a government organization formed in 1964 to protect their rights and improve their welfare. He encouraged my research and offered to come with me to visit two of their villages.

The Dongria lived in the area surrounding the district's tallest mountain, Niyamgiri (4,970 feet high). They were a small branch of one of Orissa's largest tribes, the Kondhs. The steeply pitched jungles were lush and astonishing. Waterfalls dropped hundreds of feet through tree ferns and hardwoods. Wildlife was abundant, and exotic birds proliferated. When I visited, the Dongria's principal crops were turmeric, pineapple, banana, papaya, tobacco, and sugarcane with subsidiary crops of orange, lime, mango, jackfruit, sago palm, mahua, and castor beans as well as forty-one species of millet. The Dongria did not possess firearms, but their men were avid hunters with bows and arrows. Compared with other tribal villages, these people were successful, well-fed, and happy.

The moment I entered the first village, Khajuri, I knew I was somewhere special. Children happily ran out to meet me. Men and women alike were gracious, attentive, and hospitable. Like those in many of the other tribal communities I had visited, the thatched roofs descended to within a few feet from the ground. Mohanty explained that the construction was defensive: it was easier to keep prowling tigers, leopards, and panthers from entering the home. The interior bamboo construction had been surfaced with thick mud, dried, burnished, and first painted white and then decorated with rows of red and yellow triangles in the same designs as the women's and men's embroidered clothing.

The villagers gently took my arm and guided me into their meeting hall that doubled as a temple. The Dongria did not worship any carved images of their deities. They believed that the mountain itself was Niyam Raja, the Lord of Law that governed all actions, while the forests, rocks, streams, animals, and all the mountain's produce were part of the Earth Goddess Dhartanu. Parallel rows of painted triangles covered both inside and outside walls of this meeting hall. Pairs of breasts had been carved intermittently onto its wooden roof beams. Mohanty introduced me to the Bhejjuni, the old village priestess, who told me that the paintings and carvings represented fecundity. Clay vessels on an inconspicuous altar held ritual offerings. Outside, four simply carved and pointed posts were the focal point of the Kandul Parba Festival. Once in three years, the Dongria sacrificed a buffalo to

Dhartanu, its flesh and blood buried at the corners of each cultivated plot to ensure continued fertility. It was this tribe and its sister Kuttiya Kondh tribe that had historically practiced human sacrifice. Sacrificial victims were specially appointed at birth through certain signs interpreted as gestures of the gods. Considered sacred beings, they were honored and spoiled until they reached maturity, when they were ritually killed as offerings to ensure crop fertility. The outlawing of human sacrifice by the British in the nineteenth century caused an Anglo-Kondh war that ironically resulted in the tragic massacre of thousands of Kuttiya Kondh.

Kurli, the second village, just four kilometers further up a jungled gorge beneath Niyamgiri Mountain, was fascinating. Its population combined sixty percent Dongria and forty percent Dom, a Hindu scheduled caste of weavers, traders, and moneylenders. Elsewhere in central and eastern India, the Dom are harijan tradesmen-farmers with shifting populations. In Varanasi, Dom are the only ones allowed to handle corpses and funeral pyres on the banks of the Ganges River. In Kurli and its surroundings, the Dom rented all the fruit trees at a nominal fee from their easily exploitable Dongria landowners. They then hired the naïve inhabitants to pick the tribal crops while keeping the profits from the sale themselves.

The twenty Dom houses fronting Kurli's single street heralded their economic success. A row of large verandahs was composed of clay sculpted on bamboo frameworks to create amorphous forms of chairs, benches, and loveseats. All surfaces (walls, floors, and built-in furniture) were divided into appealing rectangles and squares painted in black, dark red, and white pigments that were then burnished with smooth stones until they shone. The result was reminiscent of a Gaudi building or Mali's mud architecture—unlike anything else in India.

The treatment of Kurli's Dongria dwellings was similar to those in Khajuri—a fascinating contrast to the Dom buildings. And I had visited only the first two of approximately one hundred Dongria villages nestled onto and near the slopes of the sacred Niyamgiri Mountain. The Dongria art (embroidery, jewelry, tools, architecture, and painting) was simple but diverse, expressing their natural symbiosis with their ecosystem. In the brief time I was there, and through the few glimpses I had through S.K. Mohanty of their oral history, songs, and poetry, I became fascinated by their cultural lore and their attitude toward the sacred. The Dongria were undocumented, and the individuals I met welcomed me openly. But before I could explore this tribal culture more deeply, I had to travel back to Koraput town for my scheduled meeting with the District Collector in two days. I vowed to return the day thereafter, certain I had discovered the focus of my doctoral dissertation.

* * *

When I re-entered the District Collector's outer office on February 26, his direct subordinates seemed nervous and distracted. I could hear someone shouting behind his closed door as I waited for my appointment. After twenty minutes, two upset young men rushed out of the inner office, and I was told to enter. A squat toad of a man sat behind a large desk piled with file folders and papers. His first words were an angry "What do you want?!" When I politely told him my name and explained why I was there, he yelled that he didn't like foreigners and didn't want me to write "some soppy treatise showing how beleaguered and repressed Koraput's tribal people are." Using all my diplomatic skills, I calmly explained that I intended to honor the Adivasis and portray their traditional cultures as objectively as possible. My intentions were ethical, and my work had been approved by top officials in New Delhi and Bhubaneshwar. Upon handing him my sheaf of introductory letters, he ripped the top ones and crumpled the rest without reading even one. He threw them back into my face while screaming: "Get out of my office and get out of this district! You are not welcome here!" I had no choice but to leave.

In the outer office, I burst into tears—an extremely infrequent response for me. I could not understand what had just happened. I turned to the same junior officers who had so encouraged me three weeks earlier, but they could not intervene. They presented weak, empathetic smiles as they affirmed that I had to depart the district that same afternoon. The police had been informed and would assure that I obeyed. When, in flabbergasted confusion, I explained that all of my possessions were in disarray in my lodgings in Jeypore, they acquiesced and told me they would arrange for a grace period for the rest of that day if I agreed to leave at first light. Bewildered and defeated, unable to comprehend why the Collector had thrown me out, I returned to the Maharajah's Guest House. Anand and I packed all my belongings into boxes and arranged for their temporary storage with a friend I had met who ran Jeypore's radio station. When pressed, the latter explained that the Collector was a ruthless politician who despised the tribal people and willfully pitted them against Hindu merchants and landowners. This bureaucrat, he confided, was responsible for many hate crimes. My only possible recourse was to return to Bhubaneshwar and persuade the Collector's superiors to override my exile.

Dejected and numbed, I spent the next three weeks back in Orissa's capital city trying to arrange meetings with the same government officials with whom I had met a month earlier. It was not easy. Although I received sympathy, I felt stonewalled. The Collector was their junior in the Indian political system's established hierarchy, yet he appeared to have some sort of unexplained hold on them.

Young and energetic, I could not just mope in my room at the State Guest House during the many hours and days when these officers were unavailable. So, I rehired my driver Chand and, accompanied by Anand, spent off-hours and weekend days exploring the neighboring rural regions of that beautiful State. I fell in love with Puri District's verdant rice paddies ringed with coconut groves and interspersed with rivers and canals. I discovered miles of unpopulated beaches where the bodysurfing was unexcelled. As a native Californian, it was one of my favorite sports, and I taught its joys to both the men from Orissa. At first timid and then with growing enthusiasm, they too learned to glide on the perfect waves. I swam for hours to wash off my grief. But it was the villages that truly fed my aching soul. Resident women artists in each community adroitly painted their homes' mud walls in an endless variety of sacred and decorative designs. The white rice pigment was applied while it was still transparent and then, almost magically, dried into an explosion of creative expression. I photographed these paintings extensively and knew I had to return.

Driving by one village, I noticed a curiously sculpted planter in a farmyard. When we stopped to enquire, I realized that it had been fashioned of clay to resemble a local temple and held a sacred Indian basil plant, tulasi. The local farmer explained that it had been created by potters in the village of Balikondalo, several miles down the road (not far from the famous stone temple of Konarak). The potters were artists who had created a local industry of sculpted terracotta planters, each an individually decorated shrine for this most sacred of plants. I documented as much as I could, the seeds of a future project germinating in my mind.

But each day in Bhubaneshwar was frustrating. I felt like a clown continuously running into a doorway painted on a concrete wall, my full body repelled by the impact, only to get up again and charge into it once more. My rebuffs were endless and demoralizing. Early training had taught me that I could achieve most goals through determination and hard work. I was facing my first significant failure. Finally, one of the chief ministers recommended off the record that I return to Koraput District and aim directly for the Dongria Kondh villages. They were so remote that he believed I would be outside the Collector's radar. Just do nothing, he said, to draw attention to myself.

Anand stayed behind in Bhubaneshwar this time and a train delivered me to the coastal city of Visakhapatnam, Andhra Pradesh. In the early afternoon, my driver Ramana and his friend Venkat Rao picked me up in the Jeep. Rather than traveling on the far more populated national highway, I decided to enter Koraput District through the lesser-known Araku Pass. The switch-backed dirt road was breathtaking—dense primeval jungle with flowering trees in the radiant light of the setting sun. On reflection, our choice to begin our travel in the afternoon was a mistake. It was dark, deeply dark, soon after we crested the summit and started the long drive down into the Araku Valley. We three jammed ourselves into the narrow seat. Venkat straddled the gear shift while I held tightly to the roll bar so that I wouldn't fall out on sharp mountain turns. We passed through a few hamlets, but no other traffic punctuated our route.

The stately original-growth trees cast dense black shadows onto the road as Ramana peered ahead to navigate by the weak beams of our headlights. One of the shadows turned out to be a large black bear. We struck it hard, and its fur brushed against my body as I clung to the roll bar. Ramana stopped dead in the middle of the road, panicked with fear. I had grown up in bear country and knew well the danger of an injured animal. Despite all my entreaties, my driver would not move. The jeep remained stock still. Ramana was sure that this accident would bring bad karma into his life. We could hear the wounded bear roaring behind us, and it was making sounds of movement. Frantic, I promised Ramana that I would take full responsibility for this accident: I would absorb any bad karma that resulted. Protesting, he restarted the ignition, and we sped safely away. One mile later, we hit and killed a black cat.

It was three thirty in the morning of March 24 when we reached the tiny DKDA (Dongria Kondh Development Agency) bungalow at the bottom of the dirt road into Khajuri and Kurli. I had written ahead to S.K. Mohanty, who had assured me of his discretion and stated that we could stay in this accommodation as long as we needed it. I would begin my documentation by spending a couple of weeks in and around these two villages with the bungalow as my base. The Dongria welcomed me joyously when we drove into Khajuri the next day. I knew my decision was right. In all my experience, I had never met any group of human beings who impressed me as they did.

My learning curve in the following days was steep. The Dongria lived in small villages that rarely contained more than 300 persons, and they traveled outside their boundaries only to go to weekly markets nearby. They spoke their own mother tongue, Kuvi, a Dravidian language whose roots were similar to those of South Indian Tamil and Malayalam. As adolescents, Dongria boys and girls lived together in separate dormitories where the older youths were prepared for maturity. They learned economics, territory, sacred rituals, societal and marital customs, and environmental awareness. Dongria boys were allowed to visit the girls' dormitories by invitation, and liaisons between couples from different villages were permitted. Sex and marriage were only permissible with a Dongria from a separate village and outside the extended family. Exceptions were considered incestuous and punishable by death.

The marriage ceremony itself was straightforward, as was the case with most Adivasi marriages, and required nothing more than the couple's mutual acknowledgment. Polygamy existed, and divorce was easily obtained, with either member able to take the initiative. The only requirement for the latter was that the wife return the ornaments given to her by the groom and that her family return the gifts they received from the husband's family.

* * *

Predawn on the morning of March 30, I was awakened by the roar of a Jeep and several motorcycles, followed by pounding on my door. I blearily looked out into the barrels of several submachine guns pointed right at my head. An officious police captain barked a request for my name and passport. Several of his henchmen pushed me aside and began searching through my things. Ramana and Venkat Rao stood nervously to one side. When the captain had tediously looked at each entry in my passport, he informed me that he and the others were there to escort me out of the district. He gave me five minutes to pack. Under gunpoint, I hurriedly jammed my belongings into bags. When the captain insisted that my two companions be left behind, I grabbed a wad of bills from a pouch around my neck and confusedly paid Ramana for his services. Shaking, I was shoved into the back seat of an Ambassador car with pistol-pointing guards on either side, while the officer sat in the front near his driver. They would allow no conversation and answered no questions.

With an escort of four motorcycles, each driven by a policeman toting a machine gun, we drove two-and-a-half hours down the national highway to Orissa's border with Andhra Pradesh. At a small wayside village, we dismounted. The guards put my luggage on the roadside while the captain returned my passport and gruffly told me that a bus to Vizianagaram would arrive sometime in the next few hours. If I ever returned to Koraput District, I would be jailed. Right at that moment, unceremoniously, my hopes for a doctoral dissertation on the tribes of Orissa ended. At twenty-seven years old, I had been crushed.

Despondent and not knowing what to do, I checked into a beach hotel in Visakhapatnam and called Helene, explaining my situation. She sympathized with my plight and encouraged me to come home right away, but I felt steamrollered and reasoned that the long flight back to London would be too draining. I would wait a week. Auntie Teni Sawhney's sister, Buni, lived with her husband Sunny Pillai and their family in the nearby city of Hyderabad. Sunny was an outstanding amateur jazz pianist, Buni, a charming raconteur, and their three teenage children a breath of fresh air after the last weeks' strains. I might have recuperated well in their appealing home except for the fact that I came down with a high fever that first night, accompanied by vomiting, a severe headache, swollen glands, and painful limbs and joints. By the next day, I was delirious. When my hosts arranged for an examination by their personal physician, my fever was 107°F. He diagnosed dengue fever, a severe mosquito-borne disease. I must have been bitten on this last trip to Koraput District. Perhaps I should have been hospitalized, especially as my fever did not drop for five days. Still, the Pillai's kept me well hydrated in a comfortable bedroom and administered the prescribed care themselves. Aside from fluids and acetaminophen (Tylenol), there was no known cure.

Back in London, Helene consulted our primary care physician. When she explained my illness, he replied that they had called it "break-bone fever" in Southeast Asia during the Second World War because the patients felt like all their bones had been broken. I certainly did. When told how high my fever was, this doctor commented that it was a good thing it was no higher. At 107.6° and above, brain damage was likely. While my wife worried helplessly in London, my condition wavered on the edge of severe dengue (an often-fatal disease), and then I recovered. On the sixth day, my temperature dropped, and all my other symptoms returned to normal. Two days later, the doctor pronounced me well, although significantly depleted.

In a phone discussion with Helene, we decided that I would be better off at home, and I flew the two hours to Bombay, laid over in the terminal, and then continued for a further eleven hours back to London. By the time I arrived there, I was a wreck. Even with no fever or other symptoms, I could not function well. Finally following weeks when I felt totally lackluster, I was diagnosed as having shock and treated successfully with homeopathy.

* * *

After much deliberation, SOAS allowed me to refocus my doctoral dissertation on a comprehensive study of

Indian votive terracotta sculptures. By that point, I had been documenting terracottas in roadside shrines for eight years and had a good corpus of material already. This subject was relevant to traditional cultures in almost all districts of India and yet had also been sorely neglected. When I next returned to South Asia, I began a survey of their production and use in fourteen Indian states, resulting in my Ph.D. and my book *Gifts of Earth: Terracottas and Clay Sculptures of India*.

Three years after I was kicked out of Koraput District, Helene and I stayed at Kalakshetra, the leading classical Indian dance and music school I had visited during my first trip to India. At dinner with my mentor Rukmini Devi and close elderly friends at one of the campus's faculty homes, these sophisticated individuals discussed the tradition and current practice of black magic in India. According to them, it was an ancient and profoundly malevolent science. They insisted that one of its primary centers was the Hindu holy city of Puri, Orissa. By this point, I had already conducted intensive research in Puri District, documenting the village of Balikondalo and its surrounding communities. I had visited the sacred pilgrimage city of Puri many times and knew it to be a deeply sanctified spot. Rukmini Devi's next statement riveted me: she mentioned the Koraput Collector's family name without knowing of my connection to him. She insisted that he belonged to a small enclave of practitioners of black magic that had been honed and refined through many centuries. Rukmini claimed that this family had successfully cast curses and spells on enemies, causing immeasurable harm, even death. Had anyone else made those pronouncements, I would have discounted them without consideration. Black magic had always seemed the province of fantasy and horror fiction. However, Rukmini Devi was one of the most respected, intelligent, wise, and positively productive people I had ever met. And I remembered the wounded black bear and the black cat as I re-entered Koraput District after the Collector's banishment three years earlier, and the subsequent dengue fever that had almost killed me. I have never known how to interpret that conversation or its implications, but I still find the concept startling.

I've only returned to Koraput District once. In 1995, my Indian research assistant, Babu Mohapatra, arranged for a camping trip through Orissa's tribal districts accompanied by two close friends, Kurt and Pamela Meyer (whose field research in rural Nepal parallels mine in India). We set up tents and visited Adivasi communities throughout Orissa's coastal mountains. Our trip provided many deeply heartening and insightful experiences. At the end, we darted into Koraput District for a few hours, and briefly visited Khajuri and Kurli. Pam and Kurt were as stimulated by the architectural ornamentation of these two villages as I had been. Although my old tribal friends smilingly welcomed us, I noticed a primary change in the Dongria. Sixteen years before, they had been relaxed, open-minded, and confident of their place in the world. On this visit, they seemed nervous, defensive, and unsure.

One of the village elders explained that back in 1979, shortly before I was there, Indian mineralogists had been covertly prospecting the mountaintop of Niyamgiri, their sacred range. These geologists had discovered traces of bauxite, the source mineral for most of the world's aluminum. The Dongria had tried unsuccessfully to prevent these geological invasions. In subsequent years, a global mining corporation had attempted to muscle its way into the protected Dongria territory. These poor tribal people desperately tried to get good political representation in Bhubaneshwar and New Delhi but believed that their pleas were unheard. In recent years, they felt endangered. For the first time, I understood what might have been motivating the Collector's repressive actions. Had he worried that I might uncover and publish illicit activities that he had condoned? Was he covertly in the pocket of the mining company? I may never know the answers.

In the subsequent decades, I have closely watched the development of the Dongria Kondh's plight. They are desperate to protect their sacred lands against the incursions of strip-mining and consequential ecological devastation. At times, these Adivasis' protests have been wrongly labeled as Maoist, potentially triggering national retribution by labeling them as terrorists. But this previously remote and peaceful people have maintained their integrity and drawn together to successfully halt the destruction of Niyamgiri, their sacred mountain. Finally, on April 18, 2013, the Supreme Court issued a landmark decision recognizing the Dongria Kondh's rights to worship their sacred mountain and protect their lands in perpetuity. As wonderful as that news seems, India needs raw materials, and constant political pressure from well-paid lobbyists could still mean that the multinational corporation, Vedanta, might succeed in overturning that protective legislation. The Dongria Kondh's future remains uncertain.

I am aware from recent actions in my own country that Supreme Court rulings are not written in stone (i.e.: Roe v. Wade). I'm afraid that the shy, peaceful nature of the Dongria that I had come to admire in 1979 may have been altered forever. I find parallels to the transformation of Afghans due to a combination of international and national political manipulation. I remember with pleasure the exhilaratingly beautiful Niyamgiri Mountain, its diverse and productive forests, its waterfalls, and its bountiful wildlife and birds. Four decades ago, I felt drawn to its sacred power. Today, I pray that it will indeed remain unsullied and undefiled forever.

~ 8 ~
Abundance

Not infrequently, Indian generosity overcomes me. A profound illustration unfolded in 1980. I had invited my father and mother to join my wife and me in India to celebrate Dad's sixtieth birthday. Helene and I flew to Orissa a week ahead of their arrival. Anand, my rickshaw-wala assistant, had written that he had married and that his wife, Jumma, had given birth to a son: an answer to heartfelt prayers.

To honor this occasion, we purchased simple gifts in London that we thought they would like: jeans and a T-shirt for him, some costume jewelry for her, and an inexpensive outfit for the baby. When we arrived in their city of Bhubaneshwar, Anand and Jumma invited us for dinner. They were both scheduled caste—historically, they might have been referred to as "untouchables," and eating with them in their home was a valuable statement of acknowledgment. Their dwelling in Bhubaneshwar's slum was pitifully small: a mud-walled thatched hut about six by ten feet and not high enough inside for me to stand. A single oil lamp was the only illumination. Jumma had prepared a mouth-watering meal of several courses for us. After dinner had been served on the dirt floor on borrowed dishes, we gave Jumma our gifts. When she saw what we had brought, she screamed piercingly, violently pounded her head against the ground, and tore out her hair in bloody tufts. We were shocked and didn't know what to do. The surrounding villagers rushed in while Anand tried to comfort her. We couldn't understand what had happened. Half an hour later, when Jumma finally calmed down, Anand explained that she had just lost inconceivable "face." On seeing our gifts, this poor woman believed that Anand and she could never repay us. When we explained that the gifts were inexpensive, she was mollified to a degree.

As we talked later in the evening, and Jumma proudly showed off her son, she asked us questions through Anand. Jumma spoke neither English nor the local language of Oriya. She wanted to know how many children we had. When we said that we had none, she asked how many years we had been married. Our answer of seven years caused her to believe that we were infertile. Although she knew about birth control, she could not understand the concept of choosing childlessness. After private discussion, our two impoverished friends then offered us the ultimate gift: their firstborn son. They

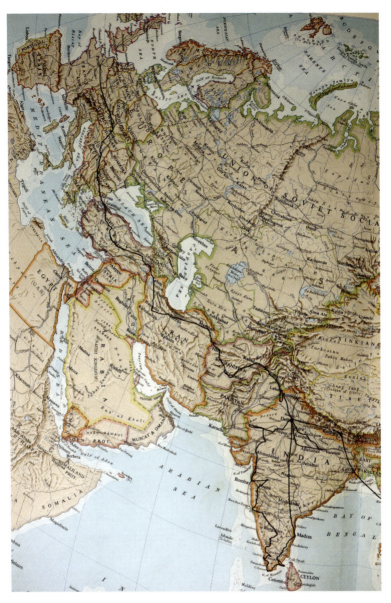

The original map of the first overland odyssey

The Huyler family at The Thacher School, 1959

Stephen and his dog Yodel, 1966

In Delhi at age 20, 1971

With Beatrice Wood, 1988

Helene Wheeler in 1968 when they met

Reunion with Helene after the first trip to India, May, 1972

Marriage portrait

Kamaladevi Chattopadhyay in the 1980s

Rukmini Devi Arundale, 1980

NT Vakani, Ahmedabad, 1972

Dinkar and Kamala Kelkar (Kaka and Kaku), 1975

Dongria Kondh girl, 1979

Documenting terracotta horses
at an Ayyanar shrine in Tamil Nadu, 1981

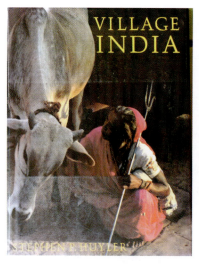 

First book, Abrams, 1985 Leading a tour, 1989

The young photographer, 1988

Maheshwar "Babu" Mohapatra, 1992

Sunithi Narayan speaking to a tour group, 1994

Jyoti Bhatt in Orissa, 1996

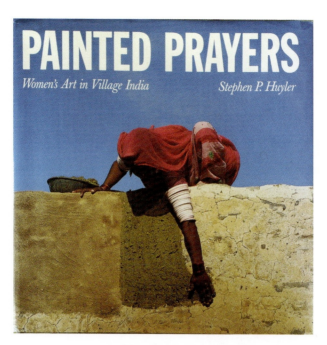

Second book, Rizzoli, 1995

Smithsonian exhibition poster, Washington, DC, 1995

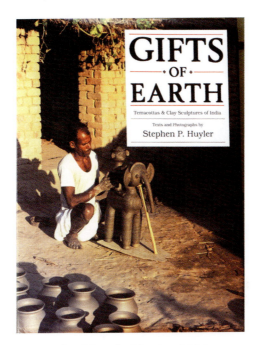

Third book, Mapin, 1996

Portrait in the Bikaner style by Mahaveer Swami, 1997

Puja exhibition at the Smithsonian, 1996-2000

Stephen and Interactive Shrine

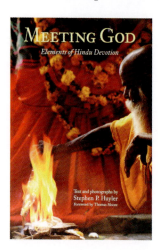

Fourth book, Yale, 1999

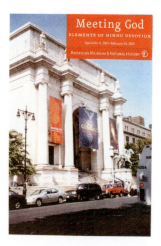

Meeting God Exhibition, American Museum of Natural History, 2001

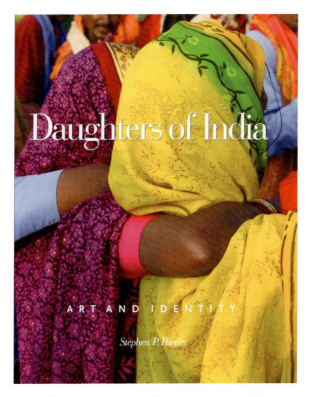

Fifth Book, Abbeville and Mapin, 2008

Sharing book with Pushpa, one of the profiled women, 2009

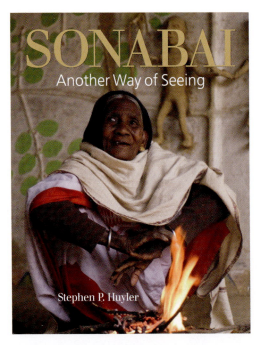

Sixth Book, Mapin, 2009

Sonabai exhibition, Mingei International Museum, 2009

Attending a wedding in Jodhpur, 2018

Writing their mystery novel, 2017

Helene and Stephen's 50th anniversary, 2023

both adored this child, but, as Jumma said, it was clear that they could have another child while we would die in old age without the pleasure of a family. What does one say in the face of such startling openheartedness? After forty-five minutes of awkwardly delicate explanations, we finally convinced them that we both were fertile but had chosen not to have children. Nevertheless, we were dumbfounded. We knew they recognized that we could provide a fine future for their child, and yet we witnessed firsthand how vital he was to their existence. We live in a society where personal possessions and family are jealously guarded. I had only met Jumma briefly the year before, while Helene knew neither of them before that night. Yet, for us, this kind couple was willing to undergo the supreme sacrifice and give us the most precious thing in their lives: their beloved son. As long as we live, this experience will remain for us the absolute pinnacle of unselfishness.

Throughout India, I have been invited into homes for meals or tea. At each level and religion of those societies, it is considered an honor and a duty to care for guests and welcome strangers. Indian hospitality is endearing and sometimes disarming, particularly when offered by a family that lives in evident poverty. How can I, whose dress and demeanor indicate relative wealth, accept charity from someone who has so little? And yet it would be a deep insult to refuse these proffered gifts. My rejection would dishonor the family and injure their pride. Hundreds of times, I have sat on the floor of tiny one-roomed huts packed with their many inhabitants while women prepared for me beverages and food. Usually, the food is offered to me alone: many Indian subcultures consider it disrespectful to eat with a guest. I worry that by feeding me, family members might go without sustenance. What can I do?

If overnighting with someone, I usually bring them a gift. But I have learned to be wary of giving too freely. It may undermine a community's or family's self-pride, and among children, can encourage begging. I prefer to find an elder to give sweets for later sharing with the young or a teacher to give pens to hand out in class.

Many Indians highly value the praise of foreigners, particularly after centuries of condescension during British rule. I try to interact with all I meet, showing proper respect for elders, appropriate deference to women, and playfulness with children. All Indian families adore their children and are grateful for compliments about them, except in those subcultures where customs mandate that praise of a child might draw bad luck (termed as "the evil eye.") All homes, however small, include objects or aspects precious to their inhabitants. I always take particular care to notice and compliment them.

Years ago, I invented a method to prevent unduly draining my hosts' resources. On my way into a remote village, I prepare first by shopping in an urban vegetable market, bartering for a broad selection of fresh vegetables and fruit that might not be available in remote communities. Upon receiving an invitation into the home of some stranger to share in a meal, a common occurrence, I inform them that I would be honored to accept, but unfortunately, I'm carrying fresh food that must be cooked. Otherwise, it will go bad. In this way, I can give to the family while still allowing them to provide hospitality. I can eat of their thoughtful and often delicious preparations without endangering their wellbeing and accept their warm generosity without harming their dignity. Nevertheless, despite all my efforts, I always feel humbled by their gifts to me.

*　*　*

After recovering from my physical depletion the year before, it took many months to decide how to proceed with my career. Was it even worthwhile pursuing my doctorate? Should Helene and I change our course and return to America? Early that summer of 1979, we spent several days near Land's End in Cornwall, Britain's most southwestern point. We felt drawn and attuned to that environment. On a second trip a month later, we unexpectedly found a seventeenth-century thatched cottage for sale in a tiny village we had particularly loved. To our utter surprise, we could afford it. Our house in London had more than doubled in value in three years and was in great demand. In late September of that year, we sold the London house and moved to a heavenly Cornish property with a refurbished thatched cottage and established garden above an estuary just a mile from the English Channel. We were to live in Helford Village, population twenty-seven, for four nourishing years.

Our only way to remain in Britain was for me to continue my doctoral studies in the UK instead of the United States. As we prepared to shift all our furniture, art, and Indian collection down to Cornwall, I searched my mind. I realized that I had found two fields of study previously undocumented: votive terracotta sculpture and women's ritual art in rural India. Although I had learned to love the latter's expressive variety, such scant scholarship on the subject existed that I would have to begin my doctoral preparations all over again. In contrast, even though no comprehensive study of terracotta sculpture in India existed, I had already collected substantial data to make a good start. I would be able to corroborate my findings with credible academic references.

South India was my first destination. Eight years earlier, Beatrice Wood and I had been captivated by the multitudinous clay sculptures of horses in the rural shrines of Tamil Nadu. I had written a research paper about them for the University of Denver. Impressed by the art and cultures of the south, I decided to begin my field research there. I found a vast undercurrent of rural Tamil beliefs and practices distinct from, and yet interwoven with, brahminical Hinduism. Rukmini Devi and I had remained in correspondence, and she invited me to use the campus of her school as my base for conducting field research.

After Christmas, 1979, I flew to Madras and moved into the same hostel at Kalakshetra where I had stayed several weeks on the first trip. Rukmini Devi Arundale welcomed me as if I was her son. That loving, elderly woman was tangentially pivotal to my future work with India. She was known by most South Asians for her cultural contributions to the nation, as a pre-eminent classical Indian dancer and choreographer, an animal welfare activist, India's first female Parliamentary Minister, and particularly as founder of Kalakshetra, India's finest school of dance and music. For me, as for thousands, perhaps millions, of others, Rukmini Devi was the preeminent teacher. She lived to help others learn. When Rukmini was a young woman, theosophical leaders proclaimed her the "World Mother," an incarnation of the Goddess, destined to lead the world into a new age. She was raised alongside the slightly older, globally famous philosopher Jiddu Krishnamurti, and both children were carefully educated and groomed together for greatness. Then, at sixteen, Rukmini scandalized many of the Indian and British old guard by marrying the Theosophical Society's English president, George Arundale, a man twenty-six years her senior. The new couple traveled the world where Anna Pavlova, the Russian prima ballerina, befriended Rukmini and encouraged her to dance.

Consequently, during the early 1930s, this young Indian woman devoted her considerable talents to studying classical South Indian dance, bharatanatyam. India's British rulers had prohibited this ancient art form decades earlier, and only a few elderly performers continued to live beneath the radar. Studying with them, Rukmini Devi learned bharatanatyam's intricate movements and highly structured rhythms. In my early years in India, I met several individuals who had attended her debut performance in 1935. All swore that Rukmini's movements on stage were like witnessing divinity in motion. Global and Indian sentiment surged to her support. Through George Arundale and his strong connections to influential Englishmen, Rukmini defied the ban against classical Indian dance and reintroduced it to an eager public.

Rukmini subsequently renounced the Theosophical Society's claim that she was a spiritual leader. Instead, in 1936, with her husband's help, she established Kalakshetra, an academy of classical Indian dance and music in a village just south of Madras. Rather than follow the predominant system of western-style education, Kalakshetra returned to the ancient Indian system of *gurukula*, whereby devotees or students live and work closely with their teacher, or guru, learning to perfect their knowledge through example, close observation, and practice. Kalakshetra was unique in India in that Rukmini drew together many leading gurus in various forms of the arts, rather than the single guru-student relationship that had earlier prevailed. She designed the campus as a series of small, thatched huts in a sandy grove of trees where each guru teaches his or her specialty. A student's well-rounded education includes academic subjects taught in affiliate schools that Rukmini founded through the guidance of Maria Montessori, who lived on campus from 1939 through the war years. I was impressed when first residing there in 1971. Returning after eight years' exploration of the Indian subcontinent, I recognized its rarity.

Through Rukmini, I hired a driver and his old Fiat to spend several months making forays into that southern state's rural regions. I discovered terracotta shrines in almost all villages—most dedicated to the God Ayyanar. Ayyanar is the Protector of Boundaries, and his shrines sit at the edge of a community just before the demarcation of a neighboring village. Although various sculptural figures are associated with him, most devotees place terracotta horses in his shrines. Local legends state that these horses are transfigured into real mounts in the spirit world for Ayyanar and his soldiers to ride in their nightly patrols to protect the community from evil.

During those four months, I interviewed priests and documented their stories, tracked down the potters who had created the sculptures, recorded their process, and spoke with devotees about their beliefs and intentions. Although I documented Ayyanar shrines alongside major highways in Tamil Nadu, I often encountered them by randomly taking rural roads. As I arrived in a village or was directed by local individuals to take further paths, frequently on foot, I would come upon a sacred grove somewhere on the community's boundary. Each was unique, captivating. Nestled beneath the tree or trees, large and small horses stood, sometimes accompanied by elephants, cows or bulls, and human figurines representing donors to the shrine, often whimsical portrayals of individual characters. With each shrine and each discovery, I seemed to step across a threshold into a different reality where the line between this world and others was faint. Sometimes I caught myself holding my breath as if the entire experience would dissolve on closer inspection. I was always welcomed in, and in the process was changed.

The variety of sculptures was broad, from simple to ornate, from purely folk in style to classical, from tiny figures to immense images. Before my research, the largest recorded terracotta sculptures in India were six to eight feet high. Occasionally one or more huge horses would frame an outdoor shrine, but authorities identified them as stucco (plaster formed on a base of fired bricks). I began to realize that some sculptures previously assumed to be stucco were, in fact, hollow clay. As time passed, I documented larger and larger fired clay horses. One day, as I passed a small, remote village, I noticed three enormous sculptures set back from the road amid trees. The two horses and one elephant were hollow, each sculpted in one piece and fired on the spot. As I photographed and recorded them, and later showed my images to archaeologists and art historians, I understood that I had discovered examples of the most massive terracotta sculptures in recorded global history. These fired clay horses and elephants were sixteen feet high, almost twice as large as the famed Chinese horses of the Xi'an excavations. (I have subsequently found other terracotta horses of a similar stature, have lectured about them globally, and no one has successfully challenged my claim.)

Typically, I spent five days or a week on the road, staying in small hotels, guest houses, or occasionally with friends of Rukmini. I would break these forays with several days on Kalakshetra's campus. Early each morning in the hostel, I awoke to meditate, often on the beach at sunrise. Then, after a light south Indian breakfast of *idly* or dosa sitting on the dining room floor alongside all the students, I would wander through a flower-filled grove to the enormous banyan tree at the heart of campus. Beneath its lofty spreading branches, Rukmini, her staff, the dance and music students, and I sang prayers in Sanskrit, Tamil, and English to the Oneness at the center of all creation—hymns that recognized the truths that similarly underlie all religions. And then the day of classes would begin. I went from hut to hut, welcomed to watch while a few students would struggle to master the intricacies of the veena, a beautiful stringed instrument, while in another, they would learn the complex Carnatic rhythms of the mridangam, or double-sided drum. Groups of small children would assemble in one class to practice the complicated steps of bharatanatyam, while elsewhere teenage boys and girls would spin, leap, and flow in perfect unison, guided by a demanding senior dancer. I was frequently in ecstasy, amazed at my good fortune in witnessing up close the astounding grace of these young performers.

By late morning, I would meet Rukmini in her office to talk. Less than three years before my visit, Prime Minister Morarji Desai offered her the post of President of India, an appointed, not elected, position. Rukmini declined, stating that Kalakshetra's students needed her more than the nation. And yet this globally recognized woman always made time for me, encouraging frequent discussions. A couple of weeks after my arrival, Rukmini asked me if I would be willing to take over her position as director of Kalakshetra. I was astounded and honored by her faith in me but refused her offer. India was still emerging from the yoke of foreign imperialism, and I knew that this national institution must continue under the direction of an insightful, capable Indian, not a foreigner. Instead, I suggested that I could spend months each year for the next four years, helping her prepare for and find her replacement.

* * *

The first four months of 1980 felt like a perfect blend of field research and learning the ropes at Kalakshetra. In late April, I joined Helene after she flew into Delhi, and we spent several days with the Sawhney family before continuing to Bhubaneshwar ahead of my parents. A few days after Jumma and Anand offered us their firstborn child, Mom and Dad arrived. That trip permanently changed my parents' attitudes toward me.

My childhood had not been easy. As my parents' third child, I broke their mold of expectations of what a Huyler should be. My interests and talents appeared outside their ken, so different from those of my older brother and sister. I had determinedly carved out my own way of doing things, often resulting in severe criticism from my family. For the first time, in India, Mom and Dad recognized me as an adult who was capable and adaptable, and I was far enough away from my difficult adolescence to appreciate their many fine qualities. My strong friendships with diverse Indians impressed them. Dad had spent six weeks in India during World War II and had looked forward to returning, but Mom was apprehensive of Indian poverty and overpopulation. Helene and I chose to bring them to beautiful, relatively peaceful Orissa first before introducing them to larger, crowded cities. Our experiences there totally allayed my mother's fears, and she learned to admire India's people and cultures. After five days exploring painted villages and carved stone temples, we flew to Delhi to stay with the Sawhneys. I enjoyed introducing them to the sites and museums of this unusual city. For successive centuries capital cities have overlaid one another there and, as one explores New and Old Delhi, relics of these earlier periods are exposed.

On an excursion to the Red Fort, the enormous walled compound that originally held the palaces and retinues of the Mughal emperors and their courts, we stopped to view a couple of art galleries in a long arcade of tourist shops inside the fort walls. In one, I noticed a rare bronze folk sculpture of Ganesha: a bust unlike anything I had ever seen. Vowing to return the next day to acquire it, I was pleased when Dad asked to accompany me.

The Red Fort is one of India's must-see tourist spots. In consequence, its shops are highly overpriced, and its vendors canny. I warned Dad that I would be playing a delicate chess game. When we arrived, I introduced my father and myself to the dealer. When he invited us for chai, we sat and conversed with him for over an hour, finding out about his family, children, and lineage as an art dealer while he asked questions about us. Intermittently, I would examine one of his artworks: a framed miniature painting, a woodcarving, an enameled box, or an inscribed vase, asking its price. Eventually, I had canvased most of the shop. At no time during that hour did I even glance at the Ganesha sculpture. When I judged enough time had passed, I told the owner I was interested in only one thing in his gallery, but that I couldn't offer him its value. He demanded to know which piece. Before pointing it out, I reminded him that I was merely a graduate student and that many of his customers had more money than I. In a self-deprecating manner, I told him of my odd superstition about numbers: specific numbers were lucky for me on certain days. (I was aware of a common Indian belief in numerology.) With the dealer's increasing pressure, I meekly told him that I liked the Ganesha. In fact, I extolled it and explained that it was far beyond my means.

By this point, although I had never asked its price, I'd calculated his relative rate of escalation by the values he put on his other inventory. I took the amount I expected he'd ask for the sculpture, cut that to 20 percent, and offered him the ridiculously low payment of 636 rupees. The shopkeeper was aghast, exclaiming that the price was 3,500 rupees. I replied that it was worth much more. I exclaimed that it was indeed a magnificent piece, unlike any other in India. Any wealthy collector, I said, would be willing to pay 4,000, perhaps even 5,000 or 6,000 rupees. He should hold on to it and sell it to one of them. When he then pressed me for my best offer, I ashamedly told him that my superstition required me to stick to my original number: 636. I thanked him, and my father and I started to walk out. The owner called after us that he had purchased the sculpture for 1500 rupees (and I believed him). After I again extolled its rarity and value, he finally agreed to my low price, and I took it home. That sculpture stands spot-lit above my desk right now. I have given away ninety percent of my Indian art collection to museums, but this one object remains a prized possession, primarily because of the manner in which I acquired it.

My father was ecstatic. As long as he lived, he told the story of that purchase again and again. As far as he was concerned, my future would be successful. The next year when I returned by myself to the Red Fort and visited the same gallery, the owner was thrilled to see me. He invited me to sit, asked the adjacent galleries' owners to join us, and then requested that I repeat my bargaining ritual. He claimed he had never been so well bested. We remain friends to this day. My rule is to never buy something by demeaning it. The transaction must be positive and uplifting for all parties involved. Otherwise, it does not interest me.

* * *

The culmination of my parent's trip was a week on the New Peony, the same houseboat in Kashmir that Helene and I had occupied five years earlier. Our experience excelled our expectations. Mom and Dad were relaxed and appreciative. It was the first time in my life that I felt fully accepted by them. The highlight was a camping voyage diametrically different from the bare bones horseback trips we'd taken in my childhood into the mountains behind Ojai. Through historical accounts, I learned that the Mughal emperors used large wooden boats for multi-day excursions down the Jhelum River and through the unsurpassably beautiful Vale of Kashmir. Although no such boats had been used in many decades, I discovered one in drydock, its primary structure still sound. For an amazingly small sum, I was able to have it outfitted with a new thatched roof and decks. Mr. Major provided all mattresses, bolsters, silk carpets and quilts, a cookstove, utensils, and crockery. Ghulam arranged for the crew and accompanied us himself.

After breakfast onboard the New Peony, we boarded our forty-two-foot wooden-hulled giant shikara. As on the smaller shikaras—the taxi boats in Kashmir—a solid wooden backrest three-feet high, with a curtain above it, divided front from rear. A third of the vessel behind us held the four oarsmen, a cook, and Ghulam, our bearer.

Mattresses covered by carpets filled the long, narrowing foredeck. All four of us sat side-by-side propped by pillows and bolsters against the backrest as the oarsmen gently paddled us through willow-lined corridors alongside garden after garden of flowering bulbs. Bright turquoise and orange kingfishers swooped down into the crystal-clear water to catch small fish. Once we joined the mainstream, the rapid current took us down into the valley far away from any other tourists.

We passed many villages with Tudor-looking half-timbered houses, their sod roofs covered in moss and flowers. Children called out and waved to us as we went by. Behind us, pots on the cooking fire bubbled with the savory scents of lamb stew. At our choice, we stopped for lunch alongside a green meadow where Ghulam leaped out to spread embroidered tablecloths, serving us a delicious meal on china dishes. Dad and Mom were exuberant. Later, we moored for the evening in a bowered cove where the cook prepared roast duck in mango sauce. Opposite us, someone had tethered a white stallion perfectly lit in the late evening sun. We encountered no other inhabitants. We slept comfortably under cozy silken quilts—a far cry from the utilitarian sleeping bags my parents still used back home. From start to finish, our experience seemed drawn from the Arabian Nights and a perfect celebration of Dad's sixtieth birthday.

Throughout history, until the last three decades, writers have extolled Kashmir. Since then, that inexpressibly beautiful region has been blown apart by strife, insidious political maneuvering, and divisive disruption. I feel about it much as I do about Afghanistan.

In my four extended explorations there, I met good, honest, well-meaning people. From what I could tell, their lives were well-balanced in relative equanimity. In recent years, confounding and seemingly unsolvable issues torment the region—similar to yet different from the complexities continuously plaguing the Middle East. It is ironic that a people whose artistic creativity and production are excelled nowhere on earth, and whose natural environment approximates paradise, are among the world's most threatened. I remember those glorious days of paddling through lakes and rivers and visiting artists' ateliers—intrigued by the intricacies of their crafts—and spending hours in Kashmiri homes drinking countless cups of cinnamon-spiced chai while we discussed their culture and world events. Days and weeks there, we slept and woke amid consummate glory. It is too dangerous now for us to return, and although I've tried to keep in touch with friends in Srinagar Valley and remain current with what is going on, whenever I think of Kashmir, my emotions shatter.

* * *

Each December for three more years, Helene and I returned to Kalakshetra in time for their dance festival right after Christmas. Seated next to Rukmini, we'd watch hours of staged productions featuring the finest dancers and musicians. Rukmini provided us with a lovely private bungalow just opposite the sacred banyan tree. We had our own kitchen but could also eat the delectable vegetarian food provided by the school's chefs. Besides short field trips out to rural areas to continue my documentation of votive terracottas, I interacted with teachers and staff at Kalakshetra. We discussed their intentions and plans for the organization's future. I carefully observed and interviewed individuals, reporting to Rukmini if I felt that their ideas might improve the curriculum or management. I also helped my elderly friend interview enterprising young and middle-aged Indians we thought might be an asset to Kalakshetra's administration. Rukmini worried that if she did not appoint a capable and forward-looking successor, the dance and music academy would be taken over by the government and institutionalized. I hope that my input eased some of her concerns. I found Rukmini's control to be absolute, and nothing could be done without her approval. Even though, in theory, she wanted to relinquish her authority, no one approached her strict expectations.

When Rukmini Devi Arundale died in 1986, just three years after we left and only a few days after her childhood friend Krishnamurti passed, Kalakshetra was left without a clear line of succession. The Indian government's Ministry of Culture took over its management, but they have done so with elan and thoughtful taste, appointing a capable and farsighted administration. In 2012, the Ministry established the Kalakshetra Foundation to manage the different schools, including the dance and music academy. Now named the Rukmini Devi College of Fine Arts, it continues to teach and train India's finest performers. My old mentor should be pleased.

* * *

Precisely ten years after I first arrived in India, I was in the northern holy city of Varanasi as part of my ongoing research into votive terracottas. I invited my Swiss friend Andrée Schlemmer to spend my thirtieth birthday with me. We had met in Switzerland when I was just eight. Andrée, a deeply spiritual person, had been a primary mentor in my early childhood at a time when I felt unappreciated by my family and community. The morning of my birthday was the first day of her first and only trip to India, and I had long prepared for the occasion.

Andrée's comment when I came to her door at 5 a.m. was: "Steve, you are all so white, so pure, so pristine!" I had just bathed, washed my hair, and dressed all in white in the traditional costume of a north Indian male: tight ankle churidar pajamas, a finely embroidered cotton kurta (tunic) reaching to my knees, and an embroidered wide wool Kashmir shawl draped around my shoulders. I responded to her comment with what I thought was modesty, but inside I felt complimented and proud. As we went downstairs and out into the cold morning air, I threw my shawl over one shoulder in a poetic gesture. I then hailed a passing bicycle rickshaw, and we both climbed into the small seat.

It was cool and still pitch-black in narrow city streets already filling with traffic. Bikes and fellow rickshaws jangled the air with the constant chorus of handlebar bells: rrrinngg-rrrinngg rrrinngg-rrrinngg! Amid the clamor, I tried to prepare Andrée for our upcoming adventure. We headed for the center of this most sacred city, the ancient heart of Hinduism. I wanted her introduction to be notable. It was. After a twenty-minute ride, we dismounted alongside a small alleyway barely lit by occasional bright windows and doorways. After I warned Andrée to stick closely to my side, we wended our way through the maze of narrow streets that comprise Varanasi's oldest section. Many are only eight feet wide, dwarfed on each side by three- and four-story buildings, some with elaborately carved and painted entrances. We passed directly by two of the most important temples, both already thronged with devotees, and next to innumerable other small shrines, many lit with tiny oil lamps and adorned with fresh flowers.

I knew my way well and made all the little turns in the dark necessary to arrive at the edge of the immense Ganges River at a place where no other foreigners would be. It was my own special spot: an ancient peepul tree stretched high above and over the river. We took off our sandals as we approached the tree, and I motioned for Andrée to sit cross-legged beside me before the ageless and holy expanse of water and riverside. Andrée again commented on how pure I looked in all my white, and I glowed with her praise. We sat in quiet contemplation as the sky began to lighten, and the river, believed by hundreds of millions of Hindus to be a goddess, turned from blackened slate to shades of lavender, pink, and gold. The sun, viewed as the God Surya, was about to rise. It was beautiful and peaceful, and I was proud to be there with my childhood mentor Andrée, introducing her to this sacred experience.

Just when the sun sent its rays to highlight all of the palaces and temples that lined the banks for miles within our view, just then as I composed myself in prayer, at that exact second, a flock of more than twenty pigeons flew into the tree above our heads and all released their excrement upon me. Wet streaks of bird dung covered me: all over my shawl, my embroidered kurta, and my pajamas, on my hands, in my hair, even one right down my glasses! Within seconds, my pristine white metamorphosed into a Jackson Pollock painting of yellows, blacks, greys, and reds. None of it, not one drop, had hit Andrée. She looked at me and burst into gales of laughter. Even the lone ascetic meditating in his shrine behind us, Homi Baba, who had not uttered a word in over forty years, looked amused. In one moment, a single cosmic gesture, my pride in my appearance had been crushed. I was taught a needed lesson in humility. And so, my thirtieth birthday remains a memory of divine humor amid the sublime and the knowledge that appearances are ever changeable.

* * *

Our years in Cornwall were nourishing and formative. Our garden there had been lovingly cherished and developed over centuries. At its edges was an ancient wood intersected by an old Roman footpath and even older druidic paths. I had always loved nature, both tended and wild, and during the months I was not in India, I immersed myself in that vibrant environment. Caring for our garden and exploring the many National Trust gardens nearby planted the seeds of my desire to design, develop, and maintain gardens. Cornwall taught me an immeasurable amount that still infuses my life today.

A diplomatic agreement between India and Britain spearheaded the Festival of India, 1982. Two dozen museums in London and elsewhere in the UK hosted innovative displays of Indian art, each specializing in a specific theme. Theaters, concert halls, and auditoriums produced signature performances of over 200 of India's top musicians, dancers, and actors. Taking the train up from Cornwall often that year, I participated in several conferences sponsored by the festival and attended openings and festival functions. Two exhibitions particularly dazzled me: *Indian Heritage* at the Victoria and Albert Museum, a sumptuous display of Mughal art, and *Aditi* at the Barbican, an insightful exploration of Indian folk art and craftsmanship. I was most closely associated with a show at the Serpentine Gallery entitled *The Living Arts of India: Craftsman at Work.*

Nine artisans, each a master craftsman in his or her own state, had been brought to London to demonstrate their production techniques and exhibit their wares. Two metal sculptors, two painters on cloth, a weaver, an embroiderer, a potter, a stone carver, and a pith sculptor arrived in London for the three-week-long exhibition before they and the show traveled on to four more galleries in England, Scotland, and Wales. None of these individuals had left India before. Many were confused, even lost in this vast foreign metropolis. As I was known to be intimately familiar with artisans in many regions of India, the organizers requested my help in easing their shock and showing them the city.

One bright Monday afternoon, the director asked me to take the nine artisans to visit nearby Kensington Palace, the residence of many of the British royal family including Princess Margaret and the recently married Charles and Diana, Prince and Princess of Wales. On that beautiful blue day in mid-May, we walked across the vast lawns of Kensington Gardens. It was hard to keep the group together. None had previously seen such expanses of green or so many beds of flowers in perfect blossom. Some wanted to linger, while others wished to run wildly. Somehow, I managed to keep them more or less within sight until we rounded the corner and approached the palace. They sobered up, wide-eyed and humbled by the enormous edifice. We were met by the palace curator, a pompous and highly restrained man appointed to show us through the public rooms of the palace in an orderly fashion.

The moment we entered the front door into the grand entrance hall, all nine Indians scattered. The lost-wax sculptor from West Bengal rushed to examine the bronze pilasters that held the banister up the grand staircase. The potter from Uttar Pradesh went for the ceremonial vases on elegant side tables, handling their glazes and intricate turnings. The curator yelped, but at that moment, the Gujarati embroiderer picked up the tapestried pillows on a majestic settee, turning them over and fingering the intricate weave. The stone sculptor from Orissa ran his experienced hands over the bust of a Moor carved of a combination of different colored marbles. In a separate room, the Rajasthani *pichwai* cloth painter had pulled the silk damask curtains out from the wall and examined the seams with her nails. The bronze sculptor from Tamil Nadu, trained in the exacting art of figural depiction, was fascinated by the life-size gilded images of Apollo and Flora standing in marble niches in the Cupola Room. Too much happened at once. The curator blew his whistle again and again to assemble as many guards as possible, directing each to cautiously intervene with the Indian guests. He harrumphed that it was his job to oversee the care of this royal collection, yet he did not want to cause a diplomatic incident. I found the situation hilarious. We never saw the breadth of public rooms that they had intended to show us, but each artist had an experience they will always remember. It remains one of my most cherished memories of our years in Britain.

* * *

A little over a year later, we moved back to the United States. Even though we loved living in London and Cornwall, we were tired of being expats and homesick for our own country. Our seven years in Britain permanently enriched our viewpoints and tastes. They also helped me understand more deeply British imperialism's devastating effect upon India, even as it helped me discern the similar impact that U.S. foreign policy has had and continues to have on many nations. The United States is so vast that unless one lives outside it for a period of time, it is difficult to understand the biases in our own world view. Those years abroad instilled in us a valuable perspective.

~ 9 ~
Grounding

All existence in India begins with mitti. *Mitti translates as earth, mud, clay, and terracotta. It is the most primal substance, that of which the world is fashioned. Mitti is the earth upon which man is born and lives. The food that sustains him and the fibers of the fabrics that clothe him are nurtured in* mitti. *Mitti is used to make the walls and roofs of his houses, the vessels for carrying, storing, washing, cooking, eating, and worship, the gifts he gives to his gods, and sometimes even the images of his gods. Numerous Indian myths and legends describe the gods as earth itself: the world is the body of the God or Goddess, composed of soil. The Mother Goddess is most closely associated with the ground and with clay. Worshiped throughout India today, it is She who bears the earth and all creation. Religious rituals equate the fashioning of a simple clay figurine with the birth of the Goddess: The Goddess is clay and clay is the Goddess. After the rituals, She is dissolved in water back into the earth: the Indian counterpart of the Christian: "Dust to dust."*

Everything has a soul in India: man and animals, plants and rocks, earth and water. All is in a state of movement, of birth and of death. Clay is the symbol of transition, of cycles of change, of impermanence and regeneration. Its plasticity makes it simple to use. It is accessible everywhere; it takes form with little effort, and its fragility assures its constant renewal. Clay objects are easily broken and as easily replaced. In India, the creation, destruction, and recreation of clay into useful forms are constant. In a land as ancient as this subcontinent, civilizations are layered one upon the other. The dust of one people becomes the ground for the next. The material for today's clay vessel is composed of a mixture of untold generations of other vessels, recent and ancient.

Divine Spirit is invited to enter sculptures made of clay. Sometimes these images represent the gods themselves and are installed in shrines as focuses for worship. More often, they are gifts to the gods, grateful responses to special favors the deities have bestowed upon the donors. They usually depict animals: horses, elephants, or cattle believed to be transformed by the gods' power into living beings in the spirit world. Whether intended as images of gods or as presents for gods, most of these sculptures are terracottas fired by potters, while some remain unfired, their impurities cleansed by Divine Energy.

Many Indian deities are associated with natural phenomena. Rivers, mountains, rocks, and trees are worshiped as specific gods and goddesses. Votive clay sculptures are placed in open shrines beneath ancient and venerable sacred trees. Often, they are given to honor the Mother Goddess in response to Her beneficence. For the duration of each donation ceremony, Her Spirit pervades the terracotta and bestows blessing upon the devotee. After the ritual, the sculpture is left to crumble beneath the tree, its purpose fulfilled. As it gradually dissolves back into the dirt, its remains mix with those of countless previous images. It is mitti, *earth, one with the Goddess, symbol of the ongoing cycles of Indian life, death, and rebirth.*

(Preface to 'Gifts of Earth: Terracottas and Clay Sculptures of India', 1995.)

* * *

Each year I traveled to new regions, seeking out sculpting potters and roadside shrines, grounded in the earth of India. It was a humbling experience. Over a decade before, I had learned the potter's craft by helping Beatrice Wood in her studio. Now I was sitting at the feet of rural masters whose ancestors had been digging and fashioning this substance for millennia.

The success of Britain's Festival of India encouraged the United States to host its own festival, broadening and enhancing the concept to include exhibitions and performances from coast to coast. I learned that two shows scheduled for the 1985–86 US Festival of India particularly pertained to my profession. The Brooklyn Museum in New York would display *From Indian Earth: Four Thousand Years of Terracotta Art* while, on the other side of the country, Mingei International Museum, near San Diego, would exhibit *Forms of Mother Earth: Contemporary Indian Terracotta*. Although I had not yet completed my doctoral research, SOAS did not stipulate that I remain in the United Kingdom after I had finished the required coursework. Organizing these two exhibitions would give me inestimable experience and credentials. They were the nudge that finally pushed us to relocate to America. I volunteered my services to both institutions and was accepted.

During our seven years in Britain, we had returned home to visit our families and friends once each year, sometimes at Christmas or Thanksgiving, or occasionally in the spring or summer. Knowing that our stay overseas was not permanent, we traveled to new parts of the States each time to ascertain what might be the best place to live. I enjoyed field research in India and was determined to make a freelance career in this work. If I could support my choice, I would not be bound by profession to a specific location. Our selection of destination was wide open.

In the autumn of 1982, we rented a car to spend two weeks driving through New England, making a loop of Massachusetts, Maine, Vermont, and New Hampshire to experience the changing foliage. Cousins in rural Maine, Taffy and Eliot Field, recommended that we check out the small coastal town of Camden. We felt at home the moment we entered this lovely community surrounded by mountains, ocean, lakes, and both deciduous and conifer forests. We wanted to spend the rest of our lives there. Upon our return to Helford, Cornwall, we put our 200-year-old house on the market.

* * *

As a devoted bibliophile from early childhood, I had always wanted to write. I naturally gravitated toward art books. Since most of what I documented in India had never been recorded, I resolutely photographed and cataloged entire environments. I spent a year working at the photography lab at SOAS learning the craft of color printing, and then set up a darkroom in our Cornish cottage. For months before our autumn trip to New England, I printed color images of a wide variety of Indian terracottas and their production and laid them out in two huge portfolios. I arranged meetings with publishers in New York at the end of our trip in an attempt to persuade one of them to publish a book on Indian terracottas in time to coincide with the new Festival of India. My life has been filled with serendipity. When we stayed with my Maine cousins, Eliot told me that he had provided legal advice to Paul Gottlieb, the editor-in-chief of Harry N. Abrams, one of the world's finest art publishers. He offered to arrange for an appointment.

When I met this CEO in his penthouse office ten days later, he sized me up, asked to see my portfolios, and began to flip through them, several pages at a time. "No...No...This subject is too specialized for our readers..." My emotions plummeted. "But...but..." Paul slowed down to look more thoroughly. "You have many interesting pictures of Indian villages. My wife and I traveled with backpacks through India about fifteen years ago, and we fell in love with the villages. By any chance, do you have more photos of them?" By this point, I had been documenting India's villages for twelve years. When he understood that I had thousands, the publisher stated that he might be interested in a book on the subject if the photographs were good enough. Did I know anyone who could write it? When I told Paul I was primarily a writer, he informed me that his leading photography editor was coming to London in three weeks. If I could choose one hundred of my best photographs of Indian village life and write a proposal, I could hand-deliver them to her. Helene and I rushed home; I scurried to put it all together and took my proposal up to the city. To my grave disappointment, Abram's photo editor refused to meet me, insisting that I leave the packet for her with the hotel concierge. Back in Cornwall, I waited three months for a response. Her reply was devastating: "Abrams is not interested. Writers can never be photographers. Thank you."

After my initial disappointment, I remembered Paul Gottlieb's enthusiasm for the project, took a gamble, and called his office. Paul's personal secretary later told me she put the call through to him only because it was long-distance from Cornwall. (In those days, we called through the international operator.) Paul listened and asked me to resubmit my proposal directly to him. Within two weeks, he had accepted. I learned a valuable lesson in listening to my intuition and, at least in some cases, refuse to take "no" as an answer. Research, writing, submissions, and responses occupied a little more than a year. In December 1983, I received a contract from Abrams for my first book: *Village India*.

* * *

At the beginning of January 1984, I purchased the first MacIntosh computer in Maine. The operating system on that initial model was 128K, so limited that it would not generate more than two to three pages of text at a time. I had to compose short files and link them together to create a complete chapter. The process was laborious, but so intuitive that I began writing the first draft of my book within a day of owning my first computer. I've used Apple products ever since. Abrams assigned me a fine editor, Sheila Franklin. I would write a chapter, send it to her, and await her suggestions. As with any good editor, Sheila improved my manuscript. I'd previously published a couple of chapters in other books. Now, for the first time, I was able to blend my heart and brain and write from my personal experience about the regions I most loved: the rural cultures of South Asia. This book enabled me to coalesce my thoughts on a wide variety of subjects and approach Indian villages in my own interdisciplinary style.

Village India began by introducing the basic tenets and norms that underline most of rural India. I then wrote a history of India beginning with prehistoric civilizations and continuing through each century and epoch solely as it pertained to rural cultures—to date, the only record of its nature and still used as a text in university courses throughout the world. The bulk of the book composed a survey of the villages and small communities of twelve Indian states, listing the unique social, cultural, and economic qualities of each.

My first book was acclaimed upon release in the fall of 1985, perfectly coordinated with the launching of the US Festival of India. Bookstores across the country and each participating museum featured it. My only disappointment was in the quality of photographic reproduction. I had chosen the photographs according to my contract's stipulation: 200 color photographs and one hundred black and white. But the finished volume reversed the number so that half the images I had selected for their color content were now black and white. I believe the visuals of the book suffered.

* * *

During the nine months that I composed that volume, I began working with Dr. Amy Poster, the curator of Asian Art at the Brooklyn Museum of Art. Amy had conceived a ground-breaking exhibition on Indian terracotta sculptures spanning five millennia. She planned to assemble an unparalleled collection drawn from many sources: the Brooklyn's archives, private American collections, and museums in India. Amy openly welcomed my participation. She recognized my unique expertise in contemporary votive terracottas and encouraged my growing appreciation of ancient Indian terracottas, particularly those sculpted between 450 BC and 400 AD. In the fall of 1984, just after I had submitted my first complete draft of *Village India*, Amy and the Indo-US Sub-commission sent me to north India. There I met with the directors and curators of leading museums throughout the Gangetic Plain to finalize which sculptures would be loaned to the Brooklyn. It was an extraordinary opportunity. I explored the terracotta collections of the National Museum in New Delhi and museums in Mathura, Lucknow, Allahabad, Varanasi, Patna, and Calcutta.

At the Lucknow Museum, the director explained that while stone sculptures, bronzes, and paintings were highly valued in India, ancient terracottas were still regarded as unimportant. The Brooklyn show was a signal opportunity to change attitudes and create respect for this overlooked field of historically relevant, highly refined art. He took me down into the basement to show me a thousand or more terracotta sculptures jumbled together in unprotected stacks several feet high on the damp floor. Most of them were at least 2,000 years old, treated as if they had no value whatsoever. As no institution had ever organized an exhibition of this nature, most museum officials reveled in the opportunity to feature some of their most outstanding works of art. I was able to handle thousands of delicate objects, many never publicly displayed. The Indian Government had given the Brooklyn Museum carte blanche to choose almost any of their best sculptures, and Amy enabled me to help facilitate that choice. I will be forever grateful.

In the ancient city of Allahabad, Amy gave me a letter of introduction to private collectors. Prabhat and Sushmita Tandan invited me over, and we became close friends almost immediately. These individuals had inherited an enormous collection of ancient terracottas and carefully expanded it. Prabhat was a professor of engineering at a local university, and Sushmita managed a family-owned pharmacy. I came to their house at teatime and stayed until late at night and was so charmed by my experience that I returned for the same length of time for the next two days. We sat cross-legged on their large bed, drinking tea and consuming delicious food while Prabhat would pull out box after box of terracotta treasures. We would handle one at a time, feeling it, discussing it, musing over its age, its use, and the iconography portrayed in minute details that often could only be seen clearly with a magnifying glass. I called Helene back in Camden that first night and confessed that while she was never in danger of my having an affair with a living Indian woman, I was in love with women of the second century BC. They were so beautiful. These tiny sculptures, most of which could fit easily in the palm of my hand, were detailed portraits of individuals who had lived near Allahabad 2,100 years earlier. Prabhat, Sushmita, and I rhapsodized about them for hours, equally entranced by these intimate glimpses into ancient, poorly documented cultures. The sculptures' immediacy, their tactile quality, and the humanity of the subjects impressed us. Many pieces bore their creators' fingerprints permanently fired into the clay—tangible links to individuals who'd lived in previous millennia. I returned to stay in the Tandan's home many times over the next two decades, reveling in our friendship and our shared passion for these easily overlooked windows into the past. We traveled together in India, and they visited us in Camden and Jackson Hole. We consider their three daughters to be our nieces.

The opening of *From Indian Earth: Four Thousand Years of Indian Art* in January 1986 was a thrill—prominently featured in the *New York Times* and elsewhere and attended by many luminaries. Color murals of my photographs of Ayyanar shrines flanked the entranceway while more murals of my images highlighted other areas of the large exhibition. The critics, art historians, and public recognized that the pieces Amy had chosen were as refined and wondrous as any of the world's greatest works of art. Alongside these historical masterpieces, she displayed folk sculptures from my collection. I contributed entries to the catalog and wrote a chapter on nineteenth- and twentieth-century terracotta traditions.

* * *

In 1984, a new version of the National Handlooms and Handicrafts Museum opened in New Delhi. An earlier and far smaller Crafts Museum had been assembled under Kamaladevi Chattopadhyay's direction and curated by Ajit Mookerjee near Cottage Industries. But this new institution had behind it the weight of a visionary central government. The contemporary Indian architect Charles Correa designed an imaginative central building and my colleague Dr. Jyotindra Jain envisioned and directed the installation of the vast collections. Jyotindra is one of the most learned, insightful, and broad-minded Indian scholars of the past half-century. Every aspect of this inspirational museum complex reflected his discerning eye and his unique comprehension of the breadth and diversity of Indian folk art, decorative art, and craft. Upon entering the main gate, the first view was a collection of dozens of large terracotta horses grouped to approximate an Ayyanar shrine. Houses representing a wide range of rustic architectural styles were reconstructed on the broad site, each adorned with the decorative art of that specific region. The main buildings held 35,000 items drawn from all regions of India and displayed in the principal galleries or viewable in the extensive study collections. Jyotindra's galleries compellingly enticed visitors into wanting to learn about Indian creativity. Behind the primary structures, he fashioned a village market of craft shops where thirty artisans and their families, each from a different area of India, would demonstrate their production techniques for a whole month. The next month they were replaced by a new set of thirty: weavers, embroiderers, painters, woodcarvers, leatherworkers, stone carvers, bronze casters, ironsmiths, potters, and many more. The inventory they brought and the items they made were for sale, and the quality was always the best. Jyotindra ensured that each artisan and family received room and board, a viable salary, and the whole proceeds from all their sales. It was an extraordinary and incomparably successful endeavor.

Beginning in the mid-eighties, the Crafts Museum, as it was always called, became one of the single most important cultural sites in a capital city filled with tourist attractions. Visitors flocked there. It was a customary part of the protocol for visiting heads of state to be brought there. Jyotindra had dozens of agents working throughout the country, contacting artisans and collecting pieces. As my work took me to remote areas and undocumented fields, it was natural that I could also help him. Increasingly, I began collecting data and sharing names with him of folk artists that I thought would benefit the museum's vision. He and I developed a deep and abiding friendship and mutual respect.

* * *

In the summer of that same year, 1984, we found a house that we liked near the center of Camden. It had been constructed in 1850 for a ship's captain and his family and now required total refurbishment. Situated at the edge of a full acre, the property had little landscaping, but included three specimen trees and several old apple trees. During the year of reconstruction, and with the talented help of many others, I designed my first real garden by converting the wide flat lawn at the back into contours and garden rooms, excavating some areas and adding dirt and natural stones to others. Many new houses were being built in the area at that time, and none of the owners wanted their abundant field stones. One hundred tons of stones were dumped for free in our back alley which we used to build a contoured landscape that looked like it had always been there. We brought in thousands of plants: trees, bushes, perennials, and annuals to morph the previously uninspired property into a secret garden, a contemplative space that has nourished my daily meditations for decades. I was coming into my own as a designer.

Helene's refined eye and taste has always complemented mine. With her constant input, she gave me carte blanche to create the gardens. Our interior spaces were a total blend of the knowledge, concepts, and artistic sensibilities of both of us. Together we created a large, yet cozy home filled with our personal visions and the art we'd collected. My wife came from a privileged family, and, in these years, we benefited from their largesse. Our increased income allowed us to create what we wanted and has enabled me to pursue my life of travel and research in India in ways that would otherwise have been impossible.

* * *

One of the first exhibitions that the Crafts Museum in Delhi held in 1984–85 was *Form and Many Forms of Mother Clay*. It was a brilliant show assembled by Haku Shah, the artist and curator I had met years earlier in Ahmedabad. The collection displayed hundreds of votive terracottas and vessels. I described my impressions to Martha Longenecker at Mingei International Museum. Martha had served with me on the board of Beatrice Wood's conceptual folk art museum, and we had remained in close touch. She flew to Delhi to see the exhibition and later persuaded the Indo-US Sub-commission to help fund its transportation to her Southern California institution. Martha then requested me to install the show with her and Haku in the summer of 1986, soon after the Brooklyn show had closed.

Gigantic wooden crates holding the terracottas were waiting, ready to be unpacked when I arrived. We only had ten days before the show opened—not much time to complete a large installation. Its creator, Haku Shah, was supposed to oversee the process, but hadn't shown up. Martha and I had no choice but to unpack and install the show ourselves. At Martha's request, I had shipped many pieces from my collection to the Mingei, and these complemented those owned by the museum. Together with the aid of a talented installation crew, we created temporary walls, niches, display cubes, and vitrines to hold over 200 objects. Martha was a seasoned exhibition designer, and my learning curve was steep, adding into the mix my visual awareness and years of recording terracottas in shrines. I suggested displays and groupings that reflected how these objects would have been placed in rural India. Once we selected some of my relevant photographs of terracotta shrines, Martha had them printed as murals and framed prints. Without Hakubhai to inform us of his original intentions, I spent each evening writing all of the descriptive panels and labels. The Indian artist/curator finally arrived in the evening before the opening. Luckily, he was pleased with how we had managed the show and made only a few minor changes. I had already learned so much the previous two years working with Amy Poster and the Brooklyn Museum. My collaboration with Martha Longenecker to design and install *Forms of Mother Earth: Contemporary Terracottas of India* instilled in me the basis for a future career as an independent curator of many exhibitions of Indian art.

Dr. Jyotindra Jain induced a succession of master potters and sculptors from regions all over India to travel to the Mingei Museum. During the show's year-long run, two to four artisans at a time demonstrated their crafts in the galleries. Martha arranged for their products to be fired in nearby kilns and then added the finished pieces to the displays. Two of the finest artists that came from rural India were Sonabai Rajawar and her son, Daroga Ram. These two were to have a profound effect on my life fifteen years later.

* * *

In the years after the Festival of India, I continued my field research on Indian terracottas. At one point, I hoped to demonstrate in my doctoral dissertation the correlation between current terracottas and many of those discovered in excavations of India's earlier civilizations. Almost no historical literary sources refer to terracottas, and their ancient purpose and use is speculative. I proposed that many ancient artifacts are so similar to those I found in contemporary shrines that they might have had similar uses and rituals. However, my advisors at SOAS correctly stated that this topic was too broad for that purpose. Instead, I focused on canvassing the rural regions of fourteen Indian states, documenting the craft and usage of pottery and votive clay sculptures. Unlike doctoral programs in American universities, the University of London had no limit on how many years I took to complete my research. I had completed all my required courses and would finish as soon as it was ready.

One evening in 1987, at dinner at a restaurant in Bhubaneshwar, Orissa, I befriended a middle-aged American tourist and his teenage son. When I explained that I was conducting research in nearby villages, they expressed interest in visiting them. The father had hired a local guide for the ancient temples of Puri District. I didn't have to work the following day and offered to accompany them. We might even stop in a village or two along the way. The next morning, I met their guide: Maheshwar "Babu" Mohapatra. I directed our driver to turn onto a dirt side road shortly before reaching the thirteenth century Konarak Sun Temple. We entered the small village of Balikondalo, which contained the potter's community I had discovered in 1979 when the Koraput Collector first threw me out of his tribal district. In the intervening years, I had bonded with the potters and their families over weeks spent observing their sculpting techniques. They modeled intricate terracotta planters for sacred tulasi plants on the architecture of local stone temples. In preparation for the UK Festival of India, I had been asked to write a chapter on craftsmanship for a book on Indian art, my first publication. Instead of making lists of the diversity in each state, I wrote a detailed description of the broad range of crafts and household arts created in Balikondalo as a paradigm for understanding the breadth of Indian rural craftsmanship. I knew this village well.

When we entered Balikondalo, our guide Babu informed us in surprise that his uncle was one of the community's leaders. The coincidence was remarkable: I'd been served meals in this man's house several times over the years. On the spot, I hired Babu Mohapatra as my research assistant. He aided me immeasurably in gathering more accurate information and details there and in nearby communities that he knew well. It was precious to work closely with an insider who was also well educated, open-minded, and informed. Over the next years, Babu and I worked together on many research projects, eventually expanding our scope to include most regions of the country.

A few weeks later in Delhi, Jerry Prillaman, the Cultural Attache of the US Embassy, and his French wife Geneviève invited me for dinner. In my experience, most American diplomats live isolated and privileged lives, remaining purposefully separate from close interaction with the people in the country that hosts them. I've always found that situation deplorable. The Prillamans were an exception: open-minded, broadly conversant in many topics, and interested in Indian history, art, and culture. During their tenure in New Delhi, I spent as much time with them as I could. As usual that evening, they had invited a diverse and intriguing mix of guests, mostly Indians. Carol Reid was a visiting representative of the Smithsonian Associates Travel Program, an offshoot of the US organization of national museums and cultural centers. She asked if I had ever considered leading tours of India. When I responded that I was not interested, Carol challenged my preconception that all tours were filled with ignorant, privileged boors. She claimed that the individuals who participated in those sponsored by her organization were carefully screened, well-educated, adaptable, and dedicated to learning about the country and people they were visiting. She promised me that if I would consider leading one, I would be allowed to create my own itinerary and introduce participants to aspects of India that few other tourists see.

The next spring, in 1988, I organized and led my first tour of India. Carol was true to her word, accompanying me personally and teaching me the ropes. Travel arrangements were made and facilitated by experienced agents. I created an itinerary that included contrasting and complementary cultures. Once the twenty-three participants plus Carol and Neil (the local agent) gathered in Delhi, we spent three weeks exploring Orissa, Tamil Nadu, and Gujarat. I prepared for that first tour and subsequent ones for months in advance, discovering a natural love of teaching. I liked almost all of the tour members (although I also found that each excursion included one or two individuals who made my life hell). Three of us worked together to facilitate each trip: the Smithsonian rep (in this case, Carol), the accompanying Indian travel agent, and I (the lecturer). The organization also provided local Indian guides for each location. As I had worked successfully with Babu Mohapatra, a trained professional guide, I insisted that they hire him for that week's exploration. In Madras and for our travels through Tamil Nadu, the Smithsonian assigned me Sunithi Narayan, an incomparable guide. Sunithi became my next primary Indian mentor. The tour was a success, and I added another string to the bow of my freelance career. For the next three decades, I limited myself to leading one tour of India each year, creating a different focus and itinerary for each.

Finally, fifteen years after I first enrolled at SOAS, I submitted my doctoral dissertation (or thesis, as it is known in Britain). It is standard for this material to be purely academic, dense, and incomprehensible to anyone unfamiliar with that specific field. I had grown uncomfortable with what I viewed as elitist scholarship. Education (learning more about any subject) should be accessible to any interested individual. I prided myself on writing material that anyone could pick up and understand. In consequence, I wrote my thesis in as clear and straightforward language as possible, avoiding or explaining terminology that might confound an uninformed reader. I intended my work to be published. I succeeded in both goals: SOAS accepted my thesis. I was fortunate that the person who read, critiqued, and approved it was Dr. George Michel, a leading scholar in the field of Indian art history and an unusually broad-minded scholar. The profusely illustrated manuscript was published jointly by Mapin Press, Ltd, and the Indira Gandhi National Centre for the Arts. Mapin, one of India's pre-eminent art publishers, had been founded jointly by Bipin Shah and his wife, Mallika Sarabhai. *Gifts of Earth: Terracottas and Clay Sculptures of India* was beautifully designed and printed, and I became Dr. Stephen P. Huyler! My parents and Helene's parents were relieved, pleased, and proud.

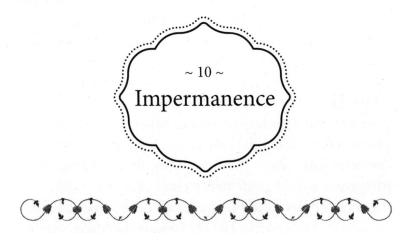

~ 10 ~
Impermanence

Bidulata's smile radiated gentle kindness. "Come! Come! Please drink some tea in my home. Or would you rather have a tender coconut? My grandson will get one for you from the tree just there." Babu and I had stopped outside her thatched home to watch as she skillfully dipped a handmade brush into a small pot of thick white rice paste and applied graceful loops, swoops, and lines to her exterior mud walls. Bidulata was refashioning her family's living space into a personal temple to Lakshmi, the Goddess of Prosperity. She stopped as she invited us in, but we protested and asked her to continue painting. We would gladly accept some chai later.

Within an hour, she had finished the exterior walls. The results were hypnotic: a treatment of lacey white on a canvas of light brown clay. Large-leafed banana trees flanked either side of the front door, peacocks and parrots roosted in the branches, and two elephants raising their trunks framed an enormous lotus representing Lakshmi. The earthen step over the threshold was marked with white lines and a set of footprints. Just inside this doorway, further sets of prints between sinuous lines of small lotuses led the way across a courtyard and into the principal room. These symbols, the Goddess's own footprints, would guide her to enter Bidulata's home. All the room's household furniture had been removed (bed, mattresses, and chairs). The aged widow, her daughter-in-law, and her granddaughters had completely resurfaced the walls with a fresh coat of clay mixed with purifying cow dung. They had then painted the entire chamber in white symbols of the Goddess to create the inner shrine, the sanctum sanctorum.

She said that, later that evening, above a lotus painted in the center of the floor, they would place a small wooden dais. At an auspicious moment, accompanied by ululating song, all the women and girls (no men present) would ceremoniously set on the wooden platform a painted terracotta pot filled to the brim with just-harvested rice. A small black stone, passed down in their family for generations, would sit atop the rice. Bidulata, as the family's elder, would invoke the spirit of the Goddess to enter this stone, garland the assemblage with fresh red hibiscus, and all of them would prostrate themselves before her. Lakshmi, the Goddess herself, would be present. Specially prepared foods placed on platters before Her would be blessed and then divided, to be eaten by family members and perhaps shared with close friends. The beneficence of the Divine Feminine would be showered upon the household and protect it from harm for the following year.

All of this we learned from that sweet old widow as we sat together in the shade of her courtyard drinking chai. The unfolding story, the details, and the richness of communion with individuals—these were the benefits of working with Babu Mohapatra, my new research assistant. I set up my tripod to photograph the art. Then I canvased all of the other houses in this tiny village not far from Babu's natal home. Each had been regenerated into a unique graphic invocation of the Goddess, as had most rural homes throughout Puri District, Orissa. All these paintings were ephemeral. They faded over the following weeks, to be washed over with a new surface of mud mixed with cow dung and replaced with different paintings for the next seasonal festival. Their impermanence intrigued me. I became obsessed with photographing the magnitude of women's creativity here and throughout the country.

* * *

Disillusioned by my photography's inconsistent quality in *Village India*, I realized that I required more nuanced instruction. We had moved to Camden, Maine, purely because we loved its environment and friendly community. To my delight, I discovered in Rockport, just a few miles from my home, one of the two most acclaimed institutions in North America for the detailed study of photography, other than universities. Each late spring through autumn, the Maine Photographic Workshops employed some of the world's best photographers to teach week-long workshops in their specialties. Although courses were also offered for beginners, it was these masterclasses that drew my attention. I could study any specific aspect of the craft with leading professionals. Beginning in 1987, I took two to three courses each summer for several years. Sam Abell, David Alan Harvey, Jay Maisel, Joe Baraban, and Joyce Tenneson were among those who shared with me their knowledge and techniques. I discovered that although I had a natural eye for beauty and composition, I needed to compose my shots more carefully and consider all elements in the frame. In each week-long workshop, I learned as much as I might otherwise in a year in the field. I was taught two practical lessons: shoot as many images as possible, varying the angle, aperture, and focal point; and, back in my studio, edit, edit, edit. Over the years, I also was tutored in valuable post-production tools such as Photoshop and Lightroom, but that knowledge was secondary to the requirement that, first, I compose my images well.

I joined classes with years of photographic experience behind me and was a fast learner. Beginning just half a decade later, from 1992–98, I taught my own masterclasses at MPW on the ethics of photographing in ethnic environments. Although I shared with my students hands-on techniques for working in the field, I also trained them to question and be clear about their motives. My experiences in India have taught me that I alone am responsible for my images, that objective photography does not exist, and that I must consciously and ethically choose what I photograph and what I share with others. My ground rule has always been never to take an image without permission. For me, the picture must be an extension of my personal relationship with the subject. Otherwise, I become a paparazzi: intrusive, offensive, and distrusted.

* * *

As I traversed India to document terracottas, I also recorded women's art. In the late 1980s, I worked on the two primary subjects simultaneously. The evanescence of each complements the another: art that was created for a short-lived purpose and then destroyed or left to decay, to be replaced by a new creative expression. I believed each topic to be worthy of a book and photographed it all. By the advent of high-quality digital photography at the turn of the millennium, and my gradual shift into that medium, I took almost 250,000 edited and cataloged transparencies of India.

Paul Gottlieb of Harry N. Abrams flatly informed me that I was "in his stable," meaning that I was one of his photographers. However, whenever I suggested he publish books on Indian terracottas and women's art, he gave me a wan smile and told me that he couldn't market them. Rizzoli International, also based in New York City, had released a series of beautiful books on ethnic women's art, most notably: *African Canvas* by Margaret Courtney-Clarke in 1990. Although the book's written narrative was limited, I loved its design, layout, and superb images. I believed that a book on rural Indian women's graphic art could be similarly presented and effectively marketed. I prepared a proposal with one hundred of my best photographs of the subject and presented it to Solveig Williams, Rizzoli's Editor-in-Chief. Solveig responded positively, gave me a contract, and offered to edit the book herself. It was an incredible honor. However, when Paul Gottlieb discovered that I had signed a contract with a competitor, he was furious, declaring that I had betrayed his trust. Honestly, I do not know how I could have proceeded differently and still published this scintillating material. Paul offered me no alternative.

By this point, I had submitted my manuscript and photographs of *Gifts of Earth* to the Indian publisher, Mapin. We were initially under contract for that book to be released in 1992, but funding issues on their part delayed the process. I could now pursue women's art wholeheartedly. What a joy that was! Throughout the twentieth century, women in India had been increasingly subjugated and ignored. Almost no one gave them the attention they deserved. My primary mentors in India had always been women: Kamaladevi, Rukmini Devi, Auntie Teni, Sushmita Tandan, and many others. Each had instilled in me a deep respect for the strength, grit, determination, intelligence, and creative productivity of Indian women. Ideally, this book would be an opportunity to bring attention to overlooked artforms and, through that, to innate feminine capabilities and achievements. I had always been a feminist. Rizzoli gave me a chance to make a difference.

* * *

The city of Jodhpur, Rajasthan, on the Thar Desert's edge, had been a destination on my first trip to India in 1972. Historically, the merchants of this city had plied their trade on the ancient camel caravan routes into and out of India. It had become a splendid royal capital, and its complex blend of cultures and arts charmed me. I returned in the early nineties as a guest of Maharajah Gaj Singh, affectionately known as "Bapji." This progressive former monarch was in the process of adapting the ancient citadel Mehrangarh Fort into a notable museum of art and culture. He requested that I help him envision and install galleries to display his collections of indigenous arts and crafts. For each of several years beginning in 1992, I spent weeks as his guest while working with the Fort and museum staff. At first, Bapji provided me a suite of rooms alongside the Fort's ramparts, but just one night as the only inhabitant of that enormous ancient edifice was enough to give me nightmares. Layers of a notoriously bloody history infiltrated any peace I might have had. In consequence, Bapji invited me to spend weeks as his personal guest at his residence, the monumental Umaid Bhawan Palace—but that experience proved to be too rich for my blood. Finally, with His Highness's blessing, I moved into a far simpler garden cottage at the nearby Ajit Bhawan. I returned there often and gladly for the several years I sporadically helped the Maharajah.

Far beneath the lofty cliff's edge of the Fort was the old residential area of Brahmapuri. I remember when I was twenty walking through its narrow, cobbled streets that wound up and down steep hills. I marveled at its whitewashed stone architecture, arched doorways, and windows, parapets, and courtyards. Brahmapuri's inhabitants were always welcoming: men in brightly coiled turbans; women dressed in brilliantly-colored saris, always veiled; and children calling out to me. I photographed this inner metropolis extensively. When I returned twenty years later, these same houses were now painted primary blue. The story, when I asked, was intriguing.

Each year in preparation for the autumn Festival of Light, Diwali, the house and its contents must be cleansed. Floors are swept, repairs made, new clothing purchased, and each household's walls repainted inside and out by the women. One year, one householder in Brahmapuri mixed too much bluing with her whitewash. (The purest white is only achieved by adding a little bit of blue.) The result was that her walls turned azure, and she and her family loved them. According to legend, her neighbors were jealous. So, the next year, they made their walls an even more dominant blue. And it spread, house to house. By the time I had returned, all of Brahmapuri had transformed into complementary shades of blue!

Now wandering the streets, as I often did before or after work in the Fort, was like entering a three-dimensional version of an M.C. Escher artwork. I never ceased to be dazzled by the geometry of bright blue stone steps rising outside indigo walls, multiple-arched windows revealing an interior of shadowed darker lapis lazuli, and the constant interplay of shape and form in each direction I turned. For my new book, I spent many hours in Brahmapuri interviewing women and, with permission, photographing their painting process. They happily encouraged me: I was giving them a voice.

When Rizzoli published my book, I referred to their neighborhood as "The Blue City." As far as I know, it had never been called that before or featured in any way. I find it amusing that now many books refer to Brahmapuri by that name as they encourage visitors to explore its wonders. I was dismayed when I was last there to witness that most houses are now reverting to plain white. Perhaps one-twentieth of the bright blue houses remain. The householders claim that it is "more modern" this way.

* * *

One early morning I was in the process of setting up my tripod and camera several miles away to photograph the early morning light on Mehrangarh, Jodhpur's fourteenth-century fort, when I noticed someone just twenty feet from me doing the same thing. Diverted, I introduced myself to Shimitsu, a young Japanese photographer who gave me a shy smile as he bowed deeply. Using gestures and his few English words, Shimitsu said that he had just arrived in India that morning for his first visit. He had flown into Delhi in the middle of the previous night and changed flights for this western desert city. These were his first pictures. Shimitsu had a friendly, compelling nature, and I asked him if he would like to accompany me later to photograph the Blue City. I explained that few tourists ever ventured there, and he gratefully accepted my offer.

The intense Indian light in the middle of the day washes out most photographs. Photographers learn to rise early to take their first images and then wait until the late afternoon to continue the process. Shimitsu and I entered the Blue City on foot at about 4:30 p.m. Most of the buildings were constructed between the fifteenth and eighteenth centuries, and many of their arched doorways and windows are intricately carved in geometric and floral patterns. The cobbled streets are too steep and narrow to allow for vehicles, but as is usual, pedestrians were ubiquitous. The startling colors of their clothes—vermilion and shocking pink veils on the women, multi-colored tie-dyed turbans on the men—were particularly vibrant when offset by the walls' pervasive blue. It was a visual feast and, as I expected, Shimitsu was enchanted. In the traditional Japanese manner, he bowed deeply from the waist to each person we met on the street, his hands touching his knees in the gesture of humility. The Indians responded with pleasure. Women framed by entrancing blue stone balconies would call down to him, and he would bow in their direction, sending them into gales of giggles. Children running along the azure rooftops to fly their paper kites catcalled, and, for their pleasure, he even bowed to them. A group of old men, playing poker on the floor of a sapphire verandah, turned to greet us. Between bows, Shimitsu took many pictures.

After half an hour of spellbound adventure through these unique streets, Shimitsu turned to me with an ecstatic expression on his face. With a sharp intake of breath, he pronounced two of his perhaps thirty words of English. He gleefully summed up his experience with the phrase: "Culture Shock!" Ever since that day, whenever the extraordinary vibrant beauty of India overcomes me,

I remember Shimitsu's response to the Blue City, and his words shout out in my mind: "Culture Shock!"

* * *

Several times I spent Holi in Jodhpur. On this spring festival, when hierarchy is set aside, everyone throws colored powders or liquid dyes on one another. I rose early in the morning to arrive in Brahmapuri before sunrise so that I might photograph the festivities: men dousing one another with buckets of bright red, orange, yellow, or purple dyes; women gently rubbing each other's faces in vermillion or acid green powders; children on the rooftops spraying anyone in the streets with bright pink dye—and all of this set against the interplaying facets of blue.

Later in the morning, the Maharajah invited me to his party at the palace. When I arrived before most of the other guests, Bapji took me aside to instruct me to stand next to the marble steps leading down into the walled garden where the royal festival would take place. When each of the many princesses arrived, I must pick her up bodily, carry her across the lawn, and dump her into one of the many zinc bathtubs of colored dye spread across the lawn. I was daunted, but my host had given me a royal command, and I did as he requested. A beautiful young Indian princess would arrive dressed all in white (as is common on that day—but in this case her outfit was couturier designed and tailored). I picked her up in my arms (she smiled and giggled as if this was normal), carried her over, and plopped her into a vat of bright purple or red. Normally, I would not even be able to touch one of these women, and here I was manhandling her and being praised for it! Throughout the garden were large brass trays on tripod feet bearing mounds of brilliantly colored powders. Servants circled with offerings of savory delicacies, alcoholic drinks, and bhang (a yogurt smoothie made with potent cannabis). As the crowd grew, live musicians and professional dancers wove among a group of perhaps sixty or seventy young princes and princesses from former kingdoms throughout western India. All were stoned on bhang and reveling in spraying one another, filling the air with puffs of dazzling colors. Such a contrast to my regular life in India spent in villages interviewing women about their art.

***

A couple of hundred miles from this palace, my four-wheeler bumped over rocks on unmarked roads as I searched for Moti-Singh-ki-Dhani, a village I heard might be painted for Diwali. Far out in the desert, past the fabled city of Jaisalmer, the landscape is bleak and dry. Less than five inches of rain falls here in a typical year, and the summer heat regularly tops 125 degrees Fahrenheit. It was just a week before the festival, and I hoped to find women preparing their homes to honor it. When I came upon the ten or twelve rough stone houses, they were almost indistinguishable from the desert. A tall stone rectangle of walls contained each plot, room enough within it to hold the family, its goats, and a few favorite camels. Only old men, women, and small children were there. All capable males were away from home for weeks at a time as they guided their herds of camels and goats far and wide searching for the scant forage. The village had no electricity, and the only well was a mile away. Several times each day, the women toted their brass pots to this limited water source, filled them, and then laboriously carried them back atop their heads, often with one or more babies strapped to their chests.

The first compound I entered was typical of the rest. A simple, one-roomed dwelling nestled against the wall opposite the entrance. Next to it was a small kitchen hut. Three charpais (basic beds composed of four legs joined by posts and interwoven with rope) stood outside the house. Inside was a carved wooden storage bin. These four items were the family's sole furniture. Phulo, the mother of the small family of inhabitants, called out to me in the forthright manner typical of these desert women. She squatted atop an interior wall and stretched her right arm down as far as she could to slap camel dung onto the surface and smooth it with her palm. This substance was precious to the family. As their only cooking and heating fuel, it was stockpiled and sparingly used. Essential water conservation and limited materials meant that the women here could only decorate their homes once each year, unlike those in many other regions of the country.

Once Phulo had resurfaced the walls of her compound and dwelling, this goatherder's wife used the flat of her hand to spread liquid white lime to cover the front of her home. She then applied swaths of yellowish-ochre pigment over the white in large, stepped rectangles. She further delineated the design by adding dark red outlines with the crushed end of a stick. Finally, she painted a rectangle of red as a counterpoint to both other shades. The result was a sophisticated geometric abstraction that might have fit into a contemporary art museum—yet neither Phulo nor any of the other women artists in the region had been exposed to modern art.

I returned each of the next several days. By the end of the week, all of the compounds in Moti-Singh-ki-Dhani displayed a different, yet complementary geometric abstraction. On Diwali, when I drove out there again, I could spot the community from a mile away. It vibrated with color and form amid the vast gray desert. When I commented to Phulo how beautiful it all was, she laughingly remarked: "Lakshmi will come only to a house that is clean and beautiful, and clean smelling. She will bring money and wealth. My house is now ready for her, and you have come this day. Do you have something you can give me? Some money or your watch, your camera, something I can sell? I think my paintings have worked. This next year will be good." I made sure my gifts pleased Phulo and her family. That evening as they lighted small camel-butter lamps along the tops of all the brightly painted walls, their home glowed with happiness and hope.

* * *

The scope of my survey throughout India was vast and varied. Rizzoli, my publisher, was most interested in portraying the graphic quality of this work. The prototype set by their other books was a large square format of beautiful color photographs complemented by brief, concise text. I would have preferred to write extensively about each region and give detailed descriptions and stories. Instead, I was bound by contract to write a text of only 10,000 words. (In comparison, this book is close to 100,000.) I worked closely with Solveig Williams to make each chapter as evocative and informative as possible and persuaded her to allow me to include illustrative captions. I loved the process of working with her. As always, the title was a long-sought prize. It must be just right to encapsulate the book's message and entice a potential reader. When I discussed the content with Lyn Donovan, an artist friend in Camden, she nailed it. *Painted Prayers: Women's Art in Village India* was a perfect choice.

Solveig was able to sell rights to three foreign publishers: Thames & Hudson in the UK, Arthaud in France, and Frederking & Thaler in Germany. Each of these companies featured my book in its 1994 Christmas catalog. For *Painted Prayers'* cover, Rizzoli had chosen a compelling photograph of Phulo bending over to resurface her wall. Thames & Hudson used the same image, but Arthaud picked a photograph of a Meena woman painting a *mandana*, while Frederking & Thaler selected one of a Kerala woman adding colored dots to her wall. Different strokes for different folks.

In 1995–96, Abrams had arranged for two or three book signings for *Village India*, but in the nineties, Rizzoli's publicity team was far more proactive. Suddenly I had signings and lectures all over the USA. The reviews were good. I printed fine enlargements of thirty-six of my best images in the book. With Rizzoli's advice and help, I created an exhibition proposal that I sent to many museums. From 1993 to 1998, I was given eighteen *Painted Prayers* exhibitions at prominent museums and galleries in the US and abroad. In each case, Rizzoli would coordinate with the institution to supply them with books and publicity materials. Life was good!

The German Government's Ministry of Cultural Affairs sponsored one of the first shows, in Munich. Solveig, Helene and I attended the opening and were gratified to be met by Andy Rossmann. During my 1968-69 senior year at The Thacher School, in Ojai, California, Andy had come from his native Germany to join me and my family for ten months as part of the academic exchange program: American Field Service. We had become close friends and remained in touch during the subsequent years. I was particularly pleased to be able to share with him this recent part of my professional life.

The Smithsonian's Arthur M. Sackler Gallery in Washington, DC, hosted an enormous *Painted Prayers* exhibition in 1995. They printed their own set of large images framed in ochre mats against walls painted in primary colors to reflect India's brilliant palette. The show was lauded by critics—including a positive personal interview on National Public Radio. Without explaining his reason, the Sackler's director, Dr. Milo Beach, suggested that Helene and I take a taxi for an evening drive up Connecticut Avenue. As we passed the White House and entered that wide boulevard, every street corner as far as we could see had a covered bus stop that featured an enormous backlit enlargement of one of my kolam (floor painting) photographs as an advertisement for my exhibition. It was one of the most thrilling moments of my life.

That same year, Dr. Jyotindra Jain displayed *Painted Prayers* at the National Crafts Museum in New Delhi. Room after room featured my photographs—but Jyotindra had added the exciting feature of inviting rural women artists from many regions of the country to paint the floors and walls of the gallery with sacred designs to complement my images. Soon after that, I traveled around the country carrying copies of this new book, returning to the villages I had photographed, and giving one to each of the featured women. They were thrilled to see themselves so honored. Even today, when I travel again to those communities, the families bring out tattered and worn copies of *Painted Prayers* to proudly show me photos of their mother, sister, or auntie decorating their home as invocations to the deities.

Rizzoli printed 15,000 copies of the volume in English (a large print run for art books at the time; today, a large run would be 6,000 to 8,000). These sold out completely within sixteen months. Over the next two years, I had over 10,000 personal requests for copies. There was nothing I could do: they were not available. Although I tried to convince Rizzoli to authorize a second printing, they refused. I never could comprehend their reasons when the handsome product they had created had been so successful and was still in demand.

* * *

Bidulata was the first featured woman to whom I gave a copy. Over the previous years, I had visited her many times. We'd become close, and she had asked me to call her "*Maushi*", the Indian word for "Auntie." In 1992, the day after I told her that I was writing a new book, Maushi urgently pressed a small piece of paper into my palm. This tiny old woman, dressed as always in a pure white cotton sari trimmed with just the suggestion of pattern at the border, broke into a sweet, tremulous smile. Her deep, wise eyes searched mine. Maushi was well educated. She had worked as a teacher and a midwife and had raised a large family. Her eldest son was an elementary school teacher himself, and now that she was widowed, she lived with him and helped to care for her many grandchildren in their simple mud-walled ancestral house in a tiny remote village in Orissa.

When I opened the paper in my hand, I found that it was covered with lines of fluid Oriya script interspersed with small drawings reminiscent of some of Maushi's wall paintings. With a look of tender intensity, she told me that these were her prayers to the Goddess Lakshmi, the deity of abundance and prosperity. She wanted me to take them and recite them every day so that this work of mine, the book I intended to write, would be successful. She hoped that the messages she had given me would be accessible to a greater world. Although I had the text translated, I could not read the Oriya script myself. And yet that paper accompanied my morning meditations and served as a link to Maushi and to the many people of India whose messages I tried to convey in my words and photographs. I believed Maushi to be old when we first met. Upon departure each of the many times we've met, I thought that I would never see her again. All these decades later, Maushi is still alive. Her portrait hangs on the wall of my meditation room in Camden, Maine. I see it every day, along with the faded and torn folded paper that contains her drawings and prayers. Even when she is finally gone, that link will remain.

~ 11 ~
Devotion

I had been to Padmapoda, a village in Eastern India, a number of times previously to visit the family of a close friend. Each time I had been taken to see the sacred tree that embodies the local goddess, the deity of community. This new experience was an unprecedented honor: being allowed to witness the ceremony of invocation in which the dynamic power of the supreme Goddess Chandi *was requested to subsume and transform that of the local deity. It was a very special ritual, enacted upon rare occasions to implore the aid of the Goddess in overcoming a difficult domestic problem. My Indian friend Babu Mohapatra, understanding my wish for insights into Hinduism as preparation for writing this book, had arranged this special* puja. *The entire ritual had already taken two priests two* hours: preparing and dressing the image of the Goddess, drawing a sacred diagram upon the ground and building a fire upon it, and feeding it with clarified butter (ghee), all the while continuously singing Her names and praises. As a middle-aged cultural anthropologist and art historian who had already spent over half my life studying India, I prided myself on my objectivity. I might feel empathy towards a particular subject or situation; but as a scholar I tried to distance myself to observe and take note.

Despite my resistance at that moment, as the fire flared brightly and the spirit of the Goddess was invoked to enter the tree and be available to the village, I actually felt Her presence. I felt a change in the atmosphere: a palpable sense of power vibrating throughout the area surrounding the sacred tree. It was a type of pulsating energy the strength of which I had never before sensed in my life. I was completely surprised, overwhelmed beyond any expectation. In that one moment I, who had come as an observer, had become a participant. That insight altered and enriched my perception, allowing me to release decades of self-identity as an objective outsider. By being fully present and receptive to an experience so very different from anything I had been raised to understand, my personal and professional life was changed. I was transformed.

... From that first experience of participating in the worship of the Goddess Chandi in the sacred tree in Orissa, my perceptions have grown immeasurably. Now when I am invited to attend a sacred ceremony, I no longer withhold myself in critical appraisal. I am fully present with all of my senses to absorb the ritual, to feel the full experience. I realize now that my earlier distance was *merely the consequence of my own limitations. The many Indians with whom I have interacted have always invited my full participation. For years I held myself apart. My Western heritage and my unconscious miscomprehension of image worship blinded me from deeper understanding. Today I believe that I can still retain a grounding in and deep respect for my American Christian background while being receptive to the many facets of Hindu spirituality. I can admire and even be in awe of the ways in which the sacred permeates the lives of the Hindu people while still maintaining strong attachments to my own home, family, friends, culture, and ideals. Awareness of one only enriches the other.*

(Preface to "Meeting God: Elements of Hindu Devotion" Yale University Press, 1999)

* * *

In the early- to mid-1990s, my career changed course a second time. I was to spend nine years attempting to convey to the western public the underlying currents of Hinduism. This metamorphosis was due to the influence of Dr. Milo Beach. Milo first befriended me in Washington, DC, during the United States Festival of India in 1985. He was a renowned professor of Indian art history, specializing in Mughal painting. In 1984, Dr. Beach was appointed as director of the new Arthur M. Sackler Gallery of Art, part of the Smithsonian Institution in Washington, DC, that was to be conjoined to the established Freer Gallery of Art. Together, these two galleries became our National Museum of Asian Art and a natural beacon for Asian studies.

The concept and design were brilliant. Urban legislation forbade any further surface buildings on the Washington Mall. The construction of the Arthur M. Sackler Gallery was fully underground against the Freer's foundation, lower galleries, and basement. Four floors were flush with the Freer, accessible both from its lower galleries and from the garden above. All galleries were illuminated by a combination of clever electric lighting and daylight effectively channeled down to even the lowest level. The architects were geniuses, but so was Dr. Beach. He masterfully planned each of the many galleries so that permanent collections from both the Freer and Sackler could seamlessly be exhibited side-by-side without viewers realizing that they were moving from one building to the next.

The Sackler contains enormous collections of Asian art that include a broad range, from awe-inspiring stone and metalworks to some of the world's most exquisite paintings. But many other items that do not belong in fine art categories are also part of its vast archived storage. In 1986, Milo hired me as a part-time consultant to help him catalog and understand Indian artworks in the collection outside the scope of classical art. He gave me an invaluable opportunity to work with a museum as it was being conceived, constructed, and refined. From the moment the Smithsonian's new National Museum of Asian Art (The Freer-Sackler) opened in 1987, it has been magnificent.

In 1992, Dr. Beach invited me to fly down from Maine to walk by myself through the Sackler's imposing storage vaults and inform him of any category that might make an appealing exhibition. I found that most of the three-dimensional Indian art in the vaults was devotional: either the object of worship or one used to facilitate worship. When I explained to Milo that they could easily become the core of a fine exhibition about Hindu art, he surprised me by asking if I would like to curate such a show. I responded positively with the caveat that the museum must agree to display the pieces in context—as they were meant to be seen rather than as items devoid of their sacred purpose. Indians criticize western museums for featuring their religious art for its artistic qualities but bereft of its spiritual essence. They find this academic approach offensive. Milo readily agreed to my terms and appointed Sarah Ridley, a member of the museum's education department, to co-curate the exhibition with me.

I was an unusual choice to conceive and curate such a show. I was not a Hindu scholar nor a specialist in Indian religions. Milo recognized that I am a lateral thinker with an unusual breadth of experience living in Hindu homes, visiting shrines and temples, and witnessing the rituals of daily devotion. I proposed to convey the daily devotion of everyday Hindu women and men, not purely through the lens of the priestly caste, the brahmins (as most other approaches to this religion did). Over the next four years, until the opening of *Puja: Expressions of Hindu Devotion*, I absorbed Hinduism. (Puja is the most common Indian word for worship.) I returned to India to immerse myself in attempting to comprehend and synthesize some of the complexities. It was not an easy task.

By this point, I had already led several tours of India. Whenever my group traveled in the south, I hired Sunithi Narayan as the guide. I was bewitched by her encyclopedic knowledge of and insights into Indian history, mythology, culture, and art, and her remarkable talent for conveying them through story and gesture. I have never met anyone like her. As a child, Sunithi had been trained in Bharatanatyam, the classical south Indian dance form championed by Rukmini Devi. With a dancer's movements and a poet's expressiveness, this professional guide lived and breathed India, bringing its illuminated past to life. Although I had studied Hindu mythology and iconography for decades, Sunithi presented them as vibrant, pertinent stories. Through her, legends carved in ancient stone cried out with passion and drama, bronze gods moved to celestial rhythms, goddesses in temple murals battled victoriously against evil.

Forty years earlier, in 1950, the Indian government had appointed Sunithi Narayan as the new nation's first official female tourist guide. Raised in a brahmin family, she had contravened centuries of caste restrictions to work openly with foreigners. Interactions with people from other cultures had broadened her mind yet strengthened her faith. I employed Sunithi to help break through my western preconceptions and truly feel the pulse of practical Hinduism. Through her, I met new individuals, entered innumerable temples and shrines normally out-of-bounds to non-Hindus, and participated in dozens of rituals that deepened my understanding of this complicated blend of beliefs often banded under the name of one religion. I also approached familiar rural and urban communities from a new angle, interviewing hundreds of individuals from a variety of occupations, ages, economic brackets, and social constructs.

When I invited Sunithi to spend a week with me at a remote sacred tree shrine in Kerala to observe the local healing rituals, the head priest asked if she was my mother. I am loomingly tall in South India, pale, and American in my demeanor. Sunithi was short, darker-skinned, and always dressed traditionally. We were so touched by this innocent question that I began to call her "*Amma*" (Mother), and she considered me her son. I will forever be grateful for the insights she shared with me.

* * *

The intense sweet smell of incense permeates my pores and dominates all my senses. For those few minutes of every day, I am fully attuned to the offering. It is early morning, and I have just entered the car, the taxi, the bus, or the motor rickshaw. It makes no difference which form of transportation I take. Each is filled with that pungent smoke as the workday commences. The scents vary from sandalwood to jasmine, but the initial impact is always the same: I am overcome.

Virtually all drivers of vehicles in India light incense to the deities of protection and safety every morning. I have seen it burning at the front of bullock carts and smelled it wafting back from the cockpits of commercial jets. Usually, a car's dashboard serves as a small shrine: a tiny bronze, plaster, or plastic image of a deity, saint, or guru adorns its center, occasionally accompanied by flowers, rosaries, or mementos of pilgrimages. For

Muslims, it is often the depiction of the Kaaba in Mecca; for Christians, Jesus or Mary or Saint Thomas; Sikhs honor their turbaned Gurus; Jains honor the naked Tirthankaras (perfect beings); while Buddhists honor Gautama or Tara. Hindus may worship any of a myriad of Gods and Goddesses, depending upon belief and inclination. Some images even strobe in multicolored lights when the ignition is turned on, while in others, the Gods' eyes light up as a constant reminder of their vigilant protection. Usually, incense is waved before the images as prayers are quietly uttered. The process is quick before the burning stick is wedged into a hole, often in the rearview mirror, and the windows opened to the relief of fresh air. It continues to burn for some time as we commence our journey, reminding the driver and me of the potent presence of the Divine.

* * *

Milo Beach had been prescient in assigning Sarah Ridley to co-curate *Puja*. Although Sarah did not know India well, she was adept at conveying information simply and evocatively. Writing the descriptive text and labels for the exhibition was the most challenging task I had ever attempted. Sarah helped me construct it to be approachable and interesting to sixth graders while still appealing to and informing scholars. I read stacks of books on Hinduism written by western scholars that missed or misinterpreted essential aspects of this vast religion. I was determined to right those wrongs and present daily Hindu devotion in ways that would correctly inform non-Hindu American audiences and still appeal to practicing Hindus. The Sackler's extraordinary staff aided Sarah and me with professional skill and insight. We were able to solicit and borrow superb art from many private collectors that enhanced the pieces I'd chosen from the museum's reserve collections.

* * *

During the summer prior to the exhibition's opening, an esteemed colleague, Dr. Susan Huntington, informed me that she had been asked to be Dean of the Graduate School at Ohio State University in Columbus. Susan and her husband John were prominent professors of South Asian art in OSU's Department of History of Art. The Huntingtons' academic program was one of the finest in the Americas, and their graduate students are esteemed. Susan asked me to teach an undergraduate/graduate course in non-classical Indian art and a graduate seminar on practical Hinduism. By this point, we had chosen all the objects for the *Puja* show, and I had written the text. The Sackler's staff handled the final stages of the exhibition, and Dr. Beach agreed that I could work and live in Columbus and commute to Washington, DC, on weekends to finalize details. It was a compelling offer.

In early January 1996, I drove from Maine to Columbus, pulling a rental trailer containing more than 400 pieces of Indian folk art and crafts, my slide projector, and 10,000 organized photographic slides. I illustrated each two-hour lecture on non-classical arts with an average of 240 selected images about one specific category, such as basket-making, brass lamps, or nomadic textiles. I would devote the last half hour to handling actual objects from my collection, letting my students learn as I had from tactile examination. Of my knowledgeable and conversant graduate students, several were South Asian. The *Puja* seminar enabled me to share personal insights, photographs, and videos, and learn as much from discussion and debate as from any of my research. I invited Amma (Sunithi Narayan) to the exhibition's grand opening. She arrived in Columbus two weeks earlier and participated in my lectures and seminars. My graduate students that semester have become leading professors and curators of Indian art. We remain in touch and not infrequently reflect on the two courses and the many insights Sunithi brought to us.

* * *

Puja opened to the public on May 6, 1996. It was a dream come true. The exhibition designers and lighting technicians were world class—and the enormous exhibition was enticing. I divided the show into three primary sections: temple, household, and community. Among the many highlights was a large installation of eleven royal rock crystal lingas set in a pink marble yoni at the bottom of the grand staircase into the primary galleries. Two bronze Chola masterpieces of the God Shiva and Goddess Parvati led into the Temple section. Just before the opening, brahmin priests blessed, dressed, and adorned each of these images so that visitors would view them as they were meant to be seen. The household section contained interactive shrines filled with the diverse elements that populate such sanctuaries throughout India. Accompanying videos conveyed the rituals of worship. A sacred tree dedicated to the rural Goddess Kali-Ma with two rounded terracotta elephants at its base was a focal point of the community section. Whenever possible, each of the hundreds of items on display was shown in context and each was accompanied by text that explained its meaning and function.

The night before the opening, we received tragic news: Helene's beloved older brother, Jim Wheeler, had died of a heart attack with no warning. We couldn't believe it. Jim and we were close friends, and we loved him dearly. Early the next morning, Helene flew west to be with Jim and his family as I readied myself for one of the most important moments of my career. My parents, other family members, and many friends and colleagues came to Washington for the opening. The dichotomy of my emotions besieged me. I was shocked by the reality of Jim's death, and yet pleased by my guests' response to the show. Perhaps my greatest joy was witnessing the many attending Hindus' enthusiastic reactions and Sunithi's pleasure in the exhibition's compelling portrayal of Hinduism. I dealt with the shock of loss in the only way I could: by compartmentalizing. I flew out to California the next day and tried to support Helene in her extreme grief, then and during the following months, while also reveling in my most significant success to that point. Juggling those opposite emotions was hard.

Network news, newspapers, and journals prominently featured and praised the *Puja* show. I had hoped to write an accompanying exhibition catalog, but, instead, we created an educational outreach program for elementary and middle school children. Sarah was truly the guiding force behind these efforts. Together, we designed packaged boxes for the schools that included an interactive guidebook about practical Hinduism, an explanatory film on VHS, and a set of Hindu posters that could be pinned to classroom walls. The Sackler distributed thousands of these packets to schools throughout DC and the bordering states.

The original intention of the Smithsonian was that *Puja* be displayed for just six months. However, the critical and public response was so positive that it remained open for four years. It was a celebratory evocation of the sacred—right in the heart of Washington, DC, less than half a mile from the Capitol Building. According to museum records, over 750,000 viewers visited the show. Tens of thousands of young American children were exposed to positive aspects of the world's third-largest religion. Local and visiting Hindus embraced the exhibition as their own, rightfully proud of their culture. Sunithi's influence had enhanced the manner in which the material was conveyed, and I felt deeply humbled.

* * *

My ruthless determination to carve away at my western preconceptions succeeded. Decades of living in Hindu homes and witnessing their daily and seasonal rituals were my foundation. For three years, I had continuously asked Sunithi, Babu, every Hindu friend, and even strangers to challenge my biases and help me more intensely feel the pulse of practical Hinduism. Composing the exhibition's text had honed my understanding—as had the insightful discussions of my graduate seminar. I resolved that if the Smithsonian could not underwrite a book on this vital material, I would do so myself. I recognized that although I had become a good photographer using natural light, I needed to learn much more about interior lighting in order to photograph inside sanctuaries. Therefore, I took three masterclasses on studio and artificial lighting at the Maine Photographic Workshops. Equipped with tripods, lights, meters, and reflectors, I returned to India in the autumn of 1996 for research and more intensive photography.

During the first four months of *Puja*, I often visited DC and watched with avid interest the responses of the exhibition's many visitors. Days of quiet observation made me aware that one of the most popular exhibits centered on a pair of wooden shrine doors I'd purchased in Rajasthan. The exhibition designers had mounted them flush to the wall with a display case inset behind them containing household Gods. Each visitor would unlatch and open the doors to reveal the inner contents and then refasten them when they departed. I watched with fascination their intrigued participation. It was as if by physically opening these doors, they simultaneously opened their own minds and hearts.

By this time, the Freer-Sackler had decided to extend the show's term and I understood the exhibition's broad appeal. Although Washington, DC, is a Mecca for tourists, and the *Puja* show was visited by hundreds, sometimes thousands, of visitors six days a week, it could not travel. Many of the objects were rare and would never be allowed to leave the museum. Others were on loan—but even if their owners agreed to lend them again, the insurance expense would be prohibitive and the paperwork monumental. Based on my observations of the *Puja* show's wooden shrine, I began to envision a second, different exhibition based on the same topic. When I returned to India that autumn, I collected old disused wooden shrines as I traveled. I also bought examples of the many accoutrements used in worship: lamps, incense holders, offering plates, and the smaller devotional images regularly sold in temple markets. I recognized that the exhibition and book were symbiotic. A new traveling show on practical Hinduism could provide a good market for a book on the subject, and a well-distributed popular publication would bring attention to the exhibition. Over the next three years, I worked intensively on creating both.

* * *

In a Kathiawar village of Gujarat, Miraben carefully scrubbed and polished all her brass and white metal kitchen vessels. She purchased a newly fired clay stove for her kitchen and a whole set of new terracotta water, storage, and serving pots from the local potter. She cleaned all her spoons, ladles, and spatulas, her colander and sieve, and the many little containers that held spices, pickles, and oils, and arranged them pristinely around the freshly whitewashed room. She even resurfaced the floor with a new layer of mud mixed with cow dung, the most common flooring material in rural India. After she had collected leaves and flowers outside, Miraben lovingly garlanded it all in fresh color and put bright spots of vermilion paste on each of the vessels and tools.

Finally, she poured ghee (clarified butter) into a small brass lamp, lighted it, and waved it with her right hand in a circular motion in front of each of these integral parts of her kitchen while she sang her prayers. At least once each year, Miraben prayed to the spirits of her home, her kitchen, and the tools she used daily to prepare the food for her family and her Gods.

I have witnessed this ritual in one form or another in innumerable homes throughout India. I am always moved by it. Annually or seasonally, depending upon local tradition, each farmer similarly honors the spirits of his plow, shovels, and hoes; the brazier his forge, and crucible, his bellows, anvil, and hammers; the weaver her loom, shuttles, and spindles; the potter his wheel and the tools for shaping and decorating his vessels; the shopkeeper his cash register and balance books; the schoolteacher her texts, blackboard, paper, and pens. Virtually every devout Hindu in the subcontinent expresses respect and gratitude for their specific relationship with the tools of their trade and for the sacred energy within them that has enabled their livelihood during the previous year.

In the West, most of us treat our tools purely as objects. We may admire their utility, design, and function, but we do not consider them to have souls. These Indian experiences of acknowledgment and respect teach me to question all my relationships, even with my laptop upon which I write these sentences.

* * *

For two years, I gathered and synthesized experiences of practical Hinduism. I interviewed priests and devotees, and witnessed and participated in innumerable humbling rituals, until I felt ready to begin composing my new book, *Meeting God: Elements of Hindu Devotion*. (The title is derived from the primary Indian word for worship: darshan, literally translated as seeing and being seen by God.)

By this time, I had already published three successful books. I felt seasoned in the field. For each of my others, I had submitted a proposal to a publisher and then fit my writing and photographs to their guidelines. For this new book, I would first compose the text as I envisioned it and submit a finished product for their consideration. Judith Joseph had become the editor-in-chief of Rizzoli International after Solveig Williams retired. We communicated well. When Judith branched out as an independent book packager, I hired her to help me create my book. Joseph Guglietti had been the gifted book designer commissioned by Rizzoli to lay out *Painted Prayers*. I hired him to design my new book. In 1998, I sent a finished 60,000-word manuscript to Judith and worked with her to perfect it. Joseph received more than 1,000 of my finest photographs organized by topic and chapter. We collaborated so that the finished volume was precisely what I wanted: 250 color images that perfectly complemented an informative, compelling text. The small trim size was preferable to the coffee-table book size of my previous volumes. It would be more affordable and fit easily into a shoulder bag. The three of us created an attractive visual proposal, and Judith effectively marketed it to leading American publishers in a sealed-bid competition. Yale University

Press gave the best offer: an unheard-of 60,000 copies printed in beautiful full color and for sale for only $35 each hardbound, $20 paperbound. I was thrilled.

In the meantime, throughout this process, I collected shrines and devotional objects and assembled a large exhibition about practical Hinduism. With my new lighting skills, and with permission of priests and householders, I had taken hundreds of new photographs of sacred Hindu images in worship. The latest technology of large-scale backlit color transparencies inspired me to conceive of placing vertical light tables at the rear wall of wooden shrines. My good friend, carpenter Ivan Stancioff, crafted the installations for me. The museum viewer would open the shrine doors into an intimate experience of darshan with a primary sculpture of a Hindu deity. I filled the space between the open doors and the God or Goddess with other elements necessary for devotion: lamps, incense holders, small sculptures, and offerings of realistic-looking fruits and flowers. The intention was that the interactive experience would open the participants' minds and hearts as they opened the doors. The eleven shrines and small temples in the exhibition were complemented by seventy-five matted and framed enlargements of intimate elements of Hindu devotion.

As I was now working on two projects simultaneously, I was unable to pursue other activities. Consequently, I hired an assistant, Cheryl Smith, to help with correspondence, pay bills, and coordinate my various projects. In the late nineties, I sent a multi-dimensional proposal to a selection of American museums. Three signed on within days: the Houston Museum of Natural

Science, which had displayed the *Painted Prayers* show, the Field Museum of Chicago, and the American Museum of Natural History in New York City. I began to work with all of them simultaneously. The *Meeting God* exhibition would start in Houston in 1999, Chicago in 2000, and New York in 2001. This assurance and the suggestion that the American Museum of Natural History might be able to travel the show further had encouraged Yale University Press to create such an unusually large print run.

Not everything went as hoped. Yale University Press failed to send any copies of my new book to India. I had created it in the belief that it would be popular there— both to interested Indians and traveling foreigners. When confronted, Yale claimed that their contractual distributor to that country specialized in medical textbooks and would not represent it. I personally took copies myself to give to Indian friends. When I showed it to the Indian distributors of my previous books, they stated that they would buy 10,000 copies, if given the chance. Yale claimed that their hands were tied. Another issue was that although the show at the Houston Museum of Natural Science was beautifully installed and well-reviewed, its administration insisted that the title be changed. While there, it was called *Touching Fire: Elements of Devotion in India*, so as not to offend intolerant Christians in the Bible Belt. Then, much to my disappointment and the chagrin of the Field Museum's curatorial staff, a new politically appointed director insisted on replacing my show in Chicago with a blockbuster about the Cubs, the city's major league baseball team. Instead of working with them, I shifted all my energies to the American Museum of Natural History (AMNH).

I had first visited that grandfather of all natural history museums when I was nine years old. Little did I know that my childhood vow to someday work there as an adult would eventually come true. The AMNH building is vast, covering four New York City blocks, and employing a full-time staff of 1,400. Under the direction of Laurel Kendall, the Curator of Asian Ethnology, and many other individuals at the top of their field, nearly one hundred specialists worked on my show. I also enlisted the advice and counsel of local Hindus. The museum gave me carte blanche to find and choose Hindu devotional items from its extensive reserve collections to enhance my exhibition. Among other fine objects, I discovered five stone sculptures of Nagas (standing cobras). Collected in Kerala in the nineteenth century, they were virtually identical to those I described in my third chapter about the snake temple of Mannarasala in 1971. I proposed grouping them beneath a sacred tree that could be the pivot for the entire show.

* * *

Late in the nineties through a series of serendipitous circumstances, I met Deepak Chopra. On a commuter flight from Boston to JFK, I noticed an Indian woman sitting across the aisle from me, one row back. When I turned to compliment her on the finely detailed gold image of the Goddess Lakshmi that she wore around her neck, she asked me why I would even recognize it? As I briefly explained about my work in India, she stated that I must speak to her husband Deepak who was sitting directly behind me. Thus began a friendship that resulted in Dr. Chopra's request for me to lecture about practical Hinduism at his institute and his publication of our ensuing interview. His own published work at that time on "synchrodestiny" resonated so deeply with my own experiences that I refer to it often in my daily life.

* * *

My friend and colleague, Dr. Jyotindra Jain invited me to install my *Meeting God* photographs at the National Crafts Museum in New Delhi in the winter of 2000. I shipped seventy-five 16" × 20" color enlargements to the museum where they were matted, framed and displayed in a large gallery. I was concerned that Hindu critics and the Hindu public might look with disdain at an American attempting to interpret their spiritual beliefs. But my photography was viewed as respectful and intimate, and the response was good. In fact, the show proved popular enough that Jyotindra arranged for it to travel to five more Indian cities: Chennai, Bangalore, Bhubaneshwar, Vadodara, and Mumbai. If only the book had been available, I believe it would have sold well.

* * *

On May 5, 2001, my wife and I were in Amsterdam to celebrate Helene's fiftieth birthday. She has always loved celebrations and, as a surprise while she slept late that morning, I sneaked fifty colorful party balloons and fifty bunches of Dutch tulips of multitudinous shades into our canal-facing hotel room. Just before Helene came into the room, I checked my email for birthday messages and discovered shocking news: Sunithi Narayan, my beloved Amma, had just died in Chennai of a massive heart attack. I was devastated. Sunithi was a superb mentor. She had helped me lead six tours of India and had joined me on more than a dozen research excursions to gather information and photographs about practical Hinduism. I had even persuaded the National Storytelling Festival in Tennessee to feature her in their next annual event—and arranged for commercial recordings of Sunithi telling the legends of India. I knew they would be easy to market. None of that was to occur. It was hard even to consider opening the new *Meeting God* exhibition without her presence. And whenever I travel in India, I still miss her insightful companionship.

* * *

The AMNH had invented the concept of lifelike natural panoramas, and its preparators are among the finest in the world. When I stated that I wanted a realistic Indian banyan tree for the show, these artists requested that I take as many photographs as I could of banyans in India and, if possible, bring them twigs, bark samples, and leaves to copy. I gladly did so. Using plywood, rebar, chicken wire, and plaster, they constructed a ten-foot-high banyan whose upper trunk and boughs appeared to reach through the ceiling. Its eight-foot-wide trunk, laterally hanging roots, and leaved branches were so realistic that unless you stood behind it during installation, it was impossible to tell it was a fake. The stone Nagas would be placed on an earthen mound next to the trunk and out of reach of the public, and an invisible laser beam alarm system would protect them from possible damage. On the day before the opening, three Hindu priests from a temple in Flushing came to consecrate them, requesting that Divine Spirit imbue them for the show's duration.

The staff of the American Museum of Natural History applied their far-reaching talents to make this exhibition the best it could be. James Hicks's design for the enormous show was inspired: viewers moved seamlessly from room to room, opening and closing a series of shrines. Photographs and text panels drew them further into personal interaction with the material. These devices deepened visitors' comprehension of this dynamic religion that underlies the lives of one in six human beings. The AMNH publicity department went overboard. The reviews after the invitation-only opening could not have been better. The positive Hindu response was deeply gratifying. On the next day, Sunday, the complete back page of the New York Times Entertainment Section was covered by my photograph of the sacred tree puja to the Goddess Chandi referred to at the beginning of this chapter. The words emblazoned across it stated emphatically: *"Meeting God!"* It was to have an irony no one foresaw. The next day the museum was closed, and Tuesday was the official opening to the public—plus a scheduled press conference where *Time*, *Newsweek*, and other magazines and papers would interview me. Those two events never occurred. Tuesday was September 11, 2001.

Early that morning, I came back to my hotel room from a jog around adjacent Central Park and called Judith Joseph to make sure she could make the press conference. Judith stated that something had just happened to the World Trade Center. I looked out across the city from my picture window and watched the second airliner crash into the second tower. As for Americans and, indeed, the world, my life was never the same again. The city and nation were in shock. The AMNH and my exhibition unceremoniously shut down.

A month later, the museum reopened to the public and extended *Meeting God* for an extra month in compensation. I flew down from Maine and a local friend and I took a taxi to Ground Zero. We stood with multitudes of grieving New Yorkers, benumbed by the still present reminders: office papers, desk ornaments, Rolodex cards strewn among the extensive rubble, remnants of so many lives lost in inconceivable violence. Later that day, when I entered my exhibition, I was overcome by the quiet peace pervading the galleries. Visitors sat or kneeled in silent reverence: hundreds of praying and meditating grievers. Some appeared to be South Asian, but most were from a broader cross-section of New Yorkers. The guards explained that every day was like this. The show was filled. Individuals placed offerings in the shrines: flowers, fruits, coins, and bills. Daily, the guards collected the money and, at my suggestion, gave it to local relief shelters. The New York Times ran an editorial describing how thousands came there for sanctuary, to sit beside the sacred tree or by the wooden shrines looking for answers and healing. The exhibition had a purpose that we never could have envisioned.

And yet, 9/11 signaled the end of a long personal trajectory. When the show closed the next spring, it closed for good. Where Americans had been open to learning about Asian customs and religions, they now felt threatened. Blinds were drawn across the minds and hearts of the American people. We were distrustful of others and even more myopic than before. Earlier, individuals at the AMNH suggested that the museum might travel the show to as many as seven other museums. Now, that interest was gone. And although my book *Meeting God* had received excellent initial reviews and had such promising sales prospects, it was now remaindered and sold on discount tables at bookstores. Quite simply, I had to reinvent my career for the third time.

***

In truth, I had a short reprieve. The initial success of the *Meeting God* exhibition encouraged me to tour it also in Britain and Europe. When I began sending proposals to museums in the UK in 2000, the New Walk Museum and Art Gallery in Leicester responded positively. A large percentage of the population of this city in the Midlands is South Asian. The museum's director, Nick Gordon, was determined to sponsor exhibitions and events that would foster the cultural pride of people of Indian descent and increase awareness and open minds of the region's other inhabitants. *Meeting God* was a perfect fit. As the show was still scheduled to travel to several museums in North America and would be prohibitively expensive to ship overseas and back, I created a second traveling exhibition for the purpose.

My assistant Cheryl Smith's husband, Ben, died unexpectedly, and she moved away from Maine. Although Helene and I missed Cheryl, I still needed an office assistant and hired Kathleen Brown in her place—an excellent choice. Kathleen was unfamiliar with Indian art or culture, but she was intensely artistic and inventive. I purchased a second series of shrines and the accoutrements in India and, with Ivan Stancioff's and Kathleen Brown's help, created a new exhibition based on the same theme but expressed differently. After it had arrived in Leicester in 2002, Kathleen, Helene, and I spent a month there installing it. The South Asian response could not have been better: they amassed at the opening and were stimulated by the interactivity of the shrines. Hindu elders took great pride bringing their offspring to the show, explaining the rituals, and recognizing in the framed photographs elements they had known as children. I will never forget coming around the corner of one of the galleries to find an aged Bengali grandmother prostrate in prayer before a Durga shrine, urging her three small grandchildren to follow her example. When they had finished their short puja, she sat cross-legged a short distance away tenderly telling Durga legends to her entranced audience. I felt that my long-held wish to build bridges of communications between India and the West was a success.

The exhibition remained crowded throughout its six-month sojourn. The next year it traveled on to Bradford in northern England—also a city with an extensive South

Asian population. It was equally popular there. But by this time, the UK and Europe were increasingly worried about Islamic terrorist attacks on their own soil. The seeds of distrust and suspicion were beginning to affect global attitudes. Nick and I could find no other institutions interested in taking the show. The Leicester Museum generously purchased it and, in 2004, it returned there permanently to remain part of their reserve collections.

~ 12 ~
Empowerment

I was nervous when I first contemplated entering the slum that surrounded much of the Mumbai airport complex. I felt that I represented all that the inhabitants could not attain. I worried that my presence would offend them, and that I would encounter filth, disease, and hostility. My experience was the exact opposite. I was as openly welcomed into those narrow streets as anywhere else in India. I found it to be impeccably clean. Yes, poverty was pervasive. The people had little. Some appeared to be near starvation. There was an open cesspool at the end of the street, but no litter anywhere. They were proud of their community and their humble homes and took the best possible care of themselves and their meager properties. Householders invited me inside wherever I walked. In this way I met Pushpa who asked me in for tea. We sat on the floor of her simple but lovely dwelling while she served me delicious chai made with milk, ginger, and cardamom, just as I like it. And as we talked, I found Pushpa to be unusually open. She wanted to tell me her story.

During that afternoon and over the next days, Pushpa told me of the indignity of living homeless for years, forced to bathe and defecate on the street in view of all passersby, raising her two small children by herself without shelter and in truly deplorable conditions. Finally, she was able to secure a unionized job as a sweeper at the international airport—and a dependable income with benefits. Pushpa was deeply proud of the simple home she and her children had built by hand, and the lifestyle she was able to guarantee them. And yet her home was threatened again. The airport was expanding and determined to bulldoze the slums, and she might be evicted. This strong, self-empowered woman was unwilling to surrender. She had circulated a petition among all her neighbors protesting the action. Over those days, and in subsequent trips, Pushpa and I became friends. She was a natural leader, admired and respected by her neighbors, resilient in the face of opposition, and determined to protect her family and their rights. To me, she epitomized characteristics that define Indian womanhood. Her tale was one I wanted to share with others.

* * *

Yet again, I had to start my career over. In reflection, I realized that I had devoted ten years to a trajectory tangential to my original intentions. I was grateful for the opportunities I had been given, for the rare doors that had opened to me, and for all that I had learned and been able to convey to others about the essence of practical Hinduism. Although I had never lost interest in my original determination to document Indian material culture, I had subsumed much of that intent as I delved into the spiritual.

India, too, had changed. In my first years there, little documentation existed about traditional rural cultures. After centuries of foreign domination, a priority had been placed on rapid economic recovery through modernization. I had been encouraged in my career by Indian mentors who were desperate to preserve valued aspects of their heritage that they feared might soon be lost irretrievably. Relatively few Indian scholars or popular media showed interest in inherited indigenous technologies, especially those commonly viewed as "backward." In my first years, I had worked almost always alone. Although I knew that my efforts were but a drop in the bucket, I had continued to conduct a cross-cultural survey of Indian arts and crafts.

But in recent decades, attitudes had changed dramatically. Indians no longer suffered from an imperially induced sense of inferiority to British and Western learning and customs. They rightfully embraced the phenomenal achievements and advances of their own culture. Universities in each Indian state developed programs to study, document, and evaluate historical and traditional knowledge. My field was now abundantly rich in Indian scholarship. The exponential growth of digital and internet technologies further altered the entire scope of study. And where for years I had been the only photographer recording many regions and subcultures, now mobile phones with cameras proliferated. Individuals in each community were now visually documenting their own lives, festivals, rituals, and arts. As I reformulated my career, I contemplated how I could best contribute.

*　*　*

My book *Painted Prayers* had been a great success, printed in several foreign editions and immediately selling out. I owned the copyright and was urged by many to reprint it, but Rizzoli had been clear that they were not interested. It would require recreating the book myself and pitching it to another publisher. Although Rizzoli had beautifully designed and printed *Painted Prayers*, I had always been aware of its limitations. The publisher had not allowed me to convey as much information about the art and the women who created it as I had wished.

In the eight years since its publication, I had become even more enthralled with the subject: the creativity expressed by Indian women. Scholars and art enthusiasts still undervalued their art. Even as I documented Hindu rituals, I continued to photograph women's creations. My visual archives were becoming immense. I had gradually succumbed to the ease of use and archival advantages of digital photography, replacing my old Nikon film cameras with newer models. On each previous trip, I had brought an average of 200 transparency films to India, making sure that they were hand-checked at each airport and appropriately stored so as not to overheat as I traveled. Developing film in India was inconsistent at that time, so I always returned home with my unprocessed films to develop and edit there.

Digital photography changed my routine. I no longer needed to carry film, but I was also bound by the requirement to download and back up my images each evening. That process could take hours. In earlier years, it was a gamble as to whether or not my photos would be worthwhile when I finally was able to view them long after I'd taken them. On one occasion, I had returned to Maine after months of field research for my doctorate only to discover that more than ninety films had been damaged! A tiny foxtail burr had blown into and behind the mirror of my reflex system when I changed lenses near the beginning of my trip. I could not see it through my viewfinder. When I processed the films at home, I discovered that a feathery piece of grass obliterated one third of each frame. I was forced to throw away over 2,000 images that otherwise would have been good. Luckily, I had used simultaneously a second camera with a different lens, so I still had visual records of at least part of every shoot. For decades, I had enjoyed long evenings in India talking with friends or reading a good book. Now the demands to edit my digital photographs each evening before moving on to a different subject or region has reduced that free time.

As I reviewed my images, I began to recognize a new theme. Preparations for my exhibitions and book about practical Hinduism had led me even deeper into relationships with Indian individuals. I had conducted hundreds of interviews and synthesized the information I had gleaned into innovative ways of portraying sacred beliefs and rituals. I understood even more fully how I could convey cultural insights best through a personal story. I determined to write a new book based solely upon the stories of individual women. For the next six years, I canvassed India, traveling to as many regions as possible, speaking with old acquaintances, and meeting numerous others for the first time. After more than a thousand interviews with different women who represented as many aspects of India's social complexity as I could find, I began to organize my material. As I did so, I realized that broad generalizations would be a disservice to the women who had opened their lives to me, and less valuable than specific stories. Many academic surveys of women's identity in India were already in publication. I decided to create a new approach that would profile diverse individuals across India whose reflections would collectively convey a picture of Indian womanhood. As the topic was immense, I chose creativity as the common thread that tied all of them together. Each woman I selected was either an artist or artisan or involved in some way in inventive visual endeavors. My book *Daughters of India: Art and Identity* was born.

* * *

The new millennium brought emotional challenges. My mother, Margaret, who had always been athletic and nimble, was diagnosed with Parkinson's Disease at the end of the century. Her condition rapidly deteriorated. In a sad trajectory, she was gone by 2005. Dad was devastated. Mom had been the single most important factor of his life, and their abiding love, demonstrated openly each day, was the stuff of legends. He had never expected to outlive her and would spend the rest of his years mourning her loss.

I am still grappling with the loss of my mother. Beyond birthing me, her character had shaped me: her humor, joy in life and other human beings, her love of nature and the outdoors, her intelligence and intellect, phenomenal strength, her inviolable sense of ethics that still allowed for unusual open-mindedness and adaptability, and, above all, her deep and abiding love.

* * *

As I traveled around India each year interviewing women, the stories I uncovered began to frame a book. I could sense them falling into place. Girija Devi, an elderly matriarch in a small village in rural Madhya Pradesh, spoke to me about her daughters-in-law and wishes for her grandchildren. She ruled her family with implacable certainty. Padma, a six-year-old girl in Tamil Nadu, wistfully watched her mother every day create kolams in the predawn light on the threshold of their home and longed to make her own. Finally, on her sixth birthday, Padma's mother consented, launching the little girl into a lifetime of daily drawings. A fourteen-year-old bride, Larku, expressed her thrill and her fears on the eve of her wedding in tribal Maharashtra. Kusima, in rural Karnataka, spoke about her son's birth deformity as she tried to protect him from local superstitions that marked him as having the evil eye.

Achamma, the bored housewife of a merchant marine in Kerala, drew on her premarital education in computer programming and developed unique software for tea plantation management. Within a few years, she had leveraged her initial investment of 25,000 rupees ($1,000) into a business she sold for $30 million! Achamma drew on skills she had adapted from the self-reliant capabilities of generations of strong women. One after another, the stories lined up. I recognized that each individual was enriched by a set of unique histories and events that had formed her. My task was to discern and draw out those specific characteristics that contributed to a collective awareness. I became fascinated by constructing the puzzle and had to provide a photographic portfolio for each that complemented and enhanced her profile.

The same serendipity that had governed most of my field research over the decades occurred again. I would arrive somewhere looking to profile a specific person or subject only to discover myself redirected to another unexpected individual and story. I traveled to Santiniketan in West Bengal, where advisors recommended a meeting with Shyamali Khastgir, only described to me as a local individual who might recommend a Bengali artist to interview. As I spoke with her and absorbed the visual environment of her art-filled home, Shyamali's own story intrigued me. This dynamic, talented daughter of a famous Bengali painter had spent her life in protest against social and environmental injustice. Although I disagreed with her modest self-opinion, she did not consider herself primarily an artist, but painted evocative protest banners that she carried in political marches. Shyamali had even been arrested when she'd traveled to Washington, DC, to subpoena David Rockefeller and President Jimmy Carter for their support of the Trident nuclear missile. Her passion and creativity were seamless; her shy but determined nature had affected many people's lives and choices, including mine. We remained good friends throughout the rest of her life.

In Delhi, Minhazz Majumdar, the writer and curator, planned to introduce me to a female *Chitrakar* from Bengal. I had thought my story would be about Jaba, a traveling female artist/bard who sang poetic versions of news and topical events as she unrolled scrolls that depicted the same incidents in her colorfully painted interpretations. Instead, I found myself photographing and writing a profile of Minhazz and her relationship with Jaba. Both were Muslim women who employed their creative talents to communicate in a mostly Hindu society. Subsequently, Minhazz has become one of my closest colleagues and a dear friend of both Helene's and mine.

Some of the profiled women I had known for years. Sunithi Narayan ("Amma"), as India's first female guide, had broken through the cultural barriers of her strict brahmin heritage to teach "unclean" foreigners about India's history, art, and culture. Bidulata ("Maushi"), the aged widow in rural Odisha, painted her home as invocations to the Goddess, as I had shown in *Painted Prayers* and *Meeting God*.

* * *

It was daunting as a white American male to publish a book about Indian women's identity and empowerment. I turned to Mallika Sarabhai, well-known throughout India and, indeed, the world, as a talented, outspoken feminist. She read my text, challenged my male perspective on many points, and helped me recraft words and phrases that had unconsciously expressed those biases. Mallika and her ex-husband Bipin Shah agreed to publish *Daughters of India: Art and Identity* under their imprint, Mapin Press, the same company that had co-published my terracotta book, *Gifts of Earth*. Abbeville Press, the esteemed American publishing house, agreed to co-publish *Daughters* through a recommendation from my close friend, author Alev Croutier. Mapin assigned their leading book designer, Paulomi Shah, to create the layout. Paulomi is a creative genius who enhanced the pages of the book with her evocative artistry.

When *Daughters of India* was released in the summer of 2008, both Abbeville and Mapin hired fine publicists to make sure of its high profile. Dozens of leading newspapers and magazines gave it good reviews, while a series of fine museums in the United States, Britain, and India exhibited my *Daughters* photographs to broad acclaim. I couldn't have been more pleased. The Indian publicists set up a lecture tour in India for me beginning the following January. I flew to Delhi, where my colleague Dr. Jyotindra Jain had arranged yet another well-designed exhibition of my photographs at the National Crafts Museum. I met top journalists as I traveled, speaking to audiences nine cities across the nation. In each, I illustrated several of the women's profiles in slide presentations tailored to that particular vicinity and subculture.

Intimidation rattled my nerves as I approached the lectern in Kolkata. West Bengal is famous for its highly motivated, outspoken feminists. My audience was filled with hundreds of women obviously out for blood. How presumptuous of a white American man to speak to them about Indian womanhood! I faced a sea of eyes seething with hostility, took a deep breath, and began relating the stories of strong, self-reliant women in regions throughout their country. By a third of the way through, I could sense them relaxing. At the half-way point, they had visibly warmed to me. When I ended, the audience gave me a standing ovation, and the same women most known for their righteous anger against male suppression came up to request selfies with me. They commented that previously they had been familiar only with the women of their region and subculture but that I had opened their eyes and minds to women's strengths and capabilities across their nation. The rest of my trip was a breeze. I had long identified myself as a feminist. I had run the gauntlet, and my work was accepted.

* * *

One in every six women in the world lives in India, more than the combined female populations of North America, the European Union, and the Middle East. Yet most people outside India know little about Indian women, who often receive confusing and inaccurate press.

...*This book makes no attempt to hide...inequalities. It conveys women's stories as they view them, in their own words. Some of the conditions these women have lived through are tragic. But they do not believe themselves to be victims. Each embodies* shakti *(power) in her own way. Each has found a means to express her own dignity and to lift her head above adversity. In this way they represent a vital characteristic common to all womankind.*

...Daughters of India *is about change in the face of almost impossible odds, personal initiative that carves out a new identity, and implacable insistence on the recognition of human rights.*

(Excerpts from Introduction to Daughters of India: Art & Identity. Abbeville Press, 2008)

* * *

The story of one of the women I had profiled, Sonabai Rajawar, kept me awake at night. The longer I knew it, the more I recognized that it warranted far more exposure than one chapter in a broader book about Indian women. I had always rejected suggestions that I focus on just one group of people or an individual. I identified myself as a cross-cultural surveyor: a person who compared and contrasted different subcultures of India. But I could not let Sonabai's story go and resolved that my next project would be about her.

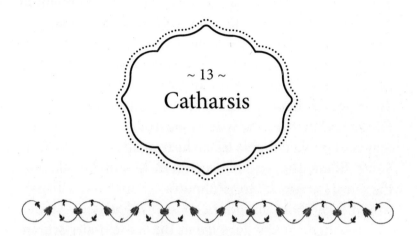

~ 13 ~
Catharsis

I entered a world of magic, of whimsy, of utter delight. This home was unlike anything I had ever experienced, visually different from all other buildings in India. It was created solely by the imaginative, inspired vision and talent of one woman in the depths of oppression. It symbolized her positive solution to an untenable position. Experiencing it changed my life.

God took me to Sonabai Rajawar's remote village—literally. I'd met the artist decades before in Delhi. She and her son, Daroga Ram, had flown to San Diego in 1986, where they lived for three months as they helped create installations for the exhibition I co-curated at Mingei International Museum, *Forms of Mother Earth: Contemporary Terracottas of India*. I had resolved years earlier to visit her home and village but had canceled each trip for one reason or another. It was now the winter of 2001, six months before the ill-fated opening of my *Meeting God* exhibition in New York. A German American friend, Ute Stebich, traveled with me for several weeks as I conducted my field research. The two of us shared a deep passion for folk art and crafts.

It was difficult to figure out how to reach Surguja District, Chhattisgarh, where Sonabai lived. I studied a map and booked flights to the nearest airport: Ranchi in South Bihar. The road between Ranchi and Ambikapur, the nearest town to Puhputra (Sonabai's village), would take about six hours, or so I calculated. As Ute and I waited for our luggage at the Ranchi airport, an arriving businessman asked me why we were there. He then declared that it was impossible to reach our destination from that location. The existing road was barely navigable, and, besides, it was besieged with dangerous dacoits (bandits). Ute and I might not make it there alive. Instead, we should return to Delhi on the next flight and transfer to Raipur, south of Ambikapur. The roads there, he claimed, were better and safer. It had taken so much effort to get this far that I hesitated and asked Ute for her opinion. She suggested that we look for a sign. My assistant, Babu Mohapatra, had come by bus from his home state of Odisha to meet us with a hired vehicle outside the Ranchi terminal. Ute and I collected our baggage and proceeded to the curb where Babu hugged me, met my companion, and then introduced us to the driver of our rented four-wheel-drive vehicle. His name was *God*—not an Indian name with a similar sound, but the English word: *God*. (I've never seen that before or since!) He explained that a foreign Christian missionary had aided his parents, and they had named their firstborn son for the man's deity. It is common for Hindus to name their children after favorite and auspicious gods and goddesses, so why not? Ute and I were amused and resolved that we could have no better sign. In consequence, we headed off on truly horrific roads toward Sonabai's village. God was a terrible driver, and it took us a day-and-a-half to reach our destination, but we arrived there safely.

Ute likened Sonabai's house to the Sistine Chapel, not in its artistic style or form, but its overwhelming beauty and otherworldly quality of serenity and deep stimulation. We were both profoundly affected by the home's exceptional grace, and yet the atmosphere also exuded humor and uplifting joy. Sonabai herself was shy and unassuming: an old, frail woman dressed in a simple cotton sari with the *palu* (endpiece) drawn over her head and hiding part of her face. Her son, Daroga, whom I had met several times before, greeted us with smiles and introduced us to his wife, Rajenbai, and their three children. They seemed not unlike many farming families I had met over decades.

The story of Sonabai's early years was disturbing, but her solutions to her difficulties inspiring. She had been married at fourteen to a far older widower. She lived with his family until she gave birth to a son, Daroga. Then, together, they built a new home on her husband's fields far outside Puhputra's boundaries, distant from any other dwellings. This type of isolation is rare in India. Most people live in tight communities for safety and companionship. The finished mud-walled dwelling with a tiled roof was typical of central Indian farmhouses. Its rooms revolved around an interior courtyard with no outside windows and only one door. When the new house was complete, Sonabai's husband, Holi Ram, closed and locked that door. His young wife was not allowed outside, and no one was permitted inside—for fifteen years! During that time, the child Daroga grew and was allowed to leave the house to play with friends and attend school, but Sonabai was locked within. As a child, Sonabai had belonged to a typical Indian extended family with siblings and cousins living in the same house and plenty of friends nearby. Now she saw no one but her husband and son. How lonely and forlorn she must have been.

Daroga was a typically active toddler, and his mother wanted him to have toys to play with, but she could not go to the market to purchase them. Instead, she took clay from the well inside her house and began to sculpt animals for him: horses, cows, bulls, and monkeys. Sonabai had no training as an artist and later claimed that no one in her family was artistic, but she enjoyed the creative process. The unfired clay animals would easily break—and so she made more. Then she had an insight: she had helped her husband build all their walls using the same clay mixed with straw and cow dung. Dry, mud walls crack frequently and must be resurfaced with fresh clay. Sonabai realized that when the clay was wet, she could add newly sculpted figures to them, thereby creating bas-relief murals. Sonabai fashioned trees with monkeys hanging from the branches to pick fruit. She added lines of horses and elephants marching along the edge of her courtyard. She sculpted human figures and depicted them dancing, playing musical instruments, and doing many of the activities that had been part of her regular life as she grew up.

In the common fashion of her region, Sonabai used white lime to cover the walls. As she painted her sculptures white, she realized that color would enhance them further. So, this untrained artist began inventing pigments in her kitchen using various spices and edible plants. She applied these new hues to her sculptures, and suddenly her artwork had shaded dimensions. Sonabai was pleased.

During India's months of sweltering weather each year, her house was like an oven with its closed door and no ventilation. Sonabai longed to trap the breezes that blew overhead. And so, she invented the concept of latticework (called *jali*). Although jali is common in other parts of India, none of the buildings in her district used it. Sonabai had never seen an example either in architecture, or in a photograph, or painting. When she and Holi Ram had built their house, they used bamboo poles for supports and ladders. Much of it was leftover. Sonabai cut lengths to create a rectangular framework between the columns that supported the awning surrounding her courtyard. With a sharp knife, she peeled strips of bamboo that she tied into circles with straw. She then joined the rings to one another and affixed them to the frame, applying thick clay to all the surfaces. Now she had a clay lattice that naturally pulled the breezes down into the courtyard and cooled the house. It was brilliant. But Sonabai did not stop there. She wanted these jalis to be beautiful, too, so she added sculpted snakes that slithered up between the circles. She placed flute and drum players inside some of the holes. In others, she put dancers, and still others, birds. Her latticework was now alive with figures, and she painted them all with the pigments she had concocted in her kitchen. Although she did not know it, this lonely young woman had invented an unprecedented style of art. Sonabai had brought into the interior of her cloistered home the outside world she missed so much.

Her life continued for more than a decade like this: lonely but creative. Then, after fifteen years of isolation, Holi Ram finally opened the door, letting Sonabai outside and the neighbors in. Sonabai and her family would never disclose the reasons for his actions. I can only imagine how curious her neighbors must have been. They told me they were astounded by what they saw. But Puhputra was an isolated village, far from any large town. Almost all its inhabitants were illiterate— they simply had no experience of the outside world. Sonabai was now able to come and go, but she was a naturally shy woman, and her long seclusion had only confirmed her introversion. For the next fifteen years, her life remained basically the same.

Sonabai's world turned upside-down in 1983. A ground-breaking museum in the capital city of Bhopal sent scouts throughout the State of Madhya Pradesh collecting regional arts and crafts. When they reached Ambikapur, someone told them about Sonabai, and they went to check her out. They'd never seen anything like it. Under the artist's protest, but with her husband's permission, these scouts took a pickax and chopped out a section of her wall to take to their museum. When they reached Bhopal, the museum's director, J. Swaminathan, was equally impressed. Without hesitation, he returned the scouts to Puhputra to commission a series of sculptures, panels, and lattices from their flabbergasted creator. The museum featured her art in a solo exhibition. Dr. Jyotindra Jain from the Crafts Museum in New Delhi came to see it—and Sonabai's life was never the same again. Within a year, she was honored with the highest award India can give an artist, the *Rashtrapati Puraskar* (The President's Award). Not long after that, she and Daroga were on a plane to San Diego and a whirlwind of travel that lasted the rest of her life. This shy, talented woman was at everyone else's beck and call to exhibit her unique sculpting techniques at museums and cultural centers throughout India.

Other artists in Puhputra were stimulated by Sonabai's success and began to copy her style. In 1991, the Government of India gave Sonabai a stipend to teach workshops of her technique to others in her vicinity. Soon, her unique art became a style associated with her broader region of Surguja. Many other artists that she trained were now called upon to travel and exhibit their products. In some ways, Sonabai's vision affected her district's economy and self-awareness.

* * *

As I gathered more and more material for *Daughters of India*, my mind kept returning to my experiences in Sonabai's extraordinary home. I decided that after I finished *Daughters*, I would write a book focused on her. Sonabai's art and home were so visually stimulating that I also planned to make a documentary film about her to pair with the book. My previous efforts had taught me that a book could be enhanced by an exhibition, and vice versa. Therefore, I decided to create all three projects simultaneously. It was a choice that would prove successful, although the process was highly demanding.

While considering how I might achieve these goals, Bruce Brown, the director of the Center for Maine Contemporary Art in nearby Rockport, offered me a huge retrospective exhibition in the summer of 2003. I used it as an opportunity to stretch my boundaries as an artist, exploring imaginative technologies to display ethnographic photographs in unusual, thought-provoking ways. This show proved to be a perfect testing ground for techniques I would later employ in my exhibition about Sonabai. I hired Duggal Visual Solutions of New York, one of the finest photo labs in the world, to help me push the limits. We printed images on burnished metal and textured cloth paper and created enormous backlit lenticular transparencies. I created a collage of photos I had printed of the working hands of Indian artisans and sculpted its frame and intersections in clay myself. I scratched off some of the reflective surface from an old Indian wood-framed mirror and placed a video screen behind it so that the surface reflected the viewer's face overlaid by successive Indian portraits. We created more than a hundred different installations, all offset by the brightly hued walls that my assistant Kathleen and I painted to reflect the colors used in Indian houses. After years of exhibiting my work elsewhere around the country and the world, I reveled in this opportunity to share it with my community.

The most effective installation of the CMCA show filled the far end of the primary gallery. Duggal had enlarged a photograph I had taken of the silhouettes of women praying to the rising sun in the Ganges River in Varanasi. It became a mural nine feet high by twenty-two feet long covering the back wall. Twelve feet out from that, we offset two nine-foot-long by five-foot-wide hanging chiffon transparencies of women lighting lamps on the riverbank. We had a fan lightly rippling these cloths, and they wafted as viewers walking through them approached the huge mural. As other viewers drew close, they would see those who had come before them stacked in layers through the transparent images of Indian women. At my specific request, Duggal Visual Solutions had invented the process of printing on chiffon. The effect heightened the viewers' responses and successfully approximated the sensation I had experienced so often on the Ganges of overlapping veils of perception. I resolved to use this same technique in my *Sonabai* show.

* * *

Throughout my research career, I had always worked solo or occasionally with a single assistant. In 2004, I returned to Puhputra with a team of five others: my two assistants, Babu Mohapatra and Kathleen Brown; a superb filmmaker friend, David Wright; and Sushmita and Shunia Tandan, a mother and daughter who were old friends from Allahabad. Babu and I were the only ones who had been there before. I planned that David and I would photograph and film; I would direct the project and conduct off-camera interviews; Babu would translate; Sushmita and Shunia would interview women on camera (Sonabai, her daughter-in-law and grandchildren, and neighbors); and Kathleen would help facilitate all our endeavors. We six worked together seamlessly. Sonabai and her family were hospitable and encouraging. We spent twelve nights in a hotel in nearby Ambikapur and each day from dawn to dusk in Puhputra. I commissioned works of art from Sonabai and Daroga, whatever they chose to make. My single request was that, if possible, the finished pieces would be strong enough to withstand shipping to America without breaking.

Those twelve days were electric. After intense discussions, Sonabai, Daroga, and a young cousin, Buddhi, began to sculpt. By this time, Sonabai was nearly eighty years old and beginning to fade. Her mind was not sharp, but her talents were undiminished. To ensure that the objects they created would not easily break, Daroga commissioned a local carpenter to cut pieces of plywood to his specifications. They planned three bas-relief sculptures, two jali (latticework) pieces, and a small version of the sculpted rice storage vessel that stood in the corner of one of their rooms. They then set to work on the first two, sculpting clay on figures made of sticks wrapped with straw and nailed to the boards. As I photographed and David filmed, we watched as a line of dancers appeared on each panel: one of men topped by turbans and pompoms and the other of women with blackened rope hair. The artists then painted the dancers in bright polychrome pigments, and the results were charming.

When asked, Daroga explained that these dances were performed during the annual autumn harvest festival. We expressed our dismay that we had missed by two months the opportunity to witness it, and Daroga offered to request Puhputra's villagers to perform the same dances for us. In the following days, while we documented the production of the four other pieces and interviewed Sonabai and her family members about their daily lives and the impact of national recognition upon them, we often heard drums and singing at a distance. The neighbors were practicing. Finally, about a week after the initial suggestion, the sounds of drums, flutes, horns, and many human voices approached Sonabai's now less-isolated home.

Over the next many hours, we witnessed an exuberant occasion. Dozens of men and women had dressed for the event: women in their most colorful saris, men mostly in white but wearing multi-hued turbans obviously created from their wives' saris and capped by jiggling pompoms. (Although turbans had been common male apparel when Sonabai was a child, now they are only worn for weddings or festivals.) While I captured the event in hundreds of photographs from as many angles as possible, David filmed the dances. Both of us even lay on the ground filming while surrounded by the men's bell-wrapped ankles stomping in striking rhythms. Each morning, David and I would arrive in Puhputra just after dawn to film and photograph the village as it awoke. We would send the car back to pick up the others from our hotel while we made visual studies of rural life. David's footage was beautiful and evocative, while my photographs showed intimate details of the inhabitants' daily existence.

The six of us also sought out and interviewed the local artists that Sonabai had taught and whose own work reflected her style. Four particularly stood out as expressing their individuality. I decided to collect their work for the exhibition and visually record them for the book and film. In the last couple of days, we hired a carpenter to create plywood crates for each sculpture. As bubble wrap and Styrofoam were not readily available in India at that time, we cut thick mattress foam into shapes to hold each piece securely. Babu accompanied a large truck loaded with crates for 1,200 kilometers (745 miles) back to Delhi. Shipped later by container truck to Mumbai, transferred to a cargo ship to Boston, and finally by truck to Maine, all the fragile sculptures arrived in perfect shape.

* * *

Back home, as I organized my photographs and notes, I recognized that our efforts had succeeded. I had been able to take some of the best photographs of my career, the sculptures were superb, and my research and our interviews had helped fill out an already intriguing story. That summer, we unpacked the sculptures and mounted them alongside printed enlargements of my new photographs. I began to sense the scope and design of an exhibition. I created proposals for the show and book and sought out a production team to make a professional film. Luckily, I found the latter close to my home in Camden, Maine. David Berez, of Post Office

Editorial, is a consummate filmmaker. I hired him to help me construct the film. David Wright supplied his footage of Puhputra and Sonabai's home and production. David Berez interviewed Kathleen and me in front of the sculptures talking about Sonabai's story, her personality, and the ways it both reflected and differed from the community in which she lived.

My beloved mother died in early September 2005. I helped deflect my grief by working on the film. By late autumn of that year, the two Davids and I had created a good short documentary about Sonabai and her life. Kathleen helped me design and assemble a full-color glossy exhibition proposal that we sent to a couple of dozen US museums.

All this was going on as I finished writing *Daughters of India* and began its launch. The most positive response to my new proposal was from Mingei International Museum in San Diego, the same institution where I had co-curated the show on Indian terracotta in 1986 and where Sonabai and Daroga had spent three months demonstrating their art. It was a perfect fit.

* * *

After decades of traveling in India, I had amassed a vast collection of Indian folk art. Experts suggested that it was the finest in this milieu in private hands in North America. I had purchased most of it for next to nothing, rescuing textiles from being cut up to make toys, brass and bronze from being melted down and refashioned, and terracotta sculptures from inevitable disintegration on discard piles. I exhibited as many pieces as possible in my two-room office, but they were jammed together on shelves or in drawers and boxes. I loved sharing these artworks with others, handling them like old friends as I told their stories to inquisitive visitors. But Helene and I had chosen to live far off the beaten track in the most northeastern corner of the country. Had we lived in an urban center where people visited all the time, perhaps I might have decided to keep this art. As it was, it seemed prudent to let a far larger public enjoy it. I considered selling it, particularly when we had financial worries, but I resisted splitting the collection up, believing that together the pieces shared cultural integrity that would be lost if they were separated.

The Mingei's founder/director Martha Longenecker and I had remained in touch ever since we'd assembled and designed the terracotta show together. Once each year, she would phone and plead with me to come work for her. As much as I admired Martha and her accomplishments at the museum, I was never tempted. Such a commitment would have significantly restricted my ability to continue my field research in India. At the beginning of the new millennium, I met the Mingei's new director, Rob Sidner. This multi-talented, gracious man had worked his way up through the museum's ranks, helping manage and improve every facet. He won my heart. I admired Rob's leadership of an institution that had become one of the two finest museums in the United States specializing in craft and folk art. In consequence, I decided to donate my Indian folk art and craft collection to it. To facilitate the transfer, Kathleen and I had to photograph and catalog each piece. I kept only a few favorite items to decorate my office but gladly gave the bulk away, including many artworks that had become close and valued friends. The Mingei accepted approximately 650 items of textile, wood, metal, terracotta, and painting, many of them priceless and irreplaceable. These pieces closely complemented the museum's existing collections. Most would remain in the facility's climate-controlled storage vaults, and, as needed, specific items would be brought out to display in various exhibitions. The Mingei has done so for years and always lets me know which of these objects they are currently showing.

* * *

Kathleen, Babu, and I returned to Sonabai's home in Puhputra two additional times before the exhibition opened. We camped in tents just outside the house so that we might be close to the family. Sonabai's health was deteriorating during our 2006 trip. In an experience that mirrored the last period of my mother's life, it was sad to watch the diminishment of the mind and body of this artist I had grown to love. We strengthened our bonds with the family and the other artists with each visit, commissioning more pieces from them for the exhibition as I took photographs I felt were missing from the full body of work.

In the summer of 2007, Sonabai died. I'll never forget receiving the sad news as I sat in my Maine home. Knowing her had changed my life. The repression in her youth had resulted in a vibrant expression that had not only brought bright hope into her imprisoning home but had grown to influence and improve the lives of many others. I still miss her.

We three came back early the next year to be with Sonabai's family. By this time, they treated us as favored relatives. We embraced one another and together mourned our loss. We had brought with us a good projector and the films David Wright had taken and edited. We whitewashed the outer wall of a neighbor's house, set up the projector in an adjacent field, and showed three short films to the locals: one about the community, a second about Sonabai, and a third about the harvest dance. The villagers were excited as they saw themselves depicted, remarking in raised voices about how much smaller their children had been at the time, laughing at how silly the men looked in their sari-turbans, and visibly sobbing as they watched our footage of Sonabai sculpting, or telling stories to her grandchildren, or sitting warming her hands over an early morning fire. They asked us to play them again and again. It was a poignant, tender visit.

***

As soon as I finished writing my last draft of *Daughters of India*, I began composing my book on Sonabai. When I told a Camden neighbor that I was searching for a title, she commented that the artist had a different way of seeing. Appropriately, I named the exhibition, book, and film *Sonabai: Another Way of Seeing*.

Suddenly, the film began to fall into place. I called Jeany Wolf, the publicist for *Painted Prayers* and *Daughters of India*, and she suggested I speak with her husband Jeffrey about it. He makes documentaries about American outsider artists. After a single conversation, I hired Jeffrey as a consultant to help us reimagine the movie. Jeffrey worked closely with David Berez and me in the summer of 2008. At his suggestion, the film now began with a veritable explosion of the photographs of Sonabai's art, portraying its particularly upbeat vision. Only then did we tell the backstory of her virtual imprisonment by her husband and how she created art to bring pleasure into what otherwise would have been a drab existence. On film, we interviewed experts on environmental artists in India and America, individuals who had altered their experiences in life by refiguring their surroundings. We ended the film on a positive note: challenging the viewer with the concept that there is no oppression or difficulty that cannot be overcome with creative solutions.

By this time, I had established a long and successful relationship with Mapin Press of Ahmedabad. Bipin Shah and Mallika Sarabhai were good friends who had published both *Gifts of Earth* and *Daughters of India*. I deeply admired the skills of their primary designer, Paulomi Shah. It was a good fit for this new book, and I signed a contract with them for *Sonabai: Another Way of Seeing*. I worked intensely with Mapin from 2007 until the book was released to coincide with the exhibition's opening in late July 2009. Paulomi's design was perfection, and the resulting book finer than I could have wished, including a DVD of the film seamlessly fit into a pocket inside the back cover.

* * *

The Mingei wanted to celebrate the gift of my art collection through an exhibition of its highlights. As I was swamped with multi-tasking three simultaneous projects, each demanding, the museum's talented staff curated the show without my help. I provided only some contextual photographs and expanded the information I had given them about the items they had chosen. *India Adorned: Selections of the Stephen P Huyler Collection* opened in late July 2008. In keeping with every exhibition I've ever seen at the Mingei, they displayed it beautifully.

The museum created a short documentary about my work in India and how I had approached collecting this art. David Berez of Post Office Editorial, the same studio producing my *Sonabai* film, created *Eye For India: Stephen Huyler's Enthusiastic Journey of Discovery*. The opening coincided with the US release of *Daughters of India*. Many friends and family came, including two of the featured *Daughters*: the protest artist, Shyamali Khastgir, and the advocate for Indian folk and tribal artists, Minhazz Majumdar. Both women flew in from India for the occasion, and it felt good to feature them there and later bring them to Ojai to spend time with us in our home.

* * *

The design and preparation of the Mingei exhibition of Sonabai's work took five years, far longer than most museum exhibitions. The results were spectacular: a collaborative effort of many talented individuals. I bounced all my ideas and concepts off Kathleen Brown, my assistant in Maine. Her inventive suggestions were inestimable. Jose Vargas, of Duggal in New York City, had been placed in charge of envisioning and overseeing the production of all the prints and designing an enormous modular display unit in burgundy enameled steel. From the beginning, I had insisted that we push the limits of exhibition design and display, employing leading-edge techniques that served our purpose while eschewing outlandish ones that would detract from the art. David Wright's films enhanced the galleries. We had collected sixty-four sculptures from Sonabai, her family, and other artists in her region. Many of them were large. We also used thirteen sculptures that Sonabai had created there at the Mingei twenty-three years earlier. I wanted my photographs to complement all the pieces and ground them in contextual settings, and yet avoid the pretense that the galleries in any way approximated what it was like to be in Puhputra. I hoped that the leading-edge technologies we employed would only underline and enhance Sonabai's innovative skills. It was a fascinating challenge.

My overall concept was to visually establish the stark difference between the village and its interconnected life and the cloistered home that separated Sonabai from it. We achieved this effect by establishing contrasting environments. An interior room that represented Sonabai's home opened into another that featured her dance panels and explanations of the harvest festival. Then the viewer entered a large gallery that conveyed the dance itself. Seven tall photographs of dancers printed on transparent chiffon hung from the ceiling, offset from one another at oblique angles. Gigantic prints of elements of the dance covered the walls: the swirling colors of saris, the stomping feet of male dancers, the bright pom-pom turbans of the men, and the fluid gestures of women. A loop of David's footage of the dancers animated one wall and filled the room with surround-sound of drums, flutes, horns, bells, and songs of the dance. The experience immersed the viewer as a participant in the sensation of being in the center of the dance. When I saw this room finally assembled and ready for the opening, I recognized fully for the first time in my life that I, too, am an artist, not merely a documenter of the visual perceptions of other artists. It was a seminal moment in my life.

The rest of the exhibition was devoted to rooms featuring six artists that Sonabai had influenced. A chamber with blackened walls spotlighted in the center a pedestal on which eight male musicians surrounded a freestanding group of ten female dancers. These sculptures were the work of Parbatibai Sarthi, an outcaste Dalit woman, untrained by Sonabai or anyone else, who had seen that we were documenting Sonabai and the other artists in 2004 and yearned to be noticed. When Kathleen, Babu, and I returned in 2006, she had insisted we come to her humble abode on the far outskirts of Puhputra. There she showed us the first three dancers she had made. Parbatibai had fashioned them in a unique style all her own: colorfully expressive, suggestive of movement in dance, yet with disproportionately large feet to keep them from falling over. Her sculptures were dynamic and evocative, and I had commissioned a complete set of dancers. Featured there at the Mingei, along with her portrait and other pieces she had created displayed outside that dark chamber, Parbatibai had shown herself an equal to any great artist. Her story, inspired by hope battling total disregard, paralleled that of Sonabai.

* * *

From my first conception of the show, I had planned for Daroga and his wife, Rajenbai, to travel to San Diego to sculpt a wall of jali latticework for the installation. They would display their techniques for visitors to witness. I had known that Sonabai was not strong enough for that international journey even years before she died. Neither of the village artists spoke English. My assistant Babu Mohapatra would accompany them and act as their facilitator and translator. Rajenbai had never even traveled outside her remote district. She was intimidated by the concept yet wanted to come. We had assumed that Babu, who had a regular income and was married with two sons in Odisha, would have no trouble getting a visa to enter the United States. But the US Consulate in Kolkata denied his application, and sadly we were unable to override their decision. In consequence, the two villagers had to travel alone. Rajenbai was literally sick with fear when they went to Mumbai to pick up their US visas. The process took longer than expected, and we had to book them later flights. Those of us awaiting their arrival in San Diego worried that the jet travel and culture shock of being in California would be too much for her.

From the moment we met Rajenbai and Daroga Ram coming out of customs at San Diego's International Terminal, that previously daunted woman was thrilled with all she experienced. Their five-day delay meant that they arrived during the annual Gay Pride Parade in San Diego. Coincidentally, its epicenter was the hotel near the museum where they and we stayed. I worried about how she would respond to the lines snaking into the lobby of scantily clad men, some of them purposefully adorned with outrageous sex symbols. She didn't even seem to notice. Rajenbai absorbed this new world with fascination. Later that afternoon, once the Indian couple had rested, we took them to the beach where they watched surfers and requested to eat nachos from a local stand. We realized they would be okay.

* * *

The opening in late July 2009 was a complete success. Many close friends and family attended, including Paulomi, who was there to launch the new book she had designed. My elderly father, accompanied by his caregiver, stayed with us a couple of nights in the same hotel with the Indian artists. Dad could not have been prouder of my show and praised my life's work. A constantly changing group of visitors admired Daroga and Rajenbai as the two villagers squatted to sculpt figures for their ceiling-tall latticework. A translator asked them a barrage of eager visitors' questions that they willingly answered. They were perfect cultural emissaries of rural India transplanted into urban America. For me, that exhibition was the culmination of my lifelong efforts to build bridges of communication between two diametrically different societies. I felt that Sonabai, her life, and her message were well represented.

The Mingei is one of seventeen museums and cultural institutions in Balboa Park. When the show closed after thirteen months, the manager of the park's information center told me that without question *Sonabai: Another Way of Seeing* was the most popular exhibition ever displayed at any of Balboa Park's institutions. It was filled with visitors throughout its long run. Soon after the opening, Rob Sidner, the director, called to ask if I had any problem with people dancing in the dance room. I replied that it should be encouraged, and every day thereafter, men, women, and children spontaneously danced there. Viewers returned to the show again and again. Many of the docents and staff have expressed in subsequent years that they wished that the exhibition could return to the Mingei. I understand why it cannot: the museum has a full roster of plans for an exciting future of good shows. But I am pleased that it had such a positive impact.

I've uploaded a short film of the Mingei installation of *Sonabai: Another Way of Seeing* at https://youtu.be/qBauxuAaZoM

* * *

In the autumn of 2009, the Camden International Film Festival featured my *Sonabai* film. It felt good to share it with the community to which Helene and I, Kathleen Brown, and both David Berez and David Wright belong. The festival's director, Ben Fowlie, suggested I submit the film to the Santa Fe Film Festival in early December. It seemed to me it might be the right fit. I had often spent time in that western city and was aware of the local admiration for folk arts and crafts. The film was accepted, and I flew out to attend the events. I love experiencing the art scene of Santa Fe. Critics acknowledge SFFF as one of America's finest, and during the days I was there, I watched a variety of excellent documentaries. I felt proud that our film was in their company.

The festival lasted through Saturday night, but I did not stay until the end. I returned on cross-country flights that day to be in Camden for a close friend's concert on Sunday evening. Sunday morning, I received a call from the organizers of the film festival asking me where I was. When I replied I was home in Maine, they spluttered: "But…but…we announced your name last night. Your film won the Award for Best Short Documentary!" A tiny puff of wind would have blown me over at that moment. The other films had been so good that I had never considered that they would honor ours. Our entire team was exhilarated.

The film *Sonabai: Another Way of Seeing* went on to win four more Best Film awards. I have posted it on YouTube so that anyone with internet can download it for free at https://youtu.be/2HL_F5C1mMg

Today, in 2024, I believe this film has even more relevance than before. During the pandemic, many of us lived in isolation and lockdown for longer than we ever thought possible. Going forward, divisiveness and discord continue to plague our world. We have so destroyed our environment that experts state that it can never recover. I believe that we could each learn from that slender, modest artist in central India. If we but use our ingenuity and innate creativity, we can invent solutions to our problems. We, too, can find another way of seeing.

* * *

My financial commitment to this exhibition was large. Once the show had closed in 2010, our expenditures had significantly depleted Helene's and my resources. I could no longer afford to employ Kathleen Brown as my assistant. She had helped keep my life organized for years. Her creative input had been essential to many projects, from creating and installing the second version of the *Meeting God* exhibition in Britain to helping conceive and manifest the *Sonabai* project. We had traveled together in India five times. Our experiences were many, varied and rich. It was hard to let Kathleen go.

* * *

I had maintained a strong relationship with the Santa Barbara Museum of Art ever since it displayed my *Painted Prayers* exhibition in 1995. This museum was only an hour from Ojai, the town where I grew up. My grandmother had taken me there as a small child as a first introduction what has become a lifelong love of art. In 2014, Susan Tai, SBMA's curator of Asian Art, asked me to work with the renowned scholar and guest curator Dr. Pratapaditya Pal to create a show for them comparing Hindu, Buddhist, and Jain art. *Puja and Piety: Hindu, Jain, and Buddhist Art from the Indian Subcontinent* opened in the spring of 2016. Dr. Pal had borrowed pieces from private collectors throughout California to complement those in Santa Barbara's permanent collections. Susan and her team had displayed them beautifully. I had added some photographs of pujas taking place and had created a film of devotional practices of all three faiths that was projected silently on a wall between galleries. The University of California Press published a catalog/book with the same title as the show. Dr. Pal wrote the introduction, and I composed the chapter on Hinduism. The material allowed me to approach a field I loved from new angles and learn more about these complex, heartfelt beliefs that continue to sustain and support more than a billion individuals in India.

* * *

When we created *Sonabai: Another Way of Seeing*, I had hoped that the show would travel to museums throughout the States. I felt its popularity would engender a great deal of interest. It was designed modularly and packed in reusable crates that could be easily and protectively shipped and reassembled without difficulty. I don't fully understand why that has never happened.

In far reduced forms, this exhibition has had three other incarnations: in 2011, at the Visual Arts Gallery on the campus of the University of Alabama in Birmingham; in 2016, at Otterbein University near Columbus, Ohio; and in 2018, in the Riverside Arts Gallery, in Ypsilanti, Michigan. In each of these venues, the exhibition filled an utterly different gallery space, and it was intriguing to adapt the material to fit. The results were stimulating.

The entire exhibition (display units, sculptures, printed murals, and chiffons) is now in climate-controlled storage units split between San Diego, California, and Ann Arbor, Michigan. The expense for all this storage is becoming prohibitive, and I hope to find a permanent home for the complete exhibition. Wherever it ends up, may it continue to serve as a beacon of hope in an increasingly beleaguered world. It has been an honor to be part of its trajectory.

* * *

Hi and I celebrated our fortieth anniversary on a secluded island in Fiji on December 20, 2013. By a fluke, we were the only guests in the tranquil and well-appointed Fiji hotel. It was a celebration of a deep love and friendship that has only grown stronger through the years of learning to open and adapt, to listen, and be attentive to the thoughts and rhythms of each other. We flew there from Ojai, where we had spent weeks caring for my rapidly failing father. Helene and I were on our way to swim beneath a waterfall on January 1, 2014, when we learned that Dad had just died. We flew home the next day.

On the long return flight, I wrote a draft of my father's obituary. What a life he had had: raised in Connecticut and Wyoming, a sophisticated cowboy, an excellent musician and raconteur who held people in his spell, a consummate teacher throughout his life, an equestrian champion, and as macho as a man could be. Dad had treated me harshly as a child, but all he wanted was that I would grow up without the social and ethical conflicts that so profoundly concerned him. We had made our peace with each other years before. In his final years, we had become friends and truly enjoyed our companionship. He had taught me many lessons, and continues to teach me, even since he is gone. I was not crushed by Dad's death the way I was with Mom's. In some ways, I felt that I had moved into his shoes. He remains with me still.

~ 14 ~
Bridges

Bidulata's face creased with smiles, her eyes twinkling as she *pranamed* in the gesture of welcome. "Namaste! Come in! Please, please, come in! You are our honored guests. Come sit…." She backed through her doorway, calling her granddaughters to bring out chairs for us. I ushered my tour group into the simple, mud-walled house and introduced them to our elderly hostess. After greeting each individual with a welcoming smile, Bidulata (whom I call "Maushi"), the retired schoolteacher who had been so good to me years before, took both my hands, searched my face, and then gently hugged me. We were old friends but were meeting now after several years. She was the one who had encouraged my documentation of her wall and floor painting and wrote out prayers to the

Goddess Lakshmi to bless my work—folded papers that remain in my meditation room to this day.

I had brought my group there so that they could experience for themselves the genuine hospitality and generosity that has been showered upon me wherever I've traveled in India. I knew that, too often, tourists see only the commercial sides of India: the hotels and restaurants, the bus and taxi drivers, the tour guides and touts, the vendors, and salespeople. They can be overcome by urban sprawl, crowds, and poverty, yet few ever visit a home or talk with the men, women, and children who populate this vast country. They never enter a classroom, walk on a rural path, or are invited to participate in any of the rituals that form the foundation of this complex culture. They are rushed from hotel to monument to temple to tourist shops and back to their hotels without ever having a chance to deeply breathe in the scents, hear the tunes, feel the textures, or taste the layered flavors that collectively compose the character of most of India. On my tours, I resolved to change that equation. My tour members would leave India as I always had: enriched by insights into at least part of that nation's intimate personality.

Right at the beginning of the tour, I took them to Maushi's home. We stayed in a favorite cottage hotel far off the usual tourist track. Our bus drove slowly along rural roads deep into the countryside of Puri District, where we watched women painting the walls of their houses with rice paste designs dedicated to Lakshmi. We took off our shoes to enter the compound of a small tree shrine I knew well, and examined the three small offerings of terracotta horses placed among its gnarly roots, as I explained why and how they were given. And then, our bus inched its way through narrow lanes to Bidulata's charming home. While my old friend oversaw the production of hot spiced chai, her three teenage granddaughters approached each of my guests and gently adorned their cheeks with cooling face powder as a ritual of honor. Then, as we drank our tea and ate a selection of sugary biscuits, they plied us all with questions about our lives and families in America and told us, in turn, about their classes, their hobbies, and their future aspirations. Each tour member had an opportunity to engage with an individual far outside the world of commercial India, and they were impressed.

That was a signature aspect of my tours that differed from most others. I returned with other groups to Bidulata's home, but my itineraries, like my life's work, covered India's breadth. India's monuments and primary sites are worthy of their reputation, and I made sure that we visited them whenever we could. But I always paired those experiences with that of everyday India—the India that has fed and infused me for the past fifty years.

I chose to introduce visitors to India's complexity by comparing and contrasting different cultures: rural and urban, dense population and open countryside, primary temple and roadside shrine, high profile industry and handmade artistry, city shops and village markets. North to south, east to west, the Indian subcontinent is more diverse than almost any comparable landmass.

I no longer lead tours of India. They require far too much work and energy and I felt that I needed to reduce my load. The almost overabundance of vitality I felt during my first seven decades has lessened. My last tour was in 2017. But I hope that I will return there with friends for the rest of my days to share with them the qualities of Indian life that I find so appealing.

* * *

Over twenty-eighty years, I led seventeen professional tours of India. I love sharing with others that which I love—and India is one of my greatest passions. My tours differed from most others in many respects. I had no desire to pontificate about India. I would diligently prepare the facts about each place we visited and try to be informed about local cultural and social values. These I would convey readily, often as much through story and example, as through academic recitation. The level of education and experience was high among my participants. Many had degrees in professions quite different from my own—medical doctors, professors, CEOs, and businesspeople—while others were experienced parents, caregivers, artists, artisans, farmers, gardeners, and active members of their communities. Most had traveled in global regions unfamiliar to me. Each brought into the mix their own history, knowledge, unique responses, and evaluations. As much as possible, I tried to draw out these individuals to share their interests with the rest of us and tell how they were responding to India.

My goal was to create traveling seminars where I learned from them as they learned from me. So, if we had a doctor or nurse accompanying us, we might visit a clinic or hospital. I would prepare and share what I knew of Indian traditional medicine and healing and contemporary medical practices. They would compare those to their own experiences and provide the rest of us with new insights. Or they might interview an Indian medical professional and share that dialog with us. Similarly, we would visit schools with teachers, businesses with entrepreneurs, farms with farmers and ranchers, and embroiderers with those that did needlepoint or knitted. Most were parents, and many were grandparents. They would bring out pictures to show our Indian hosts who gladly learned about American families' dynamics and motivations as they shared theirs with us. In these ways, at least ideally, each member of my tour was featured, each was able to meet, interact with, and learn from his or her counterpart in India. In consequence, they enhanced the experience of India for the rest of us.

I found all of my tours stimulating—the long preparations were as vital to me as the actual trip. I would try to learn the profiles of my tour members ahead of time and then spend months reading, photocopying, and creating files to take with us so that I could address their interests and concerns. As a lateral thinker fascinated with the complex interrelations of all aspects of a culture, I wanted to have at my fingertips as much cross-cultural information as possible to be able to answer questions and provide links to understanding. I had long recognized that westerners, and Americans in particular, were largely ignorant of India's long history. We tend to think of our culture as evolving independently, when, in fact, many European and American scientific inventions, theories, and medical insights had their origins in South Asia. Western economies and growth have been equally dependent for millennia upon Asian resources. I liked to point out to my tours, for example, that an acknowledged reason for the Roman Empire's economic bankruptcy was the gold sent to India to pay for cotton, silk, and spices.

My fascination with facts like these led me to create detailed timelines for each century beginning before the first millennium. I carried these charts folded in my pocket and could draw upon them as needed to explain a point. When we visited an Indian monument, say the seventh-century cave temples of Mahabalipuram, I could convey what was happening at precisely that time in each region of the world: in economics, trade, culture, religion, and politics. I could do the same thing for the 1459 founding of the Mehrangarh Fort in Jodhpur, or any date I came across. Those timelines became a trademark of my tours. My guests loved this information, and rival tour operators and guides were jealous of it.

I also photocopied recent articles and editorials, both Indian and foreign, on current affairs, politics, the arts, social developments, and religious opinions. These were reprinted and given as handouts to members to read on the long bus rides, or flights, or in their hotel rooms. At my fingertips were quotations from medieval European travelers, ancient Chinese Buddhist pilgrims, eighteenth and nineteenth-century British explorers, and twentieth-century visitors recounting their experiences and impressions of India. Comments of English imperialists, colonialist advocates, Indian freedom fighters, and contemporary revisionists elucidated points or provided context for discussions. As often as possible, Indian friends accompanied us and engaged in conversations with tour members, sometimes spurring quite lively debates. I always organized my tours through Indian agents and facilitators, encouraging these individuals to participate with their opinions. Often, they told me that no other tour leader had asked them these kinds of questions, or to speak openly to their tours, but invariably their responses enhanced our knowledge and enriched our experience. Babu Mohapatra and Sunithi Narayan were particularly adept at drawing visitors into their excitement in what it means to be an Indian. Each discussion that they led or participated in was stimulating. For me, this rich interaction between foreigners and Indians was the true pulse of each tour. I was the facilitator, and they were the builders of bridges.

* * *

I was able to take groups to visit Mannarasala, the Naga (snake) shrine in Kerala that I had found so fascinating on my first trip. Together we shared darshan with the elderly priestess directly descended from millennia of spokeswomen for the Nagaraja, the God-King of Snakes invoked for healing. In Tamil Nadu, we walked into rural tree shrines lined with terracotta horses, some of which are the largest fired clay sculptures known in global history. We rose before dawn to be out on the streets in dusky light to witness women in front of each home creating complex kolams on the ground. And I was able to introduce one group to Padma, the little girl I had profiled in *Daughters of India*, now a teenager expertly drawing an impressive large kolam.

We traveled to Ludiya, a village in Kachchh, Gujarat, that had recovered from a major earthquake. When we arrived, Samabai, an enterprising embroiderer featured in two of my books, ran out to give me a long hug—a moving experience in a veiled culture where custom dictates that visiting men remain at a distance. There, a musician spontaneously sang ballads so beautiful for us that my tour members were in tears. We traveled by jeep to Moti-Singh-ki-Dhani, the village in the remote desert past Jaisalmer, where Phulo had painted her walls in bold geometric designs. Over cups of chai, she complained about the thousands of new wind turbines now stretched across the bleak desert, through land belonging to her and her neighbors. Although these giant windmills supply electricity to much of north India, she and her community had to buy their own current at extortionate rates, while remaining unpaid for the use of their land. We visited dyers and weavers outside Jaipur, braziers in Uttar Pradesh, scroll painters in Bengal, woodcarvers in Ahmedabad, and boatbuilders in Kerala. And wherever we went, we learned from the people—who they were and what mattered to them. With their help and generosity, we opened doors and experienced free and open communication.

* * *

Not every tour was easy. Always one or more participants would cause difficulties. Usually, they were the entitled ones, those that believed that they deserved special treatment. I had to learn patience and forbearance. Smithsonian Associates, the organization that first hired me to plan and lead tours, taught me never to confront or outwardly disagree with my guests. Usually, I was able to maintain those principles. Sometimes, it was almost impossible.

* * *

In the spring of 1991, the director of a prominent art museum in New York City had heard of my unusual tours and wanted to hire my services in January of the next year. I was committed to lead my fourth Smithsonian tour the following October and told him I was not available. But as we talked, and I explained about my traveling seminars in which I interfaced closely with each participant, he insisted that I help him. To discourage him, I doubled the salary that I was getting from the Smithsonian—but he doubled that, and I could not refuse. The invitees were wealthy members of the board and donors to the museum. When I learned that the director had employed three top tour agencies to manage twenty-three tour guests for eighteen days, I was concerned about overkill. They barred no holds in the preparations. We would stay in palaces and five-star hotels, dine with royalty, and be constantly cosseted. As part of the preparations, the director flew me down to New York four different times for pre-tour lectures to the members. I'd given them a detailed reading list, and they responded eagerly. By this time, I was looking forward to a promising trip.

I was in Delhi ahead of them and achieved a feat considered impossible. I talked my way through airport security and customs to meet the new arrivals before they entered immigration and help them through passport control and baggage claim, claiming that these were VIPs. It was late at night when they climbed aboard our luxurious Mercedes bus. Once they had settled in their seats, I grabbed the mic and welcomed them to India. I had intended a brief introduction to our tour, but the director signaled me from the back with a finger across his throat and a gesture to sit down. I obeyed.

That was the last time he allowed me to speak to the tour. He never would explain his diametric reversal. I could only assume that my expertise in India threatened his ego. I had prepared a series of evening slide lectures about Indian art and culture that still occurred because the museum had published them in the guests' itineraries—but the director allowed no questions or discussions afterward. At his request, the tour facilitators simply ushered them to the next event. On all other tours, I often met with my group to draw them out and discuss our experiences. That was never permitted. I could only talk with someone if a seat beside them was empty. This experience was the exact opposite of a traveling seminar, and I was thoroughly miserable. I felt that I could not share the India I love with the participants.

The pièce de résistance occurred near the end of the tour when we arrived at the Taj Mahal. That world-renowned architectural masterwork should have been one of the highlights of the trip. It was not. Even though India's top agents had scrupulously designed our itinerary, none had realized that the only day planned for visiting the Taj coincided with the public celebrations of the 500th birthday of Shah Jahan, the Mughal emperor who had built it to honor his favorite wife. On that day only, the vast gardens and grounds were open free to the public. Close to a million ecstatic Indian tourists mobbed every available inch. When we managed to push our way through the crowds to the arched entrance gate with its classic view of the dome and minarets of the tomb in the distance, we could see it only over an endless sea of human heads. As if that were not enough, that perfect edifice described by poets and travelers as one of humanity's most sublime achievements was covered by an enormous neon portrait of its progenitor, Shah Jahan, picked out in flashing streams of bright color superimposed over the architecture. After all the tensions of that abominable trip, I fell to the ground laughing. I felt sorry for the few tour members with whom I had been able to talk but vindicated that the museum director's meticulous planning had been so vulgarly thwarted.

* * *

In 1993, Smithsonian Associates invited me to co-guide an unusual itinerary aboard a small Greek-owned luxury cruise ship, the *Aurora I*. Fifty-five paying passengers would sail in a tour entitled: *From Singapore to India's Malabar Coast*. I found the concept intriguing, especially when SA agreed to let Helene come with me in lieu of a salary. We boarded in Singapore and cruised to Borneo and then around the southern coast of India. The particular bonus was the rarely visited tribal Nicobar Islands (halfway between India and Thailand). I had always wanted to explore them. In college, I'd taken many courses on Southeast Asian history and art history, and now spent months reviewing my notes in order to give competent lectures. It was a beautiful sail. Helene and I will never forget lying abed in our cherry-paneled stateroom watching flying fish crest the waves just outside our large sea-level windows. My wife conscientiously volunteered to tell engaging Indian myths and legends and taught the female passengers how to wrap and wear a sari. Unfortunately, a political fracas prevented us from stopping in the Nicobars.

We all disembarked in Madras Harbor (not yet renamed Chennai) and boarded two luxury buses for three days and two nights ashore. I guided all the guests through the historic temples of Mahabalipuram, Kanchipuram, Tiruchirappalli, Thanjavur, and Madurai before we wended our way toward the southeastern port of Tuticorin. Dorothy Wesson, a retired schoolteacher from Minneapolis who had already been on three of my tours, suffered a heart attack when we were in Tiruchirappalli. Luckily, our staff included an American doctor who administered to her needs while the trip continued. But, as he stated, it was necessary to return to the ship's infirmary as soon as possible.

During the tour's organization, I had expressed my concerns that Tuticorin was a commercial, not a tourist, port. The Smithsonian informed me that the Indian government had issued our ship's captain special docking and boarding permits for us. Our buses arrived there just before 5:00 p.m. of the third day ashore. They offloaded all the luggage as we entered a derelict and filthy British-period waiting hall, disused for half a century. Dorothy was laid out on one of the grime-covered benches while the other tour members gingerly perched on others, and

I ran down the road after the departing buses demanding that they return. Our ship's first mate reported that he was prohibited from landing the ship's tender to deliver us aboard. The Smithsonian representative and I entered a small office with him where a white-uniformed Indian port official politely but firmly told us that our ship could not enter these waters. As I had feared, national legislation prohibited any tourist vessel from landing at that exclusively commercial port. The ship's owners had never secured permission, and we would have to return to Madras (a twelve-hour drive). The Greek first mate exploded with anger and used ripe expletives to insult the official, who grew rigid in response. As a lecturer and not an administrator, it was clearly not my position to get involved, but no one else was willing to interfere. I knelt on the floor, touched the official's feet (an Indian gesture of total submission), and implored him to let us board. I explained that one of our passengers was an eighty-year-old who urgently needed care and might not survive the long journey back to Madras. Imagine, I begged, if it was his aged grandmother? The official acquiesced and stated that if we reboarded our buses and drove to a pier a few miles away, we could take a tugboat to our ship.

We reloaded passengers and baggage, drove to a disgustingly greasy commercial pier, boarded the tug, and headed out on rough seas a full mile to our waiting ship. We only realized that the tug captain was roaringly drunk when our boat crashed at full speed into the side of the *Aurora I*. Our Greek ship's captain refused to allow us to board, fearing a further accident, but our doctor insisted that Dorothy and he must reach the infirmary without delay. Therefore, amid a rolling surf, my aged friend was literally thrown from our tug's side into the arms of two waiting Greek crew members. The doctor leaped aboard himself, and the remaining fifty-seven of us returned to the port.

Onshore, once again, our first mate lambasted the port official, calling him "a f***ing little Wog!" I could not believe it. This official was someone whose permission we required if we were ever to return to our ship. Again, I knelt and touched his feet, begging that he ignore these insults. I implored him to give us another boat, this time with a sober captain who might transfer us successfully to our vessel. After another hour of pleading, he agreed to provide a sleek motor yacht. This boat had no cabin and only a tiny deck, so all the tour members crowded on the boat's prow with only an eight-inch-high rail to which they all tried to cling. Once they had filled all the space, there was clearly no room for the luggage. The other lecturer (a naturalist), Helene, and I were left behind with the mountain of baggage as we bade farewell to our tour. It was long past sunset by this time, the sky was almost black, and the boat pitched as it moved away. We thought we would never see those people again. An hour later, the yacht returned, having transferred all of them onto our ship. Helene, the other man, and I had to load the overnight luggage for sixty passengers onto the small vessel, strap it down, hold onto the ropes ourselves, and leave. We made it aboard at about 10:30 p.m. The other tourists had already gone to bed, and we collapsed in exhaustion and mental fatigue in our stateroom.

The next morning our ship's captain called for a meeting of all hands and passengers in which he proceeded to explain that it was "the f***king Indians' fault," that they were all "slimy bastards," and that his fine crew was above reproach. I wanted to yell out in protest, but Smithsonian Associates made it clear that I could not object. I had to swallow my bile—just one of many lessons in curbing my anger whenever leading a tour.

* * *

As I became more confident of my abilities as a tour leader and organizer, I began to branch away from Smithsonian Associates to manage my own tours. My first, in 1995, was inspired by my *Painted Prayers* book. I shepherded twelve individuals through the rural regions of Orissa, Tamil Nadu, Kerala, and Gujarat, where I introduced them to women's household art. It was a lovely adventure, and I learned to prefer traveling with smaller groups.

The docents from the Smithsonian's Freer and Sackler Galleries hired me to lead a *Puja Tour* in 1998, two years after that comprehensive exhibition opened. (Remember, it ran until 2000.) Since my show's inception, I had been working closely with these individuals, preparing them to explain practical Hinduism to visitors. This trip gave Babu, Sunithi, and me many opportunities to share with them hands-on experiences of devotional rituals in roadside shrines, temples, and homes. At that time, I was still composing my book on the subject, *Meeting God*, and I learned an immeasurable amount from the participants' responses, reactions, and questions that later helped me write the text.

More than a decade later, in 2010, Babu, Kathleen, and I invited the docents of Mingei International Museum to join us on a tour of folk art, craft, and outsider art culminating in three days at Sonabai's home in Puhputra. Although we were there three years after that celebrated artist had passed, the tour members all knew her son, Daroga Ram, and his wife, Rajenbai, from having hosted them in San Diego. It was a joyous reconnection and wonderful for me to share with them in person the phenomenal art that had so stimulated me. We also visited the homes of each of the other artists, inspired by Sonabai, whose artworks we had featured in the show.

* * *

Ever since I was a small boy, I have loved to share experiences with others. I've gained a greater understanding through their responses. My family has always been at the core of my identity. It felt essential to invite them to participate in the India I love. Broad familial friendships, such as I enjoyed and benefited from, are commonplace in India. South Asians welcomed my relatives as natural extensions of me and bent over backward to make them feel at home.

Aside from two trips sharing India with my parents, many other family members have traveled with me there over the decades: my brother John and his wife DeAnne, my sister Ruth, her daughter Allison, my niece Jesse, and nephew Todd, and, most recently, Ruth's older daughter Hillary, each on individual trips coordinated with my field research. Those experiences have deepened bonds of friendship and mutual understanding, as have those with several cousins.

* * *

I've led too many tours to describe them all. Each has been instructive and demanding in its own way. Each taught me the lessons of negotiation, adaptability, innovation, and tolerance. Through Smithsonian Associates, I had met a topnotch tour facilitator, Navin Pandey. When I branched out on my own, I hired Navin to help me book and organize my tours. Beyond his refined skills and abilities to solve any challenging issue that might arise, Navin is a thoughtful gentleman, a product of generations of Old Delhi refinement. Until he retired from the business, my tours profited as much from his cool wit and warm-hearted generosity as his talents in overcoming adversity.

Through working closely with me, Babu Mohapatra founded his own tour company in the early nineties. With a degree in Indian cultural history and training as a tourist guide, Babu brought qualities into his handling of tours that I have never witnessed in another Indian. Although he is a brahmin (a member of the highest caste, which implies a high stature in India's hierarchical society), Babu never assumes any attitude of superiority and never makes any claims for special service. He has traveled with me throughout the subcontinent. As a foreigner, I am outside the Indian caste system, literally outcaste, although I am treated openly and well and make friends easily with people from all aspects of society. I have been amazed as I have observed Babu for years.

Through his natural affability and genuine acceptance of each person, all are at ease with him: aristocrats and outcastes, businessmen and laborers, priests and artisans. When Babu leads a tour with me, each participant and each person we meet feels acknowledged and included. His unassuming presence has immeasurably enhanced my tours and private travels.

Beginning in 2011, I hired my first cousin Annie Baker to help facilitate my tours. Annie studied to be a healer in many modalities. She brought her natural compassion and healing skills into each of our trips. Annie catered directly to the needs of each tour member. If Peter was sore from sitting too long in the bus or from a twisted ankle, Annie would massage his ligaments. If Marcie felt shattered by interacting with a child beggar or overcome by India's urban poverty, Annie might calm her nerves with reiki or teach her a healing meditative technique. She would intuit that Suzanne longed for her grandchildren and ask to see their pictures and compare notes as a fellow grandparent. Each participant felt seen and heard, and the compatibility of our tours together was the best of any I'd ever led. Beyond all that, Annie's infectious good humor always had us laughing.

Through years of organizing and leading tours, I've finally learned that less is truly more. Most tours of India (and of other regions of the world) are based on the belief that visitors had better see and learn as much as possible since their time in that country is limited. My early tours, organized first by Smithsonian Associates and later by me, were like that. We spent one or two nights in each place; a long sojourn was three nights. We tried to see and experience as much as we could in the time we had.

Those tours were exhausting and overwhelming. The success of my most recent tours was their slow pace. I tried to stay in each place for at least four nights, scheduling half of the day and leaving the other half free: either the morning or the afternoon, depending upon the activities available. The tour member could rest in her room if she was tired or go exploring by herself—or Annie, Babu, or I would be available to take her anywhere she wished within reason. These slow-paced days allowed the visitor to absorb what he was experiencing and to be present for the underlying subtleties that so informed all of my personal understandings of India in my early years. In this way, the homes we visited, the friends we met, the conversations they had, and the knowledge and stories that they exchanged became all the more vital. They were given adequate time to sink in.

* * *

Linda Bailey Nottingham, a participant in my *Painted Prayers Tour* of 1995, felt so transfigured by her experiences in India that she wrote the following poem. It eloquently expresses much of what that country and culture bring to me:

> Celebrate this sacred space
> Not because this space is sacred.
> Any space, in any place
> Could be.
> Celebrate because this place
> Is where the veil hiding my face
> Dropped
> And let the healing grace
> Invade my secret spaces.

~ 15 ~
Underpinnings

As I've searched my memories, notes, and photographs to compile this biography, I've recognized that India might seem an unusual choice for a boy raised in a small town in California's coastal mountains. And yet my life seemed orchestrated to travel and work there. The following chapter considers the many aspects of my formation that guided me into my unusual perspective and profession.

As a child, I fit in nowhere. My good fortune was that adults, many of them, recognized in me as-yet-unmaterialized qualities and kept me from being thwarted. My parents and most of my family were less encouraging.

Teachers formed me, literally and figuratively. Their influence is in my blood. Three of my great-grandfathers, one of my grandfathers, my father, and numerous uncles and aunts were teachers, as are my sister and many cousins. Aside from schoolwork, innumerable individuals and experiences have shaped my character. This chapter sums up those influences and their effect on my years in India. I remain an inveterate student. My primary teachers in India have been women and men who have opened their minds and hearts to me, many far off the grid and most unrecognized elsewhere as special.

I grew up in Southern California's Ojai Valley on the campus of The Thacher School, a progressive boy's preparatory school where my father taught English and horsemanship. We lived in what had been built as a dormitory for students — in a small apartment I shared with my parents and two older siblings. The school's administration required that my father eat all meals, except one each week, in a communal dining room in the company of some 150 boys, other faculty, and their families. After reaching the age of five, I joined my parents and siblings there for most meals. Students came in and out of our home all day long and often at night. We breathed a common air. This close communal living prepared me for the experience of extended families and interwoven communities that prevail in India.

We faculty children were given thorough guidance in self-care, after which we were left unsupervised. Thacher's campus flows into a two-million-acre national forest that we explored to our hearts' content after class each day. We were allowed to roam the steep mountain trails on our own, as long as we were back in time for dinner. Although my brother and sister formed strong friendships with other faculty children, I was the only one my age on campus. Playing and hiking by myself taught self-reliance that would later serve me well as an independent traveler.

Ian McDougall was my only friend on campus for many years. Two years younger, he was what is now called "on the spectrum." In my childhood, everyone regarded Ian as mentally deficient. Many belittled him, deriding his slow speech, poor articulation, and seemingly clumsy movements. I did not. Ian always fascinated me. I was a natural storyteller, constantly inventing imaginary adventures for us to pursue, and Ian endlessly traveled with me wherever I wanted to go. I loved him. Larger than me always, Ian would join me to hike the trails in search of hidden worlds, populating the mountains with fantasy cities where stones became jewels, trees bore magic fruits, bushes were dragons or monsters, and enchanted white deer stood trembling just around the next corner awaiting discovery. Ian's acceptance, his ability to be totally present in the moment, fully absorbing each offering, noticing and aware although he could not communicate his understanding in words— this friendship taught me as much, perhaps more, than any class or teacher. I have employed Ian's wisdom throughout my years in India. More than anyone else, he taught me how to absorb the insights of place. In his teenage years, science caught up with Ian and medical adjustments allowed him to catch up with his peers in school, becoming able to communicate well his unusual thoughts and observations. His perspectives astounded others but were familiar to me. After graduating from high school, my friend moved to the farthest reaches of the Yukon to become a trapper, running dogsleds for decades, immersed and infused with the mountains, forests, meadows, birds, and animal life that enveloped him, true to the unique self he had always been.

Months after I'd finished writing these memoirs, I learned that Ian was dying of cancer in the Yukon. On his deathbed, Ian managed to revive long enough for a thirty-minute conversation face-to-face through his brother's smartphone. We were able to confide that we were one another's only friends for years during our childhood and how that friendship had shaped our lives.

* * *

I learned many important lessons from my father, some as he intended, others by reacting against him. Dad (Jack Huyler) was a force to be reckoned with. Dominating, powerful, and demanding, he could also be as gentle as light rain on flower petals. He had the soul of a poet, filled with great passions that frequently expressed his many delights, yet could be volatile when confronted. Dad had strong, sure opinions and was never shy about sharing them. By all accounts, he was a brilliant teacher. He demanded excellence from all his students but earnestly helped them hone their skills to achieve it. Our lives were immersed in his work. At the breakfast table, he often read aloud the Shakespeare sonnets, the Chaucer, Donne, Keats, and Shelley he was teaching that day. He fostered in me a deep love of literature.

Dad always had yearned to be a cowboy since his early childhood spent in the authentic old West of 1920s and '30s Jackson Hole, Wyoming. He came to Thacher not only to teach grammar, syntax, and literature but to exercise his passion for riding daily a well-trained horse and raising a family of young equestrians. In my youth, each student on campus owned a horse, as did many of the faculty. Dad helped run the horse program, teaching boys the disciplines and joys of a close relationship between an individual and his horse. I can ride well. How could I not? I was on horseback before I could walk, but I deeply disappointed my father by my determined disinterest in pursuing the craft of horsemanship. My horse was foremost my friend, and although my siblings and parents were also affectionate with their horses, mine never became a well-honed tool as theirs did. It seemed an odd coincidence that a primary focus of my field research in India and a key to my doctoral thesis was the documentation of terracotta horses placed in rural shrines for the Gods of Protection to ride.

My mother taught as much through example as by word. Born and raised in Korea, Mom (Margaret Noble Appenzeller Huyler) was a profoundly compassionate soul who selflessly cared for anyone in need. Although she never received a salary in my lifetime, she worked hard as the figural mother of thousands of boarding boys during the decades of my childhood and later. Mom could listen and considerately guide without imposing her ego on another. Grounded in strong ethics and personal strength, she could be both flexible and unwavering in her sense of right and wrong. Her values shaped all three of us children. She was unquestionably available for us. Many men told me they were in love with my mother, but that they respected her commitment to my father. They proclaimed that they found her to be one of the most beautiful spirits they had ever known. The words used most often to describe her at her death were pure grace. Mom was the first of my many women mentors.

Perhaps the most precious treasure my parents offered was their example of devotion to one another. Although different in temperament and character, Mom and Dad were deeply in love for sixty-three years. They gladly shared that love with everyone they knew. Through them, I learned that trust is earned through loyalty and steadfastness, that proper acknowledgment of and attention to one another, and flexibility in the face of differing opinions, are collectively the bases of a lasting relationship. If each is willing to bend and expand and modify through the lessons of the other, then two people can successfully nourish one another for a lifetime.

I met my own life's partner when I was just sixteen at a square dance in Jackson Hole. It was kismet. The caller asked unpartnered dancers to form two circles with the men and boys in the outside ring, women and girls on the inside. When the music played, our circles revolved in opposite directions, and when it stopped, the two facing each other would then dance. I stopped opposite the most beautiful girl I'd ever beheld, my future wife: Helene Wheeler (nicknamed Hi). Years later, Indians explained that in their belief, this was the cosmic mandala, the *ras lila*. Helene became my heart's twin, the complement and balance to my perceptions. My relationship with her has informed and guided most of my decisions over the years. We are different in metabolism, nature, and viewpoint, and yet we have always held in common sensitivities and interests that continue to underscore all our activities. We view the world through symbiotic lenses. Our aesthetic impulses blend well. Daily expressions of love and affection have become a heartfelt habit that spills over into much of what I do. Without the foundation of our relationship, and Helene's unwavering support, my years of work in India would not have been the same.

* * *

My parents genuinely liked people, wherever they met them. They would often meet strangers on the street and invite them home for lunch or dinner. We met innumerable people in this way: Africans, Poles, French, Russians, Turks, Brazilians, Koreans, Japanese and Chinese, and countless others, as well as North Americans from across the States and from countries in both continents. Mom and Dad taught us that each person we meet has merit, wherever they are, whatever their background, race, or culture. Each is valuable in and of herself. I learned at an early age that most individuals yearn for recognition, to be seen and heard. With nonjudgmental attention, they blossom and shine. This maxim, this constant reaching out to listen and communicate, has underlined my experiences in India from those first minutes in the country when I negotiated with an elderly rickshaw driver to sit in the back seat of his vehicle while I cycled us both and my luggage to the nearest town. This attitude often disarms folks: It disintegrates suspicion, fear, and prejudice. Time and again, it opens the door to friendships, many of which have lasted for years.

Travel is in my bones. At no time in my life until the Covid pandemic have I resided anywhere for as long as a year. My parents insisted that travel was both educational and a way to remain in contact with far-flung friends. It was also an essential part of their job descriptions. Nine months of the year, they worked at The Thacher School in Ojai. They spent the other three in intense physical labor at my grandparents' ranch in Jackson Hole, 1,100 miles away. Travel between the two was never easy. My family always had horses to transport: only two in a trailer when I was an infant; but soon after that, we each had our own animal that could not be left behind. For many years, Dad drove an old panel delivery truck, "The Ark," carrying four horses. Mom was at the wheel of the car behind towing a two- and later a four-horse trailer. Each summer, the five of us journeyed both ways across the hot Mojave Desert, through Nevada and Utah, with the horses, a dog, and a cat. While my parents worked hard during those three months—my father haying and caring for cattle, sheep, and horses, my mother running the cabins and cooking and serving food to up to 20 people each meal—we kids were in paradise. After my grandfather died and economic necessity forced my parents to sell most of the ranch land, their workload greatly diminished, and we took three summer road trips throughout the United States visiting family and old friends. Collectively, we explored all the old forty-eight.

When I was eight years old, the school granted my father six months paid sabbatical leave. My parents wanted us to experience cultures outside the United States. Although savings from a teacher's salary would have allowed only modest travel, my grandfather's will allocated a small amount to broaden our horizons. We drove cross-country to New York City, boarded a ship, and sailed to Europe. Mom and Dad bought a Volkswagen camper bus in Munich. For the next five months, we traversed eight countries, camping wherever we could and continuously interacting with locals and fellow campers. In those months, we met only a handful of other Americans. Well-meaning friends had advised my parents to leave me behind; they believed I was too young to appreciate Europe's offerings fully. Why take on an unwarranted expense? Instead, Mom and Dad listened to their own intuitions. My experiences in those cultures effectively formed my future. I was too young to understand that foreign languages were incomprehensible without training. I easily communicated with all, while my older brother and sister were more reserved—possibly apprehensive of committing social improprieties.

For the rest of his life, my father liked to recall that first day in Munich, before we picked up the camper. We had spent the night in two rooms at a local hotel. When my parents arose the next morning, they panicked when they came to wake us three kids in the bedroom we shared, only to find that I was missing. They rushed down to the lobby and breakfast room—no Stevie. Through the revolving door and onto the street, they found me, my back against a wall, watching the passersby, in awe of all I saw. The doorman told them that I had been standing there safely since dawn. Dad and Mom realized then that

I would be okay, that I was unlikely to get into trouble. Dad recognized that I was, as I still am, fascinated by, and totally at ease with strangers.

During that trip in Europe, my youth opened societal barriers and taught me to be fearless—that if I was kind and attentive, individuals opened up to me. That lesson has carried over into all my Indian interactions. I enter communities where I am unknown, with no introduction, and am unintimidated and generally unintimidating. If I convey that I am honest, open, and genuinely appreciative of each person I meet, sensitive to their levels of shyness, reservation, or fear, barriers melt, and individuals reveal their hearts.

I have always been intensely visual: I see and notice things that many others do not. I naturally love compositions, textures, forms, and colors. Even though neither of my parents was particularly artistic, they admired beauty. Three episodes occurred in my childhood that strengthened my talents. Two were during our 1960 trip to Europe.

My father volunteered to photograph as many classical masterpieces in museums as he would be allowed for The Thacher School's art archives. Dad would present his papers at museums in each country, and then spend one or more days setting up his tripod and making studies, while we explored the galleries. This exposure made an indelible impression on my eight-year-old brain. I have appreciated museums and fine arts ever since.

The second highlight was our visit to the Lascaux Caves in rural France, where we spent an entire day exploring and viewing the archetypal Paleolithic murals, personally guided by one of the men who first discovered them when he was a young boy in 1940. What a gift. Those enthralling images still populate my dreams.

Third, the next summer when we were back in Jackson Hole, I was invited to spend a weekend in the tipi of Reginald and Gladys Laubin. Reg was the adopted son of One Bull, the Lakota chief who claimed to have killed General Custer. This elderly couple had spent their lives collecting, documenting, and living Native American ritual arts, music, and dance, particularly those of the Plains Indians. Somehow these friends of my grandparents sensed my deep interest and extended a unique invitation. I know of only two other children ever accorded that privilege! We slept in buffalo robes and tended the tipi's central fire (where Gladys cooked our meals), while both told Lakota stories and explained their traditional lore. From that moment on until I decided in my late teens to work in India, I intended to spend my life documenting native customs and art. My doctoral research into the tribal customs and arts of India described in Chapters Five, Six, and Seven was directly driven by the Laubins' mentoring.

* * *

Items made by hand intrigue me. I love holding old tools, especially well-worn ones, and as a child used to imagine the carpenter, builder, or craftsman who employed them. I have always been fascinated by the construction of things, how different elements were refined and then combined to create a new product:

pottery, sculptures, paintings, upholstery fabric, clothing (particularly costumes), and lathed or carved wood bowls, among many other things. I also loved creating assemblages: collections of interesting rocks or shells, even shelves of books. When I was about seven or eight, I bought a Chinese terracotta figurine of an old man for twenty-five cents at a rummage sale. I would happily spend hours creating shrines for him out of sticks, stems, and leaves and then adorn him with offerings of flowers. As far as I know, no one witnessed this activity. I believed that my straightlaced Protestant parents would have judged it as idolatrous.

* * *

Mom grew up in Seoul, Korea, when the Japanese ruled that country. Consequently, she spoke Korean fluently and Japanese well. Her parents were the offspring of two pioneering families of American Methodist missionaries: the Appenzellers and the Nobles. Her paternal grandparents, Henry Gerhard and Ella Dodge Appenzeller, are still recognized and admired for being the first western educators in Korea. My childhood memories are filled with references to the Korean language and culture. As I am disaffected of the overarching concept of proselytizing and missionaries, I didn't realize when I began my work in India that I owe much of my attraction to and ease in India to the paradigm of my mother's family. I've gradually recognized that we are two sides of the same coin: they brought their western Christian ethics and values to Korea, while I bring knowledge and insights about India to the West.

Dad and Mom married in 1942, just as Dad entered the army. They knew he would soon be in combat and worried that he would be killed fighting the Nazis. So, Dad applied for assignment to China, believing that sphere of action to be less dangerous. The army sent my parents to Yale, where they both took a comprehensive crash course in spoken Mandarin. Dad was then flown over the Hump into central China and served the last year-and-a-half of the conflict as an army captain of mixed American and Chinese troops. He learned to love Chinese culture and so favorably impressed a Chinese general that this dynamic leader seconded Dad into the Kuomintang (the National Chinese Army) as a lieutenant colonel under Chiang Kai-Shek. My parents spoke Mandarin when they did not want us children to understand. They both cooked with chopsticks; we learned to love exceptional Korean and Chinese food, and they always enjoyed speaking with East Asians in their own tongues. A Chinese friend who first met Dad when he was in his late eighties was amazed at how fluent he still was sixty-seven years after his sojourn in China. Those examples were formative.

* * *

Most Americans I've known live in relatively small, nuclear families. They know few cousins, aunts, or uncles well. I come from and am still in touch with an enormous extended family—well over one hundred on my father's side and more than sixty on my mother's. We genuinely like one another. We enjoy getting together. I'm closer to some than others, but I can genuinely say that there is no one I actively dislike. We keep tabs on each other's lives and careers. We celebrate new births and mutually mourn our loss of beloved elders. This deep awareness of family, of connection to my heritage, has served me well in India, where family of origin defines the identity of each human being.

Three grandmothers nurtured me as a child. Grandma (Margaret Porter Huyler) lived near us in Ojai. She could be difficult for others, but she championed me, defending me when she felt my parents, particularly my father, mistreated or misunderstood me. She regularly provided me sanctuary on weekends in her home on the other side of town. Grandma helped engender my fascination with archives. She was an inveterate storyteller, and I loved nothing more than to spend a day poring over old albums with her and learning the story behind each photograph. Grandma also taught me to admire the elderly. Each Sunday after church, she would take me to visit the residents of retirement homes where I was often the only child these wonderful old folks would ever see. I learned firsthand to deplore the rejection in America of our elderly as I sat spellbound in front of wheelchairs, listening as seniors told stories of their world from opposing perspectives to my own. Those weekly interchanges became a foundation of my later work in India.

Aunt Manie (Mary Hamilton Murdoch) was my second grandmother. Although not a blood relative, she had lived with my grandmother since she had come to America from Scotland as my father's nanny when he was just three. Aunt Manie was a loving, practical Scot with a lilt of a lowland brogue and the wit to go with it. She provided the no-nonsense counterbalance to Grandma's more outrageous excesses. Aunt Manie's exacting views on the pitfalls of privilege, entitlement, and complacency have been clear guidelines for all that I do.

My mother's mother, Grandmommy (Ruth Noble Appenzeller), was absent when I was a small child. After my grandfather died in Korea during my infancy, she remained there alone to run a home for orphans of the recent war, moving to California when I was ten to live near my uncle and his family about two hours' drive south of Ojai. She would come to stay with us for a week or two a few times each year. Grandmommy could see the humor in almost anything but would invariably respond with understatement or misdirection. When I was little, her jests escaped me, but as I grew, I learned to adore her subtle, dry wit. Ruth Noble had married into a family (the Appenzellers) more broadly recognized by Koreans for their contributions to that country than her natal family. My Noble great-grandparents followed a parallel, but less public role. In my mind, they embodied the prototype of selfless service to humanity, never seeking acknowledgment while quietly helping others to improve their lives. Through Grandmommy, I began to understand the virtues of silently listening to, witnessing, and being available for others.

My interest in art and antiques and the stories behind them was intently nurtured by my father's older brother, Uncle Coulter. We didn't see him frequently. Uncle Coulter worked for the US State Department and lived with his family on the other side of the country in Washington, DC, or farther afield in the Hague or Paris. Nevertheless, they visited us as often as possible in Ojai or at the ranch, and we stayed with them twice in DC. Uncle Coulter was a charmer and an engaging storyteller with an outrageous sense of humor, and I idolized him. Every Christmas, his gift was the one I most looked forward to opening. It was always something unexpected and unusual: handmade toys when I was a toddler, or an illustrated rare book, and later an antique sculpture or painting. Whenever he visited, he would take me aside, ask me all about my interests, encourage them, foster my hobbies, and entice me to look at things in new and intriguing ways. Uncle Coulter had lived in Bombay for two years during World War II, serving US Intelligence. He had known Mahatma Gandhi, Nehru, and other fighters for Indian independence, and many of India's royalty. His illustrious tales entranced me. His daughter, my first cousin Annie, was always a steadfast friend. Annie later became one of Helene's and my closest companions and, in recent years as I describe in Chapter Fourteen, has helped me lead tours of India.

***

Many friends of my parents also mentored me. Andrée Schlemmer befriended me in Switzerland when I was eight years old, and soon evolved into one of my primary guides to life. She and her husband, Jean, became good friends of my parents near the beginning of our travels. Jean was a well-known photographer and Andrée, a writer. She stated that she sensed unusual qualities in me and took the time to nurture them, visiting Ojai often during the next four decades and participating in many of my key moments. Andrée was a profound, perceptive, and intuitive human being who often expressed startling mystical points of view. More than anyone else during the troubling times in my adolescence, twenties, and thirties, Andrée helped me to reclarify myself and to be confident enough to follow my unusual path. It was she who (described in Chapter Eight) sat next to me on the banks of the Ganges in Varanasi beneath the spreading peepul tree on my thirtieth birthday while a flock of pigeons above us unceremoniously adorned me with their excrement.

Although the dogmatic Christianity practiced by my parents and ancestors never appealed to me, I've always been drawn to the sacred. Luckily, friends of my parents sensed and encouraged my interests. When I was about twelve, Dorothy Holroyd invited me to attend lectures at Krotona, the Theosophical Center in Ojai. Theosophists believe that the mystical teachings of all the world's religions maintain similar great truths, and that their study and comparison underline complementary ethics. Over the next several years, I learned the basic tenets of Hinduism, Buddhism, Taoism, Sufism, Bahai, and the insights and visions of Judaic and Christian mystics. The Theosophists also introduced me to yoga and meditation. When I was a junior in high school, and my mind seethed with hormones, insecurities, and confused emotions, a music teacher presented Transcendental Meditation as a means of quieting thoughts and finding peace. I was intrigued and joined a group of other students on a trip to UCLA to hear its proponent, Maharishi Mahesh Yogi, speak. It was 1967, the same year that this guru became the spiritual advisor of the Beatles and before they first traveled to India to study in his ashram. I was deeply impressed by Maharishi's message and returned the next day to receive my personal mantra directly from him. The practice of that discipline over a period of years calmed me and helped me settle more into my bones. It remained routine during my first months in India, although many experiences there have deepened and altered my methods evolving into an individual approach that I practice daily. Nevertheless, I occasionally still use the mantra given to me by the only Indian guru I ever followed– and, even in that case, only briefly.

* * *

Music runs through all my experiences, stemming from my family. Dad had a superb tenor voice. In 1940, he had helped form a college vocal group and later even made a commercial LP album singing and playing English and western ballads. He carried his guitar wherever he went and loved to be asked to sing. I grew up with family and friends harmonizing in our living room in Ojai or around the campfire at the ranch. Dad led a weekly school sing-along for all the students at Thacher, drawing from a repertoire of hundreds of traditional songs, often with designated parts and set harmonies. Music was omnipresent in our home. I inherited a good voice but was embarrassed by Dad's expansive ego in a crowd and never wanted to be center stage. I joined glee clubs, choirs, and even a madrigal group in college, but avoided singing solos. Nevertheless, I always have a tune or rhythm in my head. I sing or whistle by myself, sometimes riffing or improvising for hours, as described earlier when I traveled on Indian trains. Musical awareness has naturally extended into an appreciation of the different complex rhythms and compositions of both Indian classical and folk music. Although not core to my profession, I have worked closely with musicians there for years.

* * *

I've always been an iconoclast—and that was unacceptable in my home. Before I came along, my parents thought they knew how to handle children. My brother and sister had fit the mold they'd firmly set but I was totally different: artistic, sensitive, reflective, and perfectly happy doing things on my own. They clearly loved me, but because I didn't meet their expectations and acted so far outside their frame of reference, they feared my life would be a failure. As a child, I misread their concern as disapproval, their frequent admonitions as dislike, their efforts to make me conform to their beliefs as a rejection of my own truths. Luckily, many other adults told me I was okay. That was one of the most profound advantages of being raised on campus in a huge extended family: I had surrogate parents to validate me. While such strong parental opposition might have crushed another child, it only confirmed me in my singular path. Many teachers and contemporaries commented on my unusually strong sense of direction as a late teenager and young adult. I knew what I wanted at a young age and began to prepare for it. Once I reached middle age, my relationship with my parents softened, and we increasingly grew to appreciate one another and express our mutual love.

I was not particularly athletic, and I always eschewed violence of any kind. That and my shyness and sensitivity made me a target for bullying—from my father, who felt it his duty to prepare me for life's knocks, and from older and stronger kids. One older boy, my nemesis from earliest childhood, was frequently sadistic and shaming. I bear many scars, physical and emotional, from his tortures. My worst childhood experience was when he raped me when I was twelve. At that time, I was so distanced from and afraid of my father and my mother who clearly supported him over me that I told no one. However difficult it was for me, I never blocked that incident from my memory in the way that many other victims of assault have. It, too, shaped my future. In my late thirties and forties, I had many years of therapy and can honestly say now that I am grateful for the effect of that violence on me. It made me sympathetic toward the underdog, whatever the situation. It strengthened my belief in the value of non-violence and sharpened my determination to oppose bullying wherever I encounter it. Perhaps most importantly, it helped me empathize with the common plight of women and to guide my work as a champion of women's empowerment and rights. This empathy engendered the material for my three books about Indian women's identity. And in the past year here in Maine I have joined an organization called "Men Talking" that encourages males to speak out about patterns of abuse that have shaped their lives.

I have endured incessant physical pain since my early adolescence. I attribute it to two incidents at the Ojai Valley School, which I attended for three years. In the sixth grade, I spoke a swear word in class. I never had a foul mouth and wouldn't have dared utter more than "hell" or "damn," but my teacher sent me to the principal's office. His punishment was standard for the school but deeply damaging to me. He insisted that I swallow without water a dry teaspoon of cayenne pepper. I developed stomach ulcers overnight and have had digestive issues ever since. In the eighth grade, when I was reading a novel instead of a textbook during study hall, the monitoring teacher sneaked up behind me. With no warning, he gave me a high-voltage shock under the back of my skull with a large cattle prod. (Powered by four 'D' batteries, this electric device is used by farmers and ranchers to herd cattle). My neck, spine, and pelvis are permanently twisted because of this abuse. I had a severe headache immediately that has become a series of chronic migraines that have plagued me on average three days each week for the past 60 years. At times they last without respite for as long as 70 days and, most recently, one lasted daily for six long months. I have tried dozens of possible remedies to alter and ameliorate them. Some are palliative, but none last long. Finally, I am learning to retrain my brain to let go of pain and have good reason to believe that I have eradicated these headaches permanently. And yet, as a result of these decades of extreme discomfort, I sympathize with others who suffer.

* * *

My two years as a student at The Thacher School helped reset my path. I had been unhappy at each of my previous schools, both public and private. My antipathy with Dad had prevented me from applying to Thacher before my junior year. I regret that he made a permanent shift from teaching to full-time school administration so that we would not have to share a class. I felt guilty that the situation forced an exemplary teacher to make that choice. But I loved being at Thacher. It was the first school I ever attended that did not tolerate social cliques and bullying. In my radar-alert experience, kids there were not singled out or shamed. The faculty and students accepted and honored each boy for whatever talents he had. I have remained in close touch with Thacher through the forty-eight years since it became coeducational, and I am glad to report that the school still emphasizes these qualities today.

Before those two years, I had no abiding friends among my peers. I was a loner and deeply lonely. I did have one or two friends with whom I could spend time occasionally, but no one my age with whom I could speak to in a crisis or feel genuinely at ease. My acceptance by my classmates at Thacher precipitated a significant change of character. When I was younger, others described me as a classic introvert, but this new sensation of being accepted, acknowledged, and even liked for my unusual personality traits was transformative. I began the slow process of change into what most people now identify as extroversion. I believe I balance both sides: I am nourished as much by time on my own as by being with others.

The single most important friend in those formative years was Andreas (Andy) Rossmann. My parents correctly assessed my loneliness and arranged for us to host a German exchange student for ten months beginning the summer before my senior year. Within hours after Andy arrived at the ranch in early August 1968, we became fast friends. We lived together there and on campus at Thacher until after we graduated the following June. Motivation to introduce Andy to American folklore resulted in our attending the square dance where I first met Helene. He was a notable boy. Andy had an open and engaging excitement about all he experienced and was interested in discussing anything. He enjoyed other human beings and made light of his discomfort, adapting with grace to any challenge. All these traits helped me let go of long-held insecurities and more fully embrace life as I found it. Andy and I have continued to communicate and support one another through many episodes in our lives. He is truly my brother of the heart and remains one of my closest friends. I now count myself fortunate to have many good friends in the United States, India, and elsewhere who stimulate and sustain me, but he was my first.

My courses at Thacher were difficult and demanding. I was never a good student there but gained many skills that remain vital to me today. One of those was learning to compose and write well. I had always envisioned myself as a writer, perhaps a poet. Thacher's classes and informal tutoring helped me sharpen my tools so that when I went to college, I excelled at writing top-grade essays.

The most formative course I took at Thacher was a yearlong seminar in African American history and literature taught by the school's first Black teacher, David Lawyer. Mr. Lawyer demanded we read a wide variety of books, from the writings of Frederick Douglass, Martin Luther King, and Eldridge Cleaver to documents from the John Birch Society, Ku Klux Klan and many other sources. He encouraged us to recognize that each author wrote what they firmly believed was the truth. He urged us not to disregard any belief as categorically wrong just because it initially offended us. That class opened my mind to the realization that nothing is truly black and white. All is grey. Even though I have developed opinions based upon my own perceptions, I try to remember that the beliefs of most others, except for a few outrageous zealots, are valid in context. David Lawyer taught me to strive to be nonjudgmental and helped me open myself to another's way of thinking even though it might challenge everything I have previously believed. The essence of that acceptance underlies my continual efforts to sublimate my inherited western, Christianized attitudes and opinions to truly listen to and witness the non-Christian people I meet in India. In many ways, that ground-breaking class paved the way for my ruthless soul-searching questions illuminated in the following chapter.

***

Even as a young girl, my sister Ruth Huyler Glass refused to be boxed into the traditional American mold of the subservient woman. To me, Ruth was the perfect blend of tomboy energy (she was as athletic and capable as any boy I knew), high intelligence, and feminine warmth and intuition. Ruth's fierceness when challenged and determination to stand up to any man who attempted to stereotype or belittle her made her a role model. She helped me more fully understand the true meaning of the Sanskrit word *shakti*, or pure feminine power. An elementary teacher early in her career, Ruth soon headed a succession of independent K-8 schools. I was thrilled when she invited me repeatedly to be a guest teacher at each of those schools. Ruth always ran a tight school where each member—faculty, staff, and student—felt seen and valued for their own strengths and abilities. I taught the students in each grade about the perspectives and personalities of South Asians. The questions and perceptions of those diverse American children gave me new insights into the people of India.

My brother John was the eldest sibling, with six years difference between us. When I was a child, he often sided with Dad and could be a bully. However, when John broke away from home and went to Princeton University, he truly became his own man. Unlike our father, who had fought in the war and continued to champion aggressive masculine ideals, John recognized that he was at heart a pacifist. However, he attended Princeton on a full NROTC scholarship and was contractually bound to serve as a naval officer for five years after his graduation. After two unhappy years, the US Navy granted John an honorable discharge as a conscientious objector, one of the few officers allowed this privilege during the Vietnam War. Much to my parents' dismay, John chose to begin a lifetime career as a non-violent activist. Professionally, he became a mediator on environmental issues between communities, businesses, and governments. As practicing Quakers, he and his wife DeAnne Butterfield still work continuously to advocate peace in an increasingly militarized world. Their work inspires me. I am aware that John perpetuates the legacy of our great-grandparents, Arthur and Mattie Noble, in their determination to help create an even-tempered, less volatile, egalitarian existence.

We three siblings have an unusual relationship. Although we are each different, we share many similarities in our careers and life choices. We are devoted to our spouses and families. We each attempt to live in service to humanity. We have high ideals that we strive to honor. Our parents have both died—and yet in their passing, we have found not discord, but harmony. We genuinely enjoy one another's company. Each in our way, we embody our heritage. I had issues growing up with my siblings, parents, and others in my community, but these issues served to form and strengthen me.

* * *

"This is my gigolo, Steve Huyler." Beatrice Wood's introduction tickled me. I was eighteen years old and beginning a close friendship that lasted twenty-eight years. Her comment was intended to shock a bevy of gushing little old ladies on the main street of downtown Ojai. Her provocative humor punctuated my days. At seventy-seven, Beatrice was my new employer and before long became a significant mentor. I'd always known her. Her home was only a few hundred yards from The Thacher School gates, and I passed it daily. But, although she had frequently flirted with my grandfather before I was born, I do not think she knew who I was until I asked her for a job. During the summer after my first year in college, I was living at home alone while my parents were at our ranch in

Wyoming, and Beatrice hired me as her gardener and to clean her pottery studio and help prepare her clay. At that time, she was recognized as one of the finest ceramic artists in North America. Our relationship crystalized my profession. Among many other things, Beatrice introduced me to India.

I was mesmerized during those first months working for this captivating raconteur. I spent hours in rapt attention as she told me stories of growing up in New York and Paris and later helping to found the Dada Movement with her lover Marcel Duchamp. Books and films about Beatrice Wood abound. The unique luster glazes on her delicate vessels, achieved by reduction firing, are alchemical, reminiscent of ancient Egyptian, Greek, and Roman glass. Fine art museums and collections display her masterpieces worldwide.

Beatrice is equally as famous for her outrageous wit as for her art. But my relationship with her was deeply personal. She was a close friend and confidante for many years. Beatrice selflessly guided me to hone my talents and choose my career. Without her, I would have been someone else. Her humor was contagious. She loved to challenge preconceptions, turning expectations upside down. In this way, her life was pure Dada. But it was her unusual intelligence, her broad-minded education, and her insightful wisdom that transformed my life.

We were both plagued by a similar issue: in her teenage years, Beatrice had suffered from a neck injury from which she never recovered. Like me, she was in almost constant pain. At times, her body would hardly function—and yet she too found ways to work through her affliction. Beatrice attributed much of her abundant creativity to this challenge. In her mid-nineties, she commented: "The great artist can only be great if he suffers—because I think it's getting away from our agony that makes us want to produce, to create, to say something. We become very self-absorbed in our life because we usually do work in solitude." My own neck injury and consequent pain made me empathize with hers.

Beatrice claimed that her life had changed when, in 1962, Kamaladevi Chattopadhyay, the right hand of Gandhi and progenitor of India's crafts movement, invited her to exhibit her most outstanding pieces in galleries and museums spanning the Republic of India. Beatrice felt empathy with Indian people and cultures and fell in love with their craftsmanship. As a mark of her inward change, the garments she wore from then until she died were artfully wrapped silk saris—even when throwing vessels on her potter's wheel. Beatrice's passion for Indian arts was sealed through a second long trip through that country in 1966 as a representative of the U.S. government lecturing on the current state of American crafts.

By the time I began working for her, I had become disaffected with my long-held plan to document Native American art. I still found the subject inspirational, but I'd noticed how popular it had become with both scholars and hippies. Throughout my life, I instinctively veered away from any fads. I explained my passion for folk arts and crafts to Beatrice and that I was looking for a relatively undocumented region in which to work. It might be anywhere in the world: perhaps Africa, South America, or Southeast Asia. Beatrice suggested that I focus on India, insisting that the scope for documentation there was wide open. Indian craftsmanship and rural arts are remarkably diverse, among the finest in the world, and, through millennia of pan-Asian trade, have left an indelible imprint on western aesthetic development. She persuaded me that relatively little comprehensive scholarship existed about them (which was of course true at the time). She showed me examples in her extensive collection and the few books available and then invited me to accompany her on her third trip to India in 1971.

Beatrice took my childhood fascination with handmade tools and crafts and ritual arts and deepened my understanding of their relevance. She helped me comprehend a Dada approach—that the definitions of critics regarding what is or isn't art are artificial. She convinced me that anything that has meaning to the person who creates or uses it is worthy of being considered art. We are often blind to the beauty of the simple objects that surround us. Beatrice gave me a mission: to see, witness, and record the material cultures of India—what individuals make and use in their daily and seasonal lives. I have traveled the length and breadth of India many times pursuing that goal. My life's purpose has been precisely that, embellished over the decades to include the personal stories and insights of the many Indian women and men I have met.

* * *

As I navigate my seventies, I've made peace with my life, all of it, and it has no further power over me. The training I received in my childhood of sense of family and personal commitment, of ideals of honesty, directness, and flexibility became the foundation of my life. As best I can, I try to love and honor the other without judgment, whoever she or he might be, and to listen and quietly observe until the other person is comfortable in sharing. When I entered India on my twentieth birthday pedaling an old man's rickshaw, I carried with me a backpack of talents and skills, sensitivities, and strengths that have served me well for fifty-two years.

~ 16 ~
Puzzle

Two decades ago, an American woman I'd met during my first trip in South Asia tracked me down. Sonya was studying dance at Kalakshetra that year. She and her roommate traveled with me for a few days as we visited south Indian temples in early 1972. Sonya's letter astounded me: she stated that I had been the most entitled person she had ever known.

In the years since then, I've tried to unravel that pronouncement. I am a tall, white, fair-haired American male: attributes that for many define entitlement. My genetic composition gives me privileges that most people in the world do not have. I can make choices of where and how to live, of employment and education, of exposure or retreat. Add to that my demographic: where and how I was born and raised, my family history, and the many advantages I was given and still receive. I accepted much of that as my due without recognizing how unusual I was.

Sonya was an inner-city New Yorker whose life, as a young, Jewish woman with a family history of holocaust and immigration, had been constrained. When she knew me, I was a twenty-year-old who had traveled alone across half the world confident that I would be cared for, that I could meet any challenge and overcome any adversity. I appeared fearless and at ease in each environment I entered. For her, those qualities were unfamiliar.

When I finished my first draft of these memoirs two years ago, I was pleased with the experience of remembering, uncovering, and composing them. I expected to work on edits, submit the manuscript to publishers, and release a book in time to celebrate the fiftieth anniversary of my arrival in India in October 1971. My plans were thwarted. We were in the middle of the largest global pandemic in recorded history. Publishers, like other big and small businesses worldwide, were challenged as never before. My agent recommended that I postpone until a time of Covid recovery, when a good contract and better distribution might be more available. And so, I waited.

For me, as for others elsewhere, the lockdown facilitated deep introspection. I reevaluated my life, purpose, choices, and past actions.

During the past two years, I have carved away at my identity, attempting to strip out self-deception.

How has entitlement blinded me from the truth? I have carefully reviewed all my previous chapters, stories, and statements, altering some to fit my new awareness and removing others that are no longer appropriate. My memoirs are written sequentially, as they occurred. They reflect my mindset of the period in which they apply, but I now have caveats that must be revealed.

Like many other foreigners who successfully adapt to India, I made a choice to romanticize, or as Helene would say: "to look at India with rose-colored glasses." For years, I firmly denied her charge, maintaining that mine was the glass half-full. I countered that although I was aware of India's poverty and inequalities, I chose to champion her strengths and achievements. Now, in reflection, I wonder....

India's very complexity has spawned a plethora of academic treatises, many of which are only partially based in reality. Scholars arrive with preconceived theories and uncover data and "proof" to substantiate their premises, some of which directly contradict my own experiences. In my determination to right the wrongs and help heal the rifts of communication that have existed for generations between South Asia and the rest of the world, have I unwittingly overcompensated? Have my own entitled assumptions blinded me from concurrent truths? How can I unpack that crate?

I have attempted to absorb India unfiltered, to be a spokesperson through my books, lectures, and exhibitions for the individuals I have met, conveying their characters, perceptions, and worldviews. I've used their art and creativity as mediums for understanding deeper values, concepts, traditions, and innovations. Have I missed the forest for the trees?

As I choose to focus on one woman painting a kolam and describe her process and what it means to her family and society, I edit out her larger story. Who is she as a daughter, wife, mother, or grandmother? In her poor economy, does she perhaps forgo her own nutritional needs to feed her child? How does her family treat her? Is she truly content, or is her husband or father-in-law violent, her mother-in-law unkind? Beyond her art and its meaning, what are her personal aspirations? What does she hope for and/or sacrifice in order to be the person she is right now? By focusing on one or two aspects of her story, do I misrepresent her?

I made the decision half a century ago to create a profession of conducting cross-cultural surveys of India. By nature, this choice limits the depth with which I can record any individual or household. I'm told that my pan-Indian overviews have brought insights and awareness to many previously unrecorded aspects of South Asian culture. I've uncovered and documented styles of art unknown by either scholars or the public. My published surveys have drawn ground-breaking attention to some of the nation's cultural commonalities and exceptions.

But has this process blinded me to inequities, injustices, or human frailties that should have been brought to light? How much of my perception comes from my own unconscious assumptions of my right to be where I am, doing what I'm doing, breaking through ironclad societal barriers that have existed for centuries? Why do I think I have that right? As I've written, I always try to gain permission and honor stated restrictions and limitations. I know that I naturally put people at ease in what might otherwise be obtuse circumstances. I've been invited to participate in situations that no outsiders have ever witnessed, and I've often been encouraged to return. Can I possibly know the truth of how I am perceived? Is my feeling of acceptance at least partially based upon my entitlement?

Indians are highly hospitable to strangers and those beyond the range of their experience. As a foreigner, and particularly as an American, I am repeatedly told that my society is casteless. I know from a lifetime of experience that that statement is patently untrue. Of course, America has its own form of caste system – just more hidden and less blatant than in South Asia or in other traditional societies globally. Yet within India's highly regimented societies and defined boundaries of behavior and custom, my place in the social hierarchy is indeterminable. In the 1970s and '80s, I was frequently the only Caucasian a community had ever seen in recent history: for many, a total anomaly, an unknown. For others, British overlords were their most recent experience. Ancient Indian epics and religious tracts prioritize fair skin, and white imperial rulers capitalized on this cultural preference. As a white-skinned person, I am treated deferentially. I represent a continent that, like India, is far from England, and also successfully fought the British to create its own new identity. Educated Indians know that I was born and raised in the richest and currently the most powerful nation on earth, the home of many successful Indian immigrants. How does that affect my inclusion?

The sense of uniqueness I experienced in the last century no longer exists for me in India. Pervasive contemporary technology, widespread media, improved education, and literacy mean that virtually everyone is familiar with American culture, at least to some degree. I may still be the only foreigner to ever visit a few remote villages, but I am no longer the unknown. I feel sure that the friendships I've built in India are real, based on true human emotions and acceptance. But how much have initial impressions been generated through my tendency to filter out that which is uncomfortable?

Certainly, a large portion of entitlement is due to male hubris, the manipulation and misuse of power. As I've traveled, I've realized that this condition is a predominant characteristic of my gender everywhere, in each region of the world. Some of it may be genetic: male primates tend to dominate females of their species. But most male hubris is a conditioned, learned behavior from our earliest steps. We are taught to exert our power over individuals who are less able to defend themselves. Powerful men support one another in this suppression, sometimes overtly, often unconsciously. Of course, exceptions exist as they do in any global hypothesis. Nevertheless, most men, whether in the Americas or Europe, Africa, Asia, or Australia, assume airs of competence and superiority in front of women. We strut our stuff. How many times have I been at a table or in a meeting where either my expressed opinion or story, or that of my male companions is louder, stronger, and more insistent than whatever the women in the room want to say? I consciously try to subdue that trajectory, but it is an inbred habit.

Thirty-seven years ago, I joined a men's therapy group near my home in mid-coast Maine. Our conversations and revelations were facilitated by two strong women therapists who continuously challenged our preconceptions and called us out on behaviors, some of which they felt were unwittingly sexist. Their influence affected me immensely, teaching me to be far more sensitive to Helene and other women in my life. But so did my growing friendship with the other men in the group. Eight years later, several of us men decided that the facilitation was no longer necessary. We branched out on our own, meeting weekly for twelve years, and every two weeks since then. Our membership has changed. Four of us original participants remain while we've added in four others who have been part of our discussion group for more than two decades. Every week, each of us talks about his deepest feelings, his current story, and his insights, while encouraging honest feedback. We accept challenges when the others do not believe we are being honest with ourselves, or with them, or acting in our best interests. I cannot fully express how much I have learned in this intense but loving brotherhood. We are supported by our female partners because they realize how much more thoughtful we have become as men because of this participation. Many other women have acknowledged over the years how rare this kind of relationship is for most men and how much they wish other males could find similar groups to join.

Two years ago, during the pandemic, Helene and I were visited by a female friend who runs a non-profit to aid marginalized villagers in rural India. Over two decades, Aarti had witnessed how much I benefit from being a part of my men's group. She asked if I would be willing to help coach a selection of young Indian men on what it means to be male in the twenty-first century. I've known most of these eight young men, aged sixteen to twenty-two, since they were born. They regard me as their uncle. We met weekly online for over a year. My purpose was to create for them an environment of safety and trust so that they would feel able to ask me anything and talk about whatever concerned them, much as my own group has encouraged and supported me. To begin with, I was unsure of the parameters of our conversations. Even though I knew them well, I'd never discussed these more serious topics with them. But within a short while, I discovered that they longed to learn whatever they could. No topics were barred.

One of the subjects that most interested them was how to sustain a good relationship with a woman. None of them had even dated, much less had any prospects yet of marriage. But each of them knew what it was like to be bullied by other men, to feel less than others, and shamed by the actions or disregard of others. They knew what it felt like to be unseen and unheard. I explained to them the value of learning to listen. Why would they possibly want to mimic their own tormentors by bullying or intimidating the very person with whom they intended to spend their lives? Could they put aside their learned behavior of dominating a conversation, demanding that their future wives unhesitatingly acquiesce to their wishes? If, instead, they could draw these women out, asking them what they thought and wanted, supporting them emotionally, I believe that their relationships would be greatly improved, much as my own marriage has been enhanced by learning to listen to Helene.

To my delight, I discovered that these eight men responded in unexpected ways. Over the next weeks and months, they showed not only that they understood, but their habits began to change through this realization. In a subsequent meeting at which the community's young men and women discussed their future, one of the members of my online class was reported as stopping himself in the middle of a long story, stating that he had just realized that he was dominating the dialog. He vowed to be silent so that the women present could speak their own opinions, acknowledging the value of women's voices. Males in his region have subordinated women for centuries in ways not dissimilar to men throughout the world. Change, however slowly, can occur. I still meet online every two weeks with these eight young men. They have formed their own men's group, but I serve as an elder friend who tries to answer questions they have about life and be supportive. Although on opposite sides of the world, we sustain a mutually supportive brotherhood.

The #Me-Too movement opened my eyes to deeper aspects of sexual depredation. In the past twenty months, I have participated closely in an investigation into sexual abuse in my natal community. I have spoken out as a survivor, finding clarity and healing in owning my history. I support the organization and their process of uncovering hidden truths and finding solutions to protect potential victims in the future. Most fellow survivors are women, many still suffering from the trauma of their more recent experiences. As a senior, my years of therapy and decades of support from my men's group and others have healed my psychological wounds effectively. Recognizing this trajectory, the investigators asked me to speak in confidence to other survivors who were, at that time, unwilling to come forward. That process of listening and affirming their stories has further torn apart my complacency as a male. It has underscored my awareness of the ways in which we males groom the vulnerable to our own ends, whether sexual, racial, or any of a myriad of powerplays. More than ever, I try to distance myself from those learned traits, but the efforts require constant vigilance.

Although I have long championed women's equality and choice, I recognize my own unconscious part in devaluing women. As an American male, I make enabling choices that reinforce the polarized treatment of the sexes. Without thinking, I accept preferential treatment in social and business situations, often unaware that by condoning these actions I deny women an equal opportunity.

Endemic racism is fueled by the same assumptions and acceptance. George Floyd's brutal murder in 2020 and the rapidly developing Black Lives Matter movement riveted my attention. I had been reading books about racism in America intently since high school, but now increased my focus on the ways in which we whites support its continuation. Even though I have believed for most of my life that I am not racist, that all human beings deserve equal rights, my choices of how and where I live underline a form of separatism. I reside in a coastal community in Maine with almost no residents of color within a two-hour driving radius. Even though

I made this choice because of the natural beauty of our surroundings, I feel at ease in the social environment of my town. I justify our decision by stating that I have worked closely for half a century with South Asians who identify themselves as brown, often having no contact with other Caucasians for weeks or months at a time. These Indians are among my closest friends. How can I be racist? But as I've dissected my choices and truly tried to fathom the depths of entitlement, I recognize that my decision to live most of each year in Maine is at least partly influenced by the relative ease with which I can navigate my life in this all-white society. And racism toward indigenous inhabitants remains prevalent in this state, perpetuated by denial and inactivity. In America's northeast, as throughout the United States, housing, employment, and education are governed by self-serving whites through insidiously subtle, but damaging regulations. Many of us vote for change, but improvements are hard-earned and rare. Extensive travel and immersed experiences in regions other than my own have brought an awareness that virtually all human beings, regardless of their culture, have prejudices in one form or another: racist, sexist, and much else besides. I observe the same kind of strategizing and prioritizing in South, West, and East Asia, Europe, and South America.

So much of it is power politics: posturing and positioning ourselves, whoever we might be, to take advantages at another individual's expense. But currently we Americans lead the pack. Manifest Destiny, with all its baggage, was a primary motivation in settling North America. We justified our right to destroy and exploit indigenous civilizations for our own ends and we introduced an enslaved labor force dependent upon devaluing human lives. Although changes have been made, we white Americans continue to exploit our perceived superiority. This same assumed privilege has enabled the rapid destruction of our earth's natural resources resulting in the current disaster of global warming.

Going forward, I only know that I cannot know. I feel my life cracking open, my assuredness challenged, my assumptions have all become questions. I am male and still celebrate many of my gender's characteristics. But I vow to continue chipping away at my entitlement and to try not to not obscure reality or manipulate others to my own ends. As I sum up half a century's work in and with India, I realize that the future is unknown. I have no answers, but I find the ongoing process of uncovering the truth fascinating, and as demanding as it is difficult.

~ 17 ~
Gratitude

It is morning. I am seated on a stone slab set into a low rock wall in my garden in Camden, Maine. I gaze out at the shadows of sparse rose bushes on sun-gleaming snow. Nuthatches chirp in staccato while a church bell tolls the hour from the middle of town. Immersed in meditation, I repeat a daily routine adopted more than thirty years ago. I am simply present, as much as possible, wherever I am, preferably in nature, noticing the details of my surroundings. Depending upon season and locale, it could be wind rustling through the leaves and branches of a tree, or dewdrops sparkling on a newly budded rose, or a V of geese flying overhead—any of a myriad of possibilities, always changing. Noticing, watching, listening, quieting my mind—these are the essential qualities. This practice grounds me and opens my mind and spirit to the new.

I am a blend of East and West—mostly West, and undeniably American, genetically, culturally, and emotionally—but molded through my fifty-two-year relationship with India. India enters my daily thoughts, my responses, beliefs, and actions. Often, I write immediately after meditating; I always have, letting the words pour out fully formed within my unconscious. Or I wake up in the middle of the night with whole sentences and full stories or concepts ready to be inscribed.

Without question, I draw upon my strong Christian heritage, but my beliefs are also informed by my experiences of day-to-day Hinduism. Years of immersing myself in pujas, rituals, prayers, and festivals in India have altered and enhanced my perceptions. For me, all aspects of existence are sacred. Nothing is devoid of spirit. I attempt to honor that awareness in every part of my life. For decades, I have daily poured my prayers into our garden, trying to notice, respect, and celebrate individual elements—trees, rocks, bushes, flowering plants, grasses, birds, and animals—while Helene and I act as stewards for our property. Influenced by India, I also view my community and my environment as sacred: an extension of me, as I am of it. If they are indeed spiritual entities, how can I consciously condone anything that would damage them? I meditate to extend my awareness to my county, state, country, continent, and, indeed, our globe and beyond. My blend of beliefs is my own, positively influenced by mentors and others I have met, but also unique. I try never to proselytize.

These attitudes, insights, and perceptions are simply mine—and each other person is entitled to theirs. I have no right to judge them.

In the late nineties, Karen Lukas traded with me the painting of a sacred and healing space, my meditation room, in return for participating in my *Painted Prayers Tour*. We both believe that we got the best of that deal. Ivan Stancioff, a member of my men's group, constructed the niches that hold treasures that, for me, are receptacles of spirit. Daily, I move from the garden into this room, where I focus my attention on specific goals. Aside from honoring images of Ganesha, Lakshmi, and Durga, among others, my central shrine holds a cross, a miniature painting of Mary, a framed print of Saint Francis, and a wooden votive sculpture given to me by the priests of my favorite tree shrine in Kerala. Onto the walls of this large niche, I've pasted photographs of many of my mentors, including my father and mother, my grandmothers, Helene, Beatrice Wood, Sunithi Narayan, Karen, and all of the women I featured as *Daughters of India*. My prayers include opening my mind to all that I have learned and can still learn from them and others: my siblings and their families and many friends worldwide. Often, I've meditated there just before I write. After climbing the stairs to my office, the words just flow onto the page.

And so, this book has been a series of reflections on a long life closely involved with India. Of course, it is much more than that. By focusing on my affiliation with South Asia, I have edited out numerous aspects of my many formative experiences elsewhere, especially in the United States. As I've written about close friendships in

India, I have chosen not to feature supportive and life-changing relationships in the West. For these memoirs, most of those individuals will remain unmentioned. By intention, I try to acknowledge verbally those I care about, and hope that these individuals know of my affection and appreciation.

I had never expected to write my memoir. Friends and colleagues have encouraged it for years, but until just before I began it three months into the Covid pandemic, the concept did not interest me. Four years ago, an extraordinary man befriended me. Dr. Edward C. Crowther had been a noted Anglican bishop who had been jailed in 1965 and then deported for his critical stance against apartheid in his South African diocese. Years later, he taught and practiced Jungian psychology in Santa Barbara, California, where we met. More than any other individual, Edward encouraged me to write these memoirs, believing that these experiences should be shared with others. Although he died just sixteen months after we met, our many deep conversations were motivational.

Two other friends, Charlie and Christine Chamberlain, guided this creation. We had become good friends while spending five weeks traveling together in India six years ago. The Chamberlains wrote and designed biographies upon commission for a variety of clients. Their encouragement and advice were timely and helpful. Charlie too passed away two years ago and I feel his loss deeply.

Ongoing meetings with my men's group ground me. Ivan Stancioff, Rich Stuart, Bill Long, Michael Johnson, John Pincince, Frank Mundo, and Jeff Powell always challenge me and keep me from becoming complacent. These seven brothers have supported and improved my life, each in his own distinct way. Jeff Powell is someone with whom I discuss all that interests us. We never tire of bouncing ideas off one another and following endless rabbit holes of discovery and insight. Jeff and I met through examining perceptions of the sacred aspects of nature. After decades of friendship, we planned a trip together in India nine years ago in which I intended to share with him personal perceptions of the ways in which the Divine is honored there. Instead, at the last minute, Jeff needed open-heart surgery. As the trip was booked and prepaid, I invited another of my men's group to join me. Frank Mundo had almost no preparation before we flew together to South India. His open and appreciative nature blended with my immersion in the culture, resulting in the finest trip I had yet experienced. India genuinely transfigured Frank, and witnessing that process was humbling and informative. Through him, I understand India in new and enlightening ways.

Jeff was finally strong enough last year to travel with me through India. I created a new itinerary focused on heart healing. I was able to share with him many of the friendships and warm experiences that always have characterized much of how I view India. Daily throughout our six weeks together, I witnessed him open and transform. India continues to teach me lessons in perception.

Many others have encouraged the unfolding process of writing about my life. I contemplate a subject long before I begin typing, and then, when I am ready, compose a draft that is reasonably close to the final published version. For me, writing is pleasurable. I rarely worry about what I'm going to say—instead, I just let it spill out when it is ready. I edit each day as I go along, and often read or show that day's production to Helene for her input. But when I have finished a chapter, I understand it better when I can read it aloud to someone else. That is when the bumps are smoothed. Just after its composition, I have read aloud each chapter of every book I have written to two Maine friends, Becca Swan and Jay Leach. Their feedback and encouragement aid me in seeing the whole picture. Besides Helene, three others also have listened patiently to the full book as I find comma blunders, correct redundancies, and improve sentence structure: Jeff and Frank and Katrina Underhill. They have assisted me in honing the text. Upon request, I have sent individual chapters to several other friends for their comments. Pam Deuel Meyer, whose own work in Nepal is symbiotic with mine in India, was particularly insightful. Joan Phaup, Christine Chamberlain, Karen Lukas, and Elizabeth Garber have each helped me edit out parts that did not best serve the book. And each of my publications has been nurtured through the encouragement and advice of my friend and muse, Turkish-American author Alev Croutier.

    The book is long, but in many cases it only skims the surface of my experiences. I realized early on that I would have to write *Encyclopedia Stephennica* if I wanted to cover it all. Instead, I have loved the jigsaw puzzle of putting it all together to convey just enough story and experience of India's unique flavors to inform the reader. I attempt to balance pleasure with pain, animation with tranquility, anguish with joy, and despair with love. India has given me all that and so much more. These chapters portray many individuals who have shared their lives with me willingly, often giving me virtually all they had. I have named them and shared some of their stories as mine have unfolded. Other South Asian friends could not be named, their many kindnesses understood, their stories waiting to be told in person. I hope that they, too, know of my gratitude.

In my seventh decade, the vital longevity of my primary mentor, Beatrice Wood, often fills my thoughts. In 1981, when that artist was already eighty-eight, two leading American ceramics dealers, Garth Clark and Mark Del Vecchio, persuaded her to create new artworks for them. They displayed the results in a groundbreaking exhibition at the Garth Clark Gallery in Los Angeles. From that moment on Beatrice began to blossom, producing the finest art of her life. Garth stated: "I would say that Beatrice's nineties were the most exploratory period of her work, the most avant-garde and the most adventurous." What a model for those of us who worry about aging!

When Beatrice was ninety-four, she commented: "I get mad because everyone who comes here says: 'Are you still working?' Of course, I am!—and I will work until I'm not able to. ...I love to work, and I'm always full of ideas. ...I tell you what I've noticed: [my creativity] bubbles when I get up, and I do things—and then I'm finished, and I think: 'Goodness, I haven't an idea in my mind!' and then [I'm quiet] and up it goes again. This is the way I think life is—in rhythms... There's this duality in living where all is not on a high peak, and the fact that we're not helps us appreciate what a high peak is. Because if we were always on top, or if there was always daylight, we wouldn't know how wonderful the day is. It's the fact that there's night; it's the fact that there's suffering, all this [helps us] appreciate what life is like when it's free of its opposite."

For her 103rd birthday, I gave Beatrice a tribal comb from Borneo decorated with stick figures. She wrote that the object thrilled her, and her letter included drawings of a chalice she intended to make adorned with similar figures. It arrived three months later and became one of the most important treasures in our collection. When she died a few days after her 105th birthday, Beatrice had an unopened kiln of beautiful lusterware ready to be displayed. She had honored her dream to work until she dropped. We were bequeathed the comb after she died, and it stands next to her chalice as a reminder of the creative symbiosis with folk art she expressed.

Beatrice Wood was like her ceramics: lustrous, lit ineffably within by often surprising, always entrancing color, blending elegance and form with infectious humor. She gifted me with real friendship and guidance throughout her final twenty-eight years. Unfailingly self-effacing, never complacent, or entitled, she fully embraced life for more than a century.

Who knows how much longer I will live? I pray that I can remain as vital throughout my days as she, discovering new ways to express myself, new projects, and new creativities in this decade and, God willing, in my eighties and perhaps nineties. Beatrice's mentorship certainly nudges me forward. Helene's and my ongoing, ever-unfolding relationship enrich each day. Two years ago, we celebrated half a century of a loving marriage. What could be better?

From my first day in India, I have immersed myself: open, willing, inspired, and transformed. Although frequently challenged, my life has been blessed. I look forward to my next trip, and the ones after that....

Glossary

adivasi — generic term for the indigenous people of India, with largely tribal social structure and separate customs as well as belief systems from those of most mainstream Indians.

Ayyanar — God of the physical boundaries of a community in South India, particularly Tamil Nadu.

banyan — a member of the ficus family of trees that spreads its canopy by sending down shoots from its branches, which take root and become new trunks in their own right, allowing the tree to cover a larger area - which allows a single banyan tree to seem like a dense thicket or even a small forest. This tree is associated with the 3rd caste (vaishyas, who are often Vishnu-worshippers), but traditionally has no specific association with spirituality, unlike the peepul tree (see the entry on that in this Glossary).

Bharatanatyam — a form of *natya* (theatrical dance), whose antecedents go back at least to 13th century AD, though possibly as far as the 5th century BC. Originally called "Ekaharya Lasyanga", it focused on romantic themes. Over the centuries, under the changed name of "Dasiattam", the dance came to be associated with temple prostitution, and later, under the name "Sadirattam", with court debauchery -because of which it was banned by the British in 1932. To comply with the ban but ensure the survival of such a beautiful dance tradition, its proponents moved it out of temples and royal courts, launched a drive to get rid of its lasciviousness, created an ethically-Christianised and suitably spiritualised version of the dance, bestowed on it a faux-tradition and, to emphasis the break with the past, renamed it "Bharatanatyam" – the name deriving from 3 syllables "bha" (for *bhaava*, or emotional essence), "ra" (for *raaga*, or melodic framework) and "ta" (for *taala*, or rhythmic pattern). Today, the *natya* focuses on sacred dances performed for the glorification of the Divine and to convey epic stories and ethics.

bhejjuni – priestess for the Dongria people.

bidri — blackened steel etched with designs and inlaid with silver, brass, or gold.

biryani — the single most-ordered dish on Indian online food ordering and delivery services, and probably the most popular dish overall in India, the name is a corruption of the Farsi (Persian) " "birinj biriyan", which means, literally, "rice prepared in the biriyan way". In its most famous form, biriyani was developed in the Muslim capitals of the Deccan (central India) and consists of meat, rice, vegetables, and spices. However, since a significant proportion of India's richest people are vegetarians, entirely vegetarian versions of biryani are also available, nowadays.

brahmin — the priestly caste, the highest of the four main varnas or castes of traditional Hindu society. However, following the introduction of Western-style education from the 1830s, brahmins nowadays have taken their place in most modern professions.

Carnatic – peninsular south India between the Eastern Ghats and the Bay of Bengal, composed of four states: Andhra Pradesh, Karnataka, Kerala, and Tamilnadu.

casuarina — a native tree of Australia with soft needles, also often known as she-oak, Australian pine, or native pine.

chai — the common word in all Indian languages and dialects for tea. Although chai usually contains milk and sugar, its preparation may or may not include spices.

charpai — literally translated as 'four legs', it usually refers to a simple cot, strung with a webbing made of cloth or reed – or, earlier in history, of jute.

Chandi — the Divine Feminine in her form as the Destroyer of Evil (Bhagavati, Chamundi, and Kali).

chowkidar — guard

darshan — the moment in Hindu devotion of seeing and being seen by the Divine.

dalit — in the 1970s, the name chosen by those people for themselves who, before Indian Independence, were referred to as 'Outcaste' or 'Untouchable', and whom Gandhi had renamed 'Harijan', or children of God – so 'Harijan' was a name rejected by these communities from the 1970s.

Dhartanu— the Earth Goddess for the Dongria people

dhoti — a long, unstitched, flatwoven piece of cloth that is draped around the waist, till the remaining top end is then tucked into the waistband thus created by it.

dosa — a flat crepe most often composed of batter of fermented rice and lentil flours.

Durga — in some Indian traditions, one of the many gods in the Hindu pantheon; but, in other traditions, the Supreme Goddess, embodying the collective energy (shakti) of all the gods, and providing each of them with their inner power. Often depicted as the Divine Warrior, riding a lion or tiger, killing asuras (representatives of evil) who were in reality the original or native rulers of India.

ghat — translated as "step" but also used to describe a range of coastal mountains.

ghee — milk from a cow churned into butter, then reduced and clarified over slow heat; one of its many advantages is that it does not require refrigeration.

gurukula — traditional system of education whereby a teacher, or guru, personally hosted in his home a group of disciples or students, and instructed them as much by his words as his life.

Holi — A joyous celebration of Spring, primarily observed in central and north India, in which participants either rub powdered dyes or spray each other with colored waters. One of its many stories of origin refers to Radha, beloved of the blue-skinned Hindu God Krishna, who rubs her own face with dye in order to make the deity less self-conscious.

idli — a steamed savory rice cake

jali — lattice often used as visual screens and elements of architectural design in north India.

kolam — ephemeral diagrams drawn with rice flour or ground stone powder on the ground outside the front doors of homes in south Indian most commonly as a sign of welcome and/or as a symbol to prevent evil from entering the household.

khadi — handwoven, handspun cloth, primarily cotton; popularized in the early 20th century by Mohandas K Gandhi as a symbol of indigenous resistance to British rule.

kurta — loose-fitting tunic

Lakshmi — Hindu Goddess of Abundance and Prosperity, wife of Vishnu, often shown seated on a lotus.

Linga — the aniconic image of the primary Hindu God Shiva most commonly found in worship in his temples. Many scholarly treatises refer to the Linga's phallic form. Many Hindus find that description offensive, though other Hindus trace that prudishness to Victorian and post-Victorian influence from British times, rather than the traditional view which they claim dealt with sexuality in a totally different way as compared to the Victorians.

mandala — a circular, concentric diagram often used as a symbol to focus on for meditation.

masjid — mosque

maushi or mausi — aunt

mitti — earth, dirt, mud, and clay

naga — cobra. The species is considered semi-divine. Strong and handsome, nagas are capable of maleficence or beneficence, and of assuming either fully human or fully serpentine form. Nagas are children of Kadru, the granddaughter of the creator God, Brahma, and their birth is celebrated in the Naga-Panchami festival in the month of Shravana (July–August). Ananta Shesha or Adishesha, is the naga who supports the God, Narayana (Vishnu) as he lies on the cosmic ocean and on whom rests the whole of the created world; Vasuki is the naga who was used by gods and demons as a rope to churn the cosmic ocean of milk from which emerged several treasures and indeed the elixir of immortality but also a mortal poison, Halahala, which was entirely drunk by Lord Shiva to save the universe. Brahma banished nagas to the lower world when they became too populous on earth, though their underground kingdom is thought to be filled with resplendent palaces, beautifully ornamented with precious gems where they guard unimaginable treasures. Female nagas (naginis or nagis) are thought to be serpent princesses of striking beauty. The royal dynasties of Manipur in northeastern India, and of the Pallavas in southern India, claimed their origin in the union of a human being and a nagi. Worship of the naga is associated with many different Hindu deities, while stone images of nagas are common symbols of good health and fertility in shrines mostly in eastern and southern India.

peepul — a tree of the ficus (fig) family, considered sacred because it sheds its leaves but seems almost eternal (it has some of the longest-surviving trees on earth) and therefore is associated with eternity and spirituality. For example, the Buddha is considered to have received enlightenment while meditating under one of these. Note that this tree often gets confused with the banyan tree (see the entry on that in this Glossary).

pallu — the decorative end piece of a sari that may be worn over the head as a scarf.

pichwai — religious painting on cloth usually associated with worship of either the Hindu God Rama or Krishna.

puja — the sacred ceremonies of Hindu worship; often a word synonymous with ritual prayers

Rajput — members of a large patrilineal clan in western India who pride themselves in their descent from warriors. They comprise a large multi-component cluster of castes, kin bodies, and local groups.

ras lila – The circular dance in which the God Krishna dances with Radha and the cow maidens. It serves as a primary symbol of Bhakti, or Divine Love.

sitar — north Indian stringed instrument

sari — a wrapped and draped garment commonly worn by women throughout India and composed of 4 to 8 meters (4.5 to 9 yards) of cloth. Each region of the subcontinent identifies itself with its own sari colors, patterns, and styles of draping.

shikara — a flat-bottomed wooden boat used as a form of transportation in the waterways of Kashmir.

tabla — a pair of tonal hand drums used to supply rhythmic counterbalance in classical central and north Indian music.

tahsil — a political division of an Indian state; similar to a county

tulasi — Indian basil most often associated with worship of the Hindu God Vishnu. Most Vaishnava families grow tulasi for use in their daily devotions, unless their living conditions prohibit it.

vibhuti — sacred ash created from burnt wood or cow dung and commonly applied to the forehead during worship in a Hindu temple or shrine.

-wala (or, sometimes, -walla) — the suffix denotes a certain range of meanings. For example, it may denote a trade or profession practiced by someone or the ancestors; e.g., the term "chaiwala" refers to someone who makes or sells chai (tea). However, the suffix can also denote a person's origin or what they are associated with; for example, "Dilliwala" refers to someone from Delhi or, colloquially, "Dilli"; but "dilwala" refers to someone who is ruled by his heart and behaves with freedom and enthusiasm. But "-wala" can also denote possession. For example, "gaadiwala" could be used colloquially to refer to someone who owns a gaadi or vehicle. Further, "-wala" is often used informally to refer to a person associated with a particular thing or quality; for example, "khelwala" could be used to refer to a person who is associated with sports or with playfulness.

wallam — a word in Malayalam, the language of Kerala, signifying a flat-hulled wooden boat used for sports, for fishing, or for the transportation of cargo.

zenana — an area of the household or palace dedicated to the safety and seclusion of women.

Index

A
Achamma, software businesswoman, 288
Adivasis (Indian tribal people), 148–149; *see also* Dongria Kondh *and* Kondh
   in Koraput District, 165–166, 168–171, 181–182, 188
   marriage, 171, 184
   protests by, 189
   villages, 160, 170–171, 175–177
Afghanistan, 39–45
African Canvas (Courtney-Clarke), 239
Agra, 58, 114
Ahmedabad, 96–100, 123–125
Allahabad, 222, 223, 301
Ambikapur, 294, 298, 302
Amer Fort, 116
American Museum of Natural History, New York, 272–273, 275–276
Amritsar, 48–50, 112
Andhra Pradesh, 154, 158
Anglo-Kondh war, 177
Appenzeller, Ruth Noble, 355
Arthur M. Sackler Gallery of Art, Washington, DC, 250, 257–258
Arundale, Rukmini Devi, 62–63, 101, 187–188, 196–198, 207–208
Ayyanar (God), 70–71, 198–199, 224, 225

B
Badami, cave temples of, 92–93
Baker, Annie (Ann Huyler Baker, the author's first cousin), 338, 339, 356

Balikondalo, 181, 187, 230–231
Bangladesh, creation of, 66
Baraban, Joe, 238
Beach, Dr. Milo, 250, 257–259, 262, 263
Becherbhai, 97, 98
Bengal, scroll painters in, 328
Berez, David, 304–305, 309, 310
Bharatanatyam (classical South Indian dance), 125, 197, 201, 260
Bharatiya Lok Kala Mandal, Udaipur, Rajasthan 102
Bhubaneshwar, Orissa (now Odisha), 167, 180–181, 202, 230–231
Bidar, Karnataka, 157–158
bidriware, 158
Bidulata ("Maushi"), 235–237, 252–253, 289, 321, 323
Bissam Cuttack, 169
"The Blue City," 243–244
Blue Mosque, 30
Bombay (Mumbai), 96, 127–132, 154, 186, 281–282
Bonda tribe, 170–171, 172–173
Brahmapuri, 241–245
brassware, 158–159
Breach Candy Hospital, 127–128
Brooklyn Museum of Art, New York, 217, 222, 229, 317
Brown, Kathleen, 279, 300, 301–302, 306–307, 310–311, 312, 317, 336
Burton-Paige, Dr. John, 147

C
Calcutta, 105–106, 222, 291
Calico Museum, Ahmedabad, Gujarat, 125
Camden International Film Festival,

Maine, USA, 315
Cappadocia, 32–33
Center for Maine Contemporary Art, 300–301
Central Cottage Industries Emporium (*or* Cottage Industries *or* Cottage Emporium), New Delhi, 112–113, 225
Chamberlain, Charlie and Christine, 386
Chand, 168, 180
Chandi, Goddess, 255–256, 276
Chattopadhyay, Kamaladevi, 54–55, 112–113, 166–167, 225, 368
Chopra, Dr. Deepak, 273–274
Cochin (Kochi), 87
Cohen, Dr. Steven, 147
Connemara, Madras (now Chennai), 67–69
Correa, Charles, 225
Crafts Museum, Delhi (*see* National Crafts Museum)
Crill, Rosemary, 147
Croutier, Alev, 290, 388
Crowther, Dr. Edward C., 386
culture shock, 107–108, 115, 119, 245, 313

D
Dada Movement, 26, 367
Darpana Academy of Performing Arts, 126
darshan (eye-to-eye contact), 83, 270, 271, 327
Daughters of India: Art and Identity (Huyler), 126, 286, 290–292, 308, 310, 327, 385
Delhi, 52–58, 102–105, 112–113, 132–133, 135, 152, 162–163, 202–203, 231–232, 289, 329–330
Devi, Girija, 287
Dhartanu (Earth Goddess), 176, 177
Diwali, festival of light, 242, 248
DKDA (Dongria Kondh Development Agency), 175, 183

Dom (Hindu scheduled caste of weavers, traders, and moneylenders), 177–178
Dongria Kondh. *see also* Adivasis (Indian tribal people), DKDA *and* Kondh
art, 178
villages, 174–176, 177–178, 181–183, 188–189
Donovan, Lyn, 249
Duchamp, Marcel, 367
Duggal Visual Solutions, New York, 300–301, 311
Durga 279, 385

E
East Pakistan/Bangladesh
genocide in, 63–64
immigrants from, 105–106
independence of, 63–64
Elgood, Dr. Heather, 147

F
Festival of India, UK, 212, 231
Festival of India, USA, 217–218, 221–222, 257
Form and Many Forms of Mother Clay exhibition, 218, 228–229, 293
Franklin, Sheila, 221
Freer and Sackler Galleries, Washington, D.C., 335 (*see also* National Museum of Asian Art)
Freer Gallery of Art, Washington, D.C., 257–258 (*see also* National Museum of Asian Art)
From Indian Earth: Four Thousand Years of Terracotta Art exhibition, 217, 224–225

G
Gadaba tribe, 170–171
Gandhi, Indira, 64, 173
Gandhi, Mahatma, 356, 368
Ganesha, 203, 385

Ganges river, 59–60, 177, 210–211, 301, 357
Garber, Elizabeth, 388
Geddes, Dr. Charles, 36, 143, 144
Gifts of Earth: Terracottas and Clay Sculptures of India (Huyler), 187, 234, 239, 240, 290
Glass, Ruth Huyler (the author's sister), 364–365
Goa, 90–92
Golden Temple, Amritsar, 48–50, 112
Gordon, Nick, 278
Göreme, Turkey, 32–33
Gottlieb, Paul, 219, 239, 240
Guglietti, Joseph, 270
Gujarat, 154, 328, 335

H
Hagia Sofia, 30
Harry N. Abrams, 219–221, 239, 248, 249
healing
 rituals, 261
 skills, 338
 traditional, 324–325
Helford, Cornwall, 195, 218
Hicks, James, 276
Holi, festival of colours, 245–246
Houston Museum of Natural Science, 271–272
Huntington, Dr. John and Dr. Susan, 263
Huyler, Coulter (the author's paternal uncle), 103, 355–356
Huyler, Helene Wheeler (the author's wife), 28, 62, 64-66, 106, 109-111, 113-114, 116-117, 118-119, 126-131, 346–347
Huyler, Jack (the author's father), 319–320, 344–345, 347, 348–350, 353, 358
Huyler, John (the author's brother), 365–366
Huyler, Margaret Noble Appenzeller (the author's mother), 286–287, 345–346, 347, 348–350, 352–353
Huyler, Margaret Porter (the author's grandmother), 354
Hyderabad, 158, 185

I
India Adorned: Selections of the Stephen P Huyler Collection exhibition, 310
Indian Heritage exhibition, 212
India Office Library, 143–144
India-Pakistan war, 64, 66
Indira Gandhi National Centre for the Arts, 234
Indo-US Sub-commission on Education and Culture, 222, 228
Istanbul, 29–31

J
Jaba, Bengali chitrakar, 289
Jackson Hole, Wyoming, 224, 345, 346, 348, 351
Jain, Dr. Jyotindra, 124–125, 126, 225–226, 229, 251, 274, 290, 299
Jain-Neubauer, Dr. Jutta, 124–125
Jaipur, Rajasthan, 102, 115–116
Jaisalmer, Rajasthan, 328
Jeypore, Koraput District, Orissa (now Odisha), 168, 170, 173, 179–180
Jodhpur, Rajasthan, 241–245, 326
Joseph, Judith, 270–271, 277

K
Kachchh, Gujarat, 328
Kalakshetra (Rukmini Devi College of Fine Arts - school of classical Indian music and dance), 62, 67, 187, 196–198, 200–201, 207–208, 371
Kali-Ma, 265
Kamaladevi, 101
Kanchipuram, temple of, 332
Kandahar, 38–39, 42–43

Kanyakumari, 79–80
Karnataka, 287
Kashipur Tahsil, Uttarakhand,169, 173–174
Kashmir, 133–135, 205–207
Keating, Kenneth (American ambassador), 103–104
Kelkar, Dr. Dinkar G., 94–96, 131–132, 157 (*see also* Raja Dinkar Kelkar Museum)
Kelkar, Kaku, 95, 131, 157
Kendall, Laurel, 273
Kerala, 80–82, 288, 327, 328, 335
Khajuraho, temples of, 61
Khajuri, Koraput District, Orissa (now Odisha), Dongria Kondh village, 176, 183, 188
Khan, Ustad Vilayat, 57
Khastgir, Shyamali, 288–289, 310
kolams (powder paintings on floor), 72–74, 96, 250–251, 287, 327, 374
Kolkata, West Bengal; *see* Calcutta
Konarak Sun Temple, Orissa (now Odisha), 230–231
Kondh tribe, 166, 170–171, 175–176
Koraput District, Orissa (now Odisha), 165–166, 168–171
Kottayam, 84
Kramrisch, Dr. Stella, 125
Krishnamurti, Jiddu, 197, 208
Kurli, Dongria Kondh village, 177, 183, 188
Kusima, 287

L
Lake Palace, Udaipur, 119–123
Lakshmi, Goddess, 162, 235, 236–237, 248, 252, 321–322, 385
Lanius, Mary, 69
Larku, 287
Lascaux Caves in rural France, 350–351
latticework (*jali*), 297–298, 302, 313
Laubin, Reginald and Gladys, 149, 351

Lawyer, David, 363–364
The Living Arts of India: Craftsman at Work exhibition in London, 212
London, 144-148, 186
Longenecker, Martha, 144, 228–229, 306
Lucknow Museum, Uttar Pradesh, 222–223
Ludiya village, Gujarat, 328

M
Madhya Pradesh, 162, 287
Madras (now Chennai), 67-69, 196, 233
Madurai, temple of, 76-77, 332
Mahabalipuram, temples of, 326, 332
Maharashtra, 154, 287
Maine Photographic Workshops, 238, 267
Major, Ghulam Mohammed, 133–134, 205
Majumdar, Minhazz, 289, 310
Malkangiri Tahsil, Orissa (now Odisha), 169, 170
Mangaldas, Leena, 125, 126
Mannarasala, temple of, 81–83, 327
Manubhai, 97, 98
Mapin Press, Ahmedabad, 126, 234, 240, 290, 309
Marshall, Heather, 147
Mathura, 222
McDougall, Ian, 343–344
Mecca, 30
meditation, 103–104, 200, 322, 357–358, 383–384
Meeting God: Elements of Hindu Devotion (Huyler), 257, 270, 289, 335
Meeting God exhibition, 272–273, 275–278
  in UK, 278–280, 317
Mehrangarh Fort, Jodhpur, 241, 243, 326
metalwares, 157–158
Meyer, Kurt and Pamela, 188, 388

Michel, Dr. George, 233–234
Mingei International Museum, San Diego, 124, 144, 217–218, 228–229, 293, 305, 307, 310–312, 315, 336
mitti, 215–216
Mohanty, S.K., 175–176, 178, 183
Mohapatra, Maheshwar "Babu," 188, 230–231, 233, 237, 255, 294, 301–302, 312, 313, 327, 335, 336, 337–338, 339
Mohapatra, Sitakant, 168, 175
Montessori, Maria, 125, 198
Mookerjee, Ajit, 56, 225
Moti-Singh-ki-Dhani village, Jaisalmer, Rajasthan, 246–248, 328
Mumbai (*see* Bombay)
Mundo, Frank, 386–387
Murdoch, Mary Hamilton, 354–355
Museum of Art and Photography, Bengaluru, 112
Muswell Hill, London, UK, 145, 147

N
Nagaraja (King of the Snakes), 81, 327
Nagas (standing cobras), 273
Nagini, the Snake Goddess, 81–82
Nagin Lake, Kashmir, 133
Nair, K. Nanu, Mr., 84
Naqqash, Bhai Gian Singh, 51
Narayan, Sunithi, ("Amma"), 233, 260–261, 264, 266–267, 275, 289, 327, 335, 385
National Crafts Museum (National Handlooms and Handicrafts Museum), New Delhi, 225–226, 228, 251, 274, 290
National Museum of Asian Art, Washington, D. C., 257, 258; *see also* Freer and Sackler Galleries, *and* Freer Gallery of Art
Nehru, Jawaharlal, 356
New Walk Museum, Leicester, UK, 278, 280

New York Times, 224, 276, 277
Nishat Bagh, Kashmir, 134
Niyamgiri Mountain, Orissa (now Odisha) 175, 177, 178, 188–190
Nottingham, Linda Bailey, 339

O
Ohio State University, 263
Ojai, California, 131, 144, 310, 317, 319, 342, 348, 354, 355, 356, 357, 358, 360
Orient Express, 29
Orissa (now Odisha), 161–162, 165, 335
Otterbein University, 318

P
Padmapoda village, 255
Painted Prayers: Women's Art in Village India (Huyler), 74, 249–250, 270–271, 284, 289, 335
Painted Prayers exhibition, 250–251, 272, 339, 385
painting(s), wall, 176, 177–178, 235–237, 247–248, 297–298, 321–322, 328; *see also* kolams (powder paintings on floor)
Pakistan, 45–46 kolams
Pal, Dr. Pratapaditya, 317–318
Pandey, Navin, 337
Parvati, Goddess, 264
Pathnaik, Anand, 167, 168–169, 170, 172, 179, 191–192
Pathnaik, Jumma, 191–192
Periyar National Park and Wildlife Sanctuary, Kerala, 84–86
Phulo, 247–248
Pillai, Sunny and Buni, 185
Poster, Dr. Amy, 222–223, 225, 229
Post Office Editorial, 304–305, 310
Powell, Jeff, 386–387
Prillaman, Jerry and Geneviève, 231–232
Puhputra (Sonabai's village), 294–299,

302–305
Puja: Expressions of Hindu Devotion exhibition, 259, 262, 263–268, 335
Puja and Piety: Hindu, Jain, and Buddhist Art from the Indian Subcontinent exhibition, 317–318
Pune, 94, 157
Puri District, Orissa (now Odisha), 180–181, 187, 237, 322
Pushpa Pawar, 282

R
Raja Dinkar Kelkar Museum, 94, 157; *see also* Kelkar
Rajasthan, 102, 115, 154, 155–156
Rajawar, Daroga Ram, 229, 293, 295–296, 302–303, 305, 313–314, 336
Rajawar, Rajenbai, 295, 313–314, 336
Rajawar, Sonabai, 229, 292–299, 302, 336
Rao, Ramana, 170, 172, 182, 184
Rao, Venkat, 182, 184
Rashtrapati Puraskar (The President's Award), 299
Ravi Shankar, 101
Reid, Carol, 232–233
Ridley, Sarah, 259, 262
Riverside Arts Gallery, Ypsilanti, Michigan, 318
Rizzoli International, 239–240, 243, 248, 249–250, 251, 270, 284
Rossmann, Andreas (Andy), 250, 362–363
Rukmini Devi, *see under* Arundale
Rukmini Devi College of Fine Arts (*see under* Kalakshetra)

S
Samabai, 328
Samar, Dr. Devi Lal, 102
Santa Barbara Museum of Art, 317–318
Santa Fe Film Festival, 315–316

Santiniketan, West Bengal, 288
Sarabhai, Giraben, 125
Sarabhai, Dr. Mallika, 126, 234, 290, 309
Sarthi, Parbatibai, 312–313
Sathya Sai Baba, 103–105
Saurashtra Handicraft, 97, 124
Sawhney, Shami and Teni, 56–57, 112, 127, 132–133, 152, 185, 202, 240
Schlemmer, Andrée, 209–210, 356–357
School of Oriental and African Studies (SOAS), London, UK, 143, 144–147, 186–187, 218, 233–234
Serpentine Gallery, London, UK, 212
Shah, Bipin, 126, 234, 290, 309
Shah, Haku, 124–125, 228
Shah, Paulomi, 290, 309, 314
Shalimar Gardens, Lahore, Pakistan, 45,
Shalimar Gardens, Srinagar, Kashmir, India, 134
Sidner, Rob, 306, 315
Silverstein, John, 147–148, 158–160
Singh, Maharajah Gaj, 241, 245
Singh, G.S. Sohan, Sri, 50–51, 112
Smith, Cheryl, 271
Smithsonian Associates Travel Program, 232–233, 328–329, 331, 332, 333, 335, 337, 338
Sonabai: Another Way of Seeing exhibition, 311–313, 314–315, 318–319
Sonabai: Another Way of Seeing (film), 308–309, 315–316
Srinivasulu, K., 69–70
Stancioff, Ivan, 271, 279, 385, 386–387
Stebich, Ute, 294
Surguja District, Chhattisgarh, 294, 299

T
Taj Mahal, 114–115, 330, 331
Taj Mahal Hotel, 129–132

Tandan, Prabhat and Sushmita, 223–224, 301–302
Tandan, Shunia, 301–302
Tehran, 36–37
Thacher School, Ojai, 250, 342–343, 345, 348, 350, 361–364, 366
Thampi, K.P. Padmanabhan, Sri, 80–83
Thanjavur, temple of, 332
Thar Desert, 241
Theosophical Center, Ojai, 357
Theosophical Society, 197
Tiruchirappalli, temple of, 332
Touching Fire: Elements of Devotion in India, 272
Transcendental Meditation, 357

U
Udaipur, Rajasthan, 100–102, 119–123
Udwadia, Dr. Farokh E., 128–129, 130
Umaid Bhawan Palace, Udaipur, Rajasthan, 241
University of Denver, 26, 27, 196
University of London, 143
Urdu language, 147

V
V&A (*see* Victoria and Albert Museum)
Vakani, N.T., 95–100, 124
Valai Amma (high priestess), 82, 83
Varanasi, 59–60, 177, 209–211, 222, 301, 357
Victoria and Albert Museum, 144–146, 147, 212
Village India (Huyler), 219–222

W
West Bengal, 162–163
Williams, Solveig, 240, 249, 250, 270
Wolf, Jeany, 308–309
Wolf, Jeffrey, 309
Wood, Beatrice, 67–68, 196, 217, 366–369, 385, 389–390
    in Calcutta, 106
    folk art museum, 111, 228
    illness, 57–58, 61
    lecture tour through major Indian cities, 71
    letters to Stephen Huyler, 110
    road trips in Tamil Nadu, 69–70
    Rukmini Devi and, 62, 64
    Stephen Huyler working for, 26–27, 109, 366–369
    visit to Delhi, 57–58
Wright, David, 301–305, 308, 311, 312

Y
Yogi, Mahesh, Maharishi, 103, 357–358

Pippa Rann Books
and
Global Resilience Publishing
(imprints of **Salt Desert Media Group Ltd., U.K.***)*

SALT DESERT MEDIA GROUP LTD., U.K., was established in 2019, and currently publishes under the imprints, Pippa Rann Books and Media and Global Resilience Publishing.

Pippa Rann Books and Media publishes books about India and the Indian diaspora, for everyone who has an interest in the sub-Continent, it's peoples and cultures. At a time of political challenge, Pippa Rann books aim to nurture the values of democracy, liberty, equality and fraternity that inspired the founders of the modern state of India.

Titles on the Global Resilience Publishing list explore how global challenges can be addressed and resolved with an inter-disciplinary and transnational approach. The imprint focuses on subjects such as Climate Change, the Global Financial System, Multilateral and Corporate Governance, etc. In addition to its own publications, Salt Desert Media provides distribution services in English-speaking territories for several authors and publishers.

Sales and Distribution:
- India and SE Asia: Penguin Random House India
- Canada and the USA: Trafalgar Square Press (https://www.ipgbook.com/)
- UK: LSS (Sales) Contact: Andrew Wormleighton (andrew@lionsalesservices.com)
- Rest of World/Rights: Prologue Sales Contact: Rob Wendover (rob@prologuesales.com) Distribution: Marston Book Services above